COMMUNITIES ON THE WAY

Communities on the Way

Rebuilding Local Economies in the United States and Canada

STEWART E. PERRY

State University of New York Press

Published by
State University of New York Press, Albany

©1987 State University of New York

For information, address State University of New York
Press, State University Plaza, Albany, N.Y., 12246

Library of Congress Cataloging in Publication Data

Perry, Stewart E.
Communities on the way.

Bibliography: p.
Includes index.
1. Community development—United States.
2. Community development—Canada. 3. Community
development corporations—United States.
4. Community development corporations—
Canada. I. Title.
HN90.C6P47 1987   307.1′4′0971   86-30069
ISBN 0-88706-526-0
ISBN 0-88706-525-2 (pbk.)

10 9 8 7 6 5 4 3 2 1

Contents

Acknowledgements

E ACH book I publish joyfully entails my affectionate acknowledgement of the crucial aid, astute criticism, and warm encouragement of Helen Swick Perry. I am, as always, deeply indebted and ever grateful for her intellectual contribution to my work as well as her steady support.

No foundation grants, university salary, or other subsidy underwrote the preparation of this book, but an unrestricted gift to the Institute for New Enterprise Development from Grace M. Dingee made it possible to pay for typing, editing, and other INED expenses for this and other publications, as well as for INED operational expenses. Her gift was as unexpected as it was heartwarming and made it possible for me to concentrate on the book rather than on INED's financial needs. I want to tell her once more of my deep appreciation for that generous surprise.

I am of course especially indebted to the many community leaders, who as my constant colleagues in the field of community economic development over the past twenty years, taught me so much. This book is as much theirs, in that sense, as it is mine. I want to single out two especially, though many more could be named. Greg MacLeod, activist, teacher, conversationalist par excellence, has for the years of our association in community economic development offered valuable ideas and stimulating interaction. I want to take this occasion to express my appreciation on many different levels for his friendship and colleaguial support, not just with respect to this book but also in general throughout our work together. DeForest Brown gave me my first introduction to what it means to try to get a forgotten community started on its way. I garnered much understanding and knowledge from working with him in a number of different settings, and I will always appreciate that.

On an early draft, my friend John Hanratty, who is now editor of the *Atlantic Cooperator*, gave me detailed, wise, and friendly comments and corrections, especially with regard to the Canadian context. I am very, very grateful for his generous help.

Along the way of writing (and seeking a publisher) I received special encouragement from Herbert Vetter and Nelson Foote and Arthur Rosenthal. Their belief in the value of what I had written was important when I needed it. It was also a special encouragement to have the interest and the sophisticated aid of Martha Goodman, who was able to decipher quasi-inscrutable passages while typing my manuscript.

I hope this book, despite the limitations I have imposed upon it, will justify the help I have gotten from all these people. I especially want to reiterate my dependence upon the practitioners of community economic development and hope that they will feel free to contact me about any mistakes of fact or interpretation they may see in the book—and thus continue the collaboration that has been so important to me.

Institute for New Enterprise Development
Harvard Square, Box 360
Cambridge, Massachusetts 02138

Prologue

T HIS book tells the story of how forgotten communities in Canada and the United States have taken up the struggle to reverse the despair of their deep economic depression. It tells the story as I watched it unfold over almost twenty years. In 1967, virtually by accident, I had the chance to observe firsthand a new wellspring of concentrated social energy that expressed itself in crucial community inventions. These social inventions spread throughout much of North America, and today they mobilize and redirect underused local resources and bring back hope to a scene from which it had long departed. I somehow knew at the time that I was a participant observer of a potentially very important social episode, but only now am I able to look back upon this time and try to lay out systematically what it can mean.

I have to admit that I had had no professional interest in the problems of the forgotten community until they were thrust upon me by a change in work sites. I had worked as a social scientist in one of the more hopeful arenas of behavior—how health care can be more effectively offered in hospitals and clinics. But I moved from a university medical center to a federal planning office, where I intended to work on health care for the poor. That move soon led me further afield than I could have predicted, into a new scene of hope and struggle, where the tools are not medical but broadly human, where the main actors are not highly trained specialists though just as highly committed, and where, paradoxically, recalcitrant economic problems become translated into resolvable human issues of organization and pragmatic action. I was taught by the people in depleted communities that the revitalization of a local economy, if it is to occur at all, must be tackled by local efforts.

Once I had encountered that wellspring of energy, I sought to follow it wherever it appeared in distressed communities, rural and urban, Canadian and American. Sometimes I worked directly with these communities; at other times I worked indirectly, as when I was involved in helping design national programs and legislation in support of their struggle.

This book, then, focuses on economic development in a variety of local areas. One locality might be an inner-city neighborhood of a great metropolitan center, such as New York City's Hunts Point or Montreal's Point St. Charles. Another might be a relatively circumscribed, mostly rural district of small towns and villages, like the Northern Kingdom district of Vermont and New Hampshire or like Nova Scotia's Cape Breton Island. Or again, the locality might be a single county, like Hancock County, Georgia, or an even smaller community, like the village of Sebastopol, Ontario. All of these communities will figure to some degree in this book (with other communities as well), because all of them have helped to evolve an innovative approach to local productivity, an approach to be called "community economic development." Paradoxically, this approach to the improvement of local productivity and of the local way of life cannot be understood as being fundamentally economic. On the contrary, it has to be understood initially in social, psychological, and political terms; it is thus an *institution-building* process for strengthening or creating the practices and organizations of local productivity. I hope to make this distinction very clear.

For the past twenty years, practitioners at the local level, wielding the tools of new specialized community organizations, have been working with many conventional specialists from other fields. Yet strangely enough, this field of practice has not yet been examined systematically; it has not yet developed the well-rounded established literature* or detailed conceptualization of a well-researched discipline. Although it has remained a vital practical activity, it has received no explicit and thorough rationale and analysis. This book aims to present an introduction to the field in the hope that other students in urban and rural planning and development will critically examine this new community-based

---

*Any bibliographical references will be cited in the section "Notes and Sources" at the end of the book. This practice is designed to avoid any interruption of the text and yet to furnish necessary formal citations and to provide a useful foundation or context for each unit of the book. The chapter-by-chapter notes also permit running commentaries on particular points. Only some of the leading published materials will be cited; in this way I hope to encourage the reader to do his or her own explorations, without being put off by an exhaustive list of citations.

economic development strategy and move beyond the preparatory formulations I offer.

The broader significance of this account lies in what it can suggest to other distressed localities and also in what it implies for rethinking national economic policy in Canada and the United States. The success of the community-based approach and the necessary redefinition of the problem of local economic development as I try to lay it out offer a missing element in current national economic policy concerns. This element—community-based development—can bridge the gap between the macroeconomic measures of national fiscal and monetary policy and the microeconomics of conventional business activity. The community-based approach also has a relevance for underdeveloped nations.

In Part One I describe how my own initiation into the field began. This sort of examination can reveal the constraints and biases in one's approach, and I hope it will encourage the reader to consider also how she or he has come to be involved in the field. New ideas can evolve only from examined personal experience of the history through which we live, and this sort of analysis helps to cross-check and validate experiences and conclusions. Since historical events led to the critical social innovations that made community-based economic development possible and that provided the energy for local economic growth, I begin with history and personal history.

I then present two disparate cases, one from the United States and one from Canada, of the invention of the key institutional tool—what has come to be called a "community development corporation," or "CDC." Since this social invention requires a different conceptualization of the problem of the distressed local economy, I review that conceptualization in detail and review some of the misleading ideas and strategies for local redevelopment that have to be avoided in order to give the community-based approach a real chance. I then examine all the terms that describe the alternative strategy of community-based economic development, for these serve to introduce systematically how local programs are conceived. For example, what indeed is meant by *community* in this context?

Part Two is more descriptive. What are the steps by which a community is likely to arrive at its own specialized invention for designing and carrying out its strategy? And what is the role of outsiders in this discovery and creation process? The core institution, or CDC, merits special attention, and I portray its most likely internal structure, together with frequently found variations. I then review the two major thrusts of local economic strategy—business development and infrastructure development. These, of course, have required various forms and sources of capital, which CDCs have learned to mobilize in imaginative ways from within and without the community; I describe these financial elements and comment on the difference between community development finance and conventional finance. I conclude this section by reviewing the internal difficulties of the new strategy—what might be called the "inherent" or "existential" tensions that are encountered along the way.

Finally, in order to provide a basis for policy options, in Part Three I review the available systematic evidence in evaluation studies that assess the effectiveness of community economic development as an alternative development strategy. I then move away from the community arena to consider the relevance of transcommunity institutions the CDCs have involved or actually created whenever they were necessary. These have included national institutions, as well as state and provincial or regional resources. This discussion leads to consideration of policy issues at national, state or provincial, and municipal levels.

Looking back, I am somewhat puzzled that the desperation of the forgotten community, sometimes clamorous, sometimes quiet, has received so little sustained attention. I suppose that in an otherwise abundant land, dilapidated city neighborhoods or abandoned rural districts are as awkward to encounter as a mumbling bag-lady in an upscale shopping mall. So perhaps it is not surprising that the distress of impoverished communities is more often ignored than relieved. After all, their problems seem so recalcitrant and long-standing. How then did a change take place, at the local level itself, in such a discouraging picture? How have the forgotten communities begun to rise on their own efforts? This book hopes to tell part of that story.

PART ONE

ONE

The Wellsprings

T ODAY'S hope for rebuilding urban and rural communities in deep economic distress can be discovered in the tangled history of the United States in the 1960s, truly a knotted skein of both despair and hopeful new beginnings: The black ghettos of America's inner cities were exploding with rage and fire and bullets just as the civil rights movement was reaching its most significant victories. The nation was engaged in a vicious war in Vietnam, but somehow those young people who might have been expected to be caught up in chauvinistic passion were instead proclaiming peace and love and justice, borne too by new themes in art, music, and social thought. Too many leaders for those new times were felled by an assassain's bullet—John Kennedy, Malcolm X, Martin Luther King, Robert Kennedy—and yet other leaders carried on their vision.

Certainly I was not immune to what was happening around me. I was struggling too to find a meaningful thread through a seemingly irrational pattern. For much of the 1960s I was working at the University of California in San Francisco and Berkeley, and surely that setting then did not permit any insulation from the social upheavals of my country. I tried and did manage to carry on the regular tasks of teaching, research, and the administration of a fellowship program, while at the same time becoming involved locally in the anti-war campaign, in civil rights activities, and even in the burgeoning counterculture of the Haight-Ashbury.

At that time I was studying the phenomenon of "dirty work," socially derogated work, particularly in the medical setting at the University's medical center, and wondering how it could be transformed by appropriate organizational innovation into appreciated duties. That might seem far removed from what shortly came to be my preoccupation with the distressed community, but it strangely led that way. Beginning in 1966, as a part of the research on dirty work, I was riding the trucks and working with the men of a worker-owned garbage company, for the garbageman is the archetypal dirty worker anywhere in the world. But in San Francisco, the garbagemen, for about forty years, had shared equally in the ownership of their own firm; and this economic and organizational innovation had seemed to make all the difference in the way they and others regarded their work—and in the high quality of the service in the city. I wanted to take a close look at that phenomenon, and it took me into the dark and early mornings of garbage collection in different areas of the city.

Most especially I went into the Haight-Ashbury just as that neighborhood was becoming the symbol of a social rethinking for the nation. From all over the country, and from outside it as well, even from Vancouver and Paris, Toronto and The Hague, young people were descending upon the neighborhood that had become known as a place of new beginnings. They were coming to celebrate life and to reaffirm the meaning of love, peace, justice, and friendship across all the boundaries that can separate people. Among the goals shared by many of the young wanderers was to find new ways of organizing the necessary exchange of money and goods that would bring people together rather than set them apart. Utopian communes, restaurant and art cooperatives, a "black peoples' free store," and other forms of economic innovation were rediscovered and tried again. And, as I went about the district with the garbagemen, I was getting an inside (or perhaps better, an underside) view of the Haight-Ashbury phenomenon as it began.

To young people, precursors in history are not so important as their own present moment of experimentation and discovery. Yet there were young people in the Haight-Ashbury district who did reach back into the very beginnings of America. They recognized their roots, for example, in Governor John Winthrop's utopian hopes of "A Model of Christian Charity"—the "city upon a hill" that had energized the early settlers of the Massachusetts Bay Colony, organized then as a communally owned company for development of the New World. The gentleness of the early hippie values that sought to include all people also granted a hearing even to those "over thirty" who told tales of the kibbutzim of Israel, the kolkhozy of Russia, the *ejidos* of Mexico, the syndicalist factories of France, and especially the Oneidas of America—all showing how people found new ways to live and produce together. Within this context and the context of the civil rights movement, it was relatively easy in the (then) economically and racially integrated Haight-Ashbury neighborhood for the white, middle-class young wanderers to seek and find relationships with the local and less advantaged blacks whose music was so much a part of the American youth culture.

The phenomenon of the hippies and the close cross-racial relations of the middle-class wanderers and the local blacks insulated many of us from the racial disorders elsewhere and perhaps inoculated the city itself against the more virulent strains of the plague that was infecting other metropolitan areas that were falling prey to the racial disturbances of the inner city. Yet in the fall of 1966, shortly after I began my garbagemen study, San Francisco had had its own racial trouble, when a white policeman wrongfully shot and killed a black youth. The police department rather quickly acknowledged the responsibility, and perhaps the disturbances in San Francisco's black districts were therefore mild by comparison to elsewhere. But it had occasioned a six-day curfew in some poor neighborhoods, including the Haight. In the Haight an interracial countercultural group, the Diggers, began their practice of preparing food and serving it free to all comers; they were particularly concerned for those in the Haight who might not be able to get food because of the curfew. Later, in the following summer, in what the media called the Summer of Love, which attracted so many more wanderers, the Diggers and other local activists strove to handle the social stresses consequent upon the enormous influx of people who came to find San Francisco's vaunted magic. But the so-called Summer of Love collapsed into another tangle of despair and new hope symbolic of those times, a hype of drugs and commercialization of the young peoples' energies and ideas. The hippie leaders were overwhelmed by their task, but perhaps the failure was not as bad as what was happening elsewhere.

Elsewhere in the country in the metropolitan centers the nation, divided white and black, confronted the question of whether a riot of death and fire in the poorest black neighborhoods was to come that summer. The last few summers had seemed to be the danger time, when youthful black males, out of school, out of work, not yet drafted for a war that still had eight long years to go, would light the tinder of rage and despair that most blacks, rich or poor, feel in a racist society. There had been so many conflagrations that, to a disbelieving white society, they seemed mysteriously contagious. In the three previous years at least twelve major disorders had occurred in large metropolitan centers. In 1965, a racial disorder in Los Angeles had been the worst that the country had seen since 1943, when the massive World War II riots had taken place in Detroit. Yet in 1967, Detroit again went through a disastrous episode, when another forty-three people were killed. Despite its undeniable slums, San Francisco came through that summer unscathed, and like other residents I could have breathed a sigh of relief and concentrated on other local issues. But I was catapulted into a different perspective by a new job.

I moved to Washington, D.C., that fall, where it shortly became part of my responsibility, in the planning office of the so-called War on Poverty (more formally, the federal Office of Economic Opportunity), to consider how the government's antipoverty efforts could prevent any further explosions in the black ghettos around the country. Already in that one year, major riots had occurred in 8 cities, with serious disturbances in 33 more, and lesser disorders in still 123 more. Some people had hoped that once a city had gone through such an upset, it would not happen again—as if it were a case of reducing the level of steam pressure. But even in that same year, 25 cities suffered at least twice, and New York City suffered five times. In Cleveland and Rochester, the second episode of that year was a major riot, involving loss of life.

Meanwhile, the President's Commission on Civil Disorders was soon to issue its report; in response, the planning section at the Office of Economic Opportunity (OEO), then a part of the Executive Office of the President, had to be ready with some new ideas about what the agency could do. And so the "urban ghetto seminar," an informal interracial study group, was organized in our office, and we began to review what we knew about the black ghettos and what we believed was missing or beside the point in the current antipoverty programs in those neighborhoods. Some of us had visited a site of a previous disturbance and had talked with leaders of the young male blacks of the street. We also combed through the so-called quick-and-dirty interview surveys that had been made in several of the urban black ghettos—surveys that might not have met all the requirements of scientific research but which were needed to bring swift, new, if rough, information to bear on our questions.

After several weeks, our seminar concluded that however useful the poverty programs were, they had little meaning for the young black males who were in the forefront of the riots. What did seem to interest those blacks was a growing black consciousness movement which looked toward local self-determination that would include control of the economic institutions in the black community.

Both the aspirations and the discontents of black community residents had risen in tandem just as the beginning successes of the past ten years of the civil rights movement were taking hold. Those successes had not brought any ultimate satisfaction to blacks; they had merely highlighted how much was still wrong. Moreover, the antipoverty programs seemed only to emphasize the basic vulnerability of the black person as an individual trying to get ahead in a racist society. If the resentment of the discriminated against, the left out, was not to destroy their own neighborhoods, it would have to be mobilized to build those neighborhoods. And to build them required a comprehensive approach based on a sense of black unity.

The ideas of black unity and collective economic action were not new to black Americans. It was a tradition that reached back at least to the convulsions after the Civil War, when former slaves sought to plan a new life. But one hundred years later, that tradition took on new strength in the aftermath of the convulsions of the inner city. From the street leaders of the young men, we learned that the urge toward black self-determination and unity was the one major motive held by almost all blacks, older or younger, male or female, professional, business, blue-collar, or unemployed.

The postriot movement for black self-determination and "Black Power" was expressed in an amazing variety of groups and ideas, ranging from Marcus-Garvey-like campaigns considering a return en masse to Africa, to a rash of cooperatives for the shared buying of food in the cities and the shared marketing of farm products in the countryside, to buy-black campaigns, and to plans to cut out some territory within the United States as an independent black republic. There were even a few tiny armed bands that carried their inner-city suspicions to the point of awaiting invasions from white armies to level the black neighborhoods of America; their fears were fed, of course, by the tiny private organizations of armed whites who openly considered such invasions.

Somewhere in this period of time, an institution now known as the "community development corporation," or "CDC," was invented.* Like many other inventions, even in science and technology, it was not invented just once but more or less simultaneously in a number of different black ghettos in America, where desperate need, combined with ingenuity, opportunity, and talent, brought forth the new institution. What caught our attention in Washington was that this innovation—distinct from others that were appearing in this time of social foment and social creativity—appeared to bring together all elements of the black inner-city community, even attracting blacks who had migrated to the middle class in the suburbs.

The CDC, as it appeared then, was a black coalition of welfare-mother activists, young street leaders, lawyers, shopkeepers, ministers, taxi drivers, and so on. In each instance, the CDC seemed to have been a direct reaction to the local disasters of an inner-city riot. I did not understand at first the urgency of the feelings which made it possible for a neighborhood to submerge many differences in a CDC coalition. Nevertheless, my co-workers and I set about designing an agency program that would undergrid such coalitions for development. Only later did we discover how excruciatingly necessary it could be for a group to come together on its own, after a major disorder, to see what could be done about its neighborhood.

My own discovery happened a few months later, in the spring of 1968, the evening of the day that Martin Luther King, Jr., was assassinated. I looked out of my Washington apartment window that evening and in the near distance saw a huge wall of fire, many blocks long and deep, flaming hundreds of feet in the air. It burned for hours and hours, a beacon for general looting and vandalism that swept through the black slum and, a block or so away, onto my own street. Even some days later, my eyes would smart from the tear gas still lingering in the neighborhood supermarket where I shopped. At OEO we learned then in a personal way what awesome energies had been released and had to be redirected in neighborhood coalitions.

A successful black professional man in Buffalo, New York, later told me about his own experience: "My children asked me what I had been doing to prevent the riot here and help my fellow

---

*I will be examining the CDC in detail, but for the reader's convenience now a quick definition would be "a coalition organization of neighborhood residents to carry out their own comprehensive program of local renewal activities, especially including business development."

blacks, and there was nothing I could tell them." That was when he and others in Buffalo and in the other riot cities shifted their perspective from an individuated legal concept of black civil rights to the social-psychological-economic concept of the black community. It was, after all, the black citizens of all classes who were suffering most from the riots. The urge to burn was destroying their own neighborhoods. That is why middle-class and working-class blacks were swiftly mobilized by the riots into a new and different kind of struggle, and why they joined poorer folk and the more alienated in reassessing the black agenda. All over the stricken areas, independent neighborhood groups formed to piece out meaning from the events and to light a different beacon.

In each city, as each neighborhood puzzled out its local scene, the pieces of the answer fell into the same pattern. Whatever was wrong, it went far beyond the acts of those who set the fires or looted or taunted the police and firemen—or shot at them. The community itself had not taken enough responsibility to direct its own destiny and to counteract the systemic inattention, derogation, or exploitation by the larger society. If their community had been forgotten by the rest of society, it also seemed that it had been forgotten by the residents themselves. Suddenly it became clear that the stricken neighborhood would never improve because of natural and spontaneous market forces or because government agencies would eventually do something; a neighborhood would have to consciously take its destiny in its own hands and build all of the necessary resources—the institutions and social tools that make a community work. This neighborhood would incude businesses that created jobs and incomes, political networks, housing, schools, recreational facilities, and all the patterned practices that build a new sense of self-respect and self-determination. Out of a recognition of the systemic problems that the forgotten community faced, a new social and economic tool was invented that would act systematically. The CDC represented and directed a community approach to comprehensive revitalization of a unified neighborhood.

In a few years the idea of community economic development and the CDC institution itself spread from the urban centers to rural areas, from black neighborhoods to other ethnic groups and to white communities—as a more hopeful means for distressed communities of all kinds to take their destiny in their own hands. The idea of the CDC caught on in both the United States and Canada because the concept of community-based economic direction was vague enough to fit each local situation. But it was also definite enough to focus on the core problem of the depleted community: how is it possible to spur development under terms that fit local circumstances and needs and, for this purpose, to mobilize the single significant available resource—the people, the residents of the area? The CDC became the specialized tool for answering that question.

In Washington, however, the idea of community-based economic development for an impoverished community was not popular. Poverty was mainly conceptualized as a problem of individuals, not a problem of communities. Fix up the individual person, and he would take care of himself. He would leave the horror of the slum behind; and then the slum itself could be torn down and rebuilt as a completely new district with a different function—say, to house the professionals and clerks of the downtown firms. So the preferred programs of assistance sought, in effect, to rebuild people, by providing medical services that would make them healthier, by training them for better jobs, by giving them a head start with adequate nursery school care, and especially by offering them employment training programs. However meaningful those programs were (and are today), the communities where poor people live were bypassed.

Even those who promoted the national community action program with its local Community Action Agencies (CAAs), each an amalgam of city or county government officials, social agency people, and low-income neighborhood representatives, seemed to think of the CAAs mostly as an instrument by which individual-centered programs (job counseling, Head Start, health counseling, and so on) could be "delivered" to needy persons. Earlier, it was true, the CAAs had been considered a potential instrument for social and community change, but over time, pressures of one sort or another had constricted that function of the CAA in order to prevent it from disturbing local government leaders.

Thus what the new neighborhood organizations as CDCs represented did not have a ready federal audience, and those of us in OEO who believed they were a key invention cast around for a way to support them. There was already one new showpiece economic development project, which in a way expressed something of what we had in mind. Yet even it was not a direct OEO program, although it was funded out of a special OEO appropriation. It was a program administered, by agency delegation agreement, by the

Department of Labor, which sponsored that single project and used the rest of the appropriation for employment counseling and referrals in low-income areas. That economic development project was the Bedford-Stuyvesant Restoration Corporation (Restoration), organized in 1967 to serve Brooklyn's Bedford-Stuyvesant ghetto. It envisioned a comprehensive renewal of the area in social and economic terms, and it was run by eminent black leaders. However, quite clearly it had not arisen from Bedford-Stuyvesant itself. It had been put together on the impetus of Senators Robert Kennedy and Jacob Javits, with the collaboration of New York City's Mayor John Lindsey. The original board of directors had been handpicked by a prominent and well-respected black judge, who had been approached by Senator Kennedy. Moreover, the redevelopment of Bedford-Stuyvesant was posited on responsibility being assumed by major New-York-based corporations to provide financial and other assistance; and these corporations were organized for this task in a separate renewal group parallel to Restoration and named the D&S Corporation (*d*evelopment and *s*ervice). Major funding came from New York foundations, such as Astor and Ford. The federal government, through the Department of Labor, participated by means of a multimillion-dollar grant initiated under the so-called Special Impact legislation sponsored originally by Javits and Kennedy.

Some of our urban ghetto seminar members had visited the Bedford-Stuyvesant project and were tremendously impressed by its scope, not to mention its prime executives—Franklin Thomas (president of Restoration) and John Doar (president of D&S). But obviously such a powerhouse of leadership and of political, financial, and other backing could not be a model for the forgotten communities elsewhere in the United States. Most especially, the project was not the broad coalition of local neighborhood activism that we felt had to be the base of a self-run program.

The conclusion of our seminar, that local self-initiated groups should have agency support in their drive toward autonomously directed economic development, found few ready ears at the agency, which had not even been prepared to sponsor the Bedford-Stuyvesant project. In addition, "black separatist" overtones were imputed to our program concept, and many whites (and some blacks) worried that black consciousness and black community self-development would only increase the racial segregation of American society. All this, together with an agency priority on employment and training programs as presumably being the most cost-efficient way to aid the poor, meant that our analysis was initially ignored.

Then an unexpected source of leverage came from outside the agency. A U.S. Senate committee pressed for more vigorous use of the existing Special Impact authority for ghetto programs, and this pressure provided the opportunity to get approval of our design for at least an experimental test of inner-city economic development under local resident control. Thereupon began a period of some twelve years of federal support by the agency (and its successor) for community-controlled CDCs.

This bit of bureaucratic history helps correct any impression that the community economic development groups in the low-income areas of the United States were somehow a creation of a federal program. Of course, federal money encouraged such groups, and in fact the recognition that early groups received through the federal response was a crucial confirmation of their perspective and plans. Moreover, the model they represented was adopted and adapted by other groups hopeful of receiving federal support. But it was specifically a neighborhood initiative, occurring simultaneously in many neighborhoods, to which OEO responded. In retrospect, the antipoverty agency can be seen to have played only one specific but critical part in sketching in the new institutional pattern. Although the CDC was born as a local innovation to handle local problems, it did require some outside resources. The role of OEO essentially was to organize some new formal practices to allocate resources—namely, federal funds—for capital investment by the new local institution, the CDC.

The total financial support from the antipoverty agency was never very large—it usually hovered at $20-$40 million a year and rose once to a peak of about $55 million. But the federal recognition and later some specific legislation that took the program out of the experimental category helped to swiftly institutionalize and make credible the basic concept of comprehensive, locally controlled, community economic development. Within a short time, a network of leading CDCs were receiving ongoing federal support; an independent, private, nonprofit think tank had been organized, as well as a national legal services support center, technical assistance groups, and a training institute; and a national association of CDCs was formed to monitor the agency, lobby Congress, and exchange information on problem solving at the local project level. All this activity gave local groups a kind of outside confirmation that their efforts and their ideas had a basic validity. Eventually, when other federal government agencies also began targeting some support for local development groups, the CDC idea gained greater visibility.

When the CDC idea was taken up in Canada, again it was not at first through government sponsorship but by depressed Canadian communities. Although it was not racial disorders that gave impetus to local initiatives and locally controlled community economic development, there was the same kind of increasing discontent over what was perceived as outside exploitation and unresponsive governments.

In 1975 a legal services unit at Dalhousie University, originally established to aid low-income people in one of the most depressed provinces, Nova Scotia, helped to publicize the idea of the CDC nationally by sponsoring a conference to bring together government representatives and informal community leaders. The ostensible focus was on the troubled Atlantic Provinces (Newfoundland, New Brunswick, Prince Edward Island, and Nova Scotia), but the community leaders expressed a feeling that was also recognizable from Quebec to British Columbia. They came to describe their discontent with federal and provincial actions and to report their search for economic alternatives. And they invited me and others to report on what was happening in the United States.

However, Canada had long had its own strong traditions of locally controlled and locally initiated economic development activities. Much more widely than in the United States, producer and consumer cooperatives, had played a central role for economically distressed communities, especially the smaller ones. As a matter of fact, one spur of the Canadian cooperative tradition, the so-called Antigonish movement, had become internationally known. This movement took its name from the tiny town of Antigonish, Nova Scotia, where the extension service of St. Francis Xavier University was the base of a highly successful cooperative organizing effort during the Great Depression. In that period, co-ops were clearly a tool for counteracting the power of economic interests outside each community and indeed outside the province and the country; they were defined as a means of self-determination. Eventually, a reputation for success in building fishing co-ops, credit unions, co-op grocery stores, and so forth, spread abroad, especially to Latin America, and attracted many community activists to study at the university.

Credit unions were even more successful and widespread in

Quebec, where the *caisses populaires,* as people-based banking institutions, provided an essential alternative to English-oriented national banks that turned a cold eye on the credit needs of Francophones. Today the *caisses populaires* represent about $6 billion Canadian dollars in deposits at local institutions. Many other different forms of communal ownership and sponsorship of economic institutions grew up in the provinces of Western Canada. So the idea of a comprehensive development institution like the CDC could find fertile ground in Canada. The Dalhousie conference sought to till that ground.

The significance of this conference for a new Canadian ferment in community economic development probably cannot be overemphasized. For the community group representatives, it was an opportunity to hear of each other's experience and of progress being made by comparable groups in the United States. This kind of interchange is crucial in the early stages of organization for depressed communities, where local things matter so much that it is difficult to relate to distant events. For this reason, the function of leadership in local development includes reaching outside the community to find resources and ideas elsewhere. The Dalhousie conference provided a context for that process of interchange. One conference participant, Father Gregory J. MacLeod, who had studied at Antigonish as well as in European universities, returned home to northernmost Nova Scotia, to Cape Breton Island, to tell his associates that he had discovered the name (CDC) for what they wanted to do. That outside confirmation of their own efforts spurred the Cape Breton group to plan more comprehensively for a broader local program—and later on to take the lead in encouraging CDCs throughout the country by launching the Federation of Community Development Corporations of Canada.

The conference, which provided simultaneous translation in English and French, had a further significance on a national level. As it helped to transcend the national pattern of local isolation because of cultural differences and population dispersal, it also offered the community leaders a chance to teach the federal and provincial government representatives to think in different terms and to bring those terms into the national discourse at Ottawa and the provincial capitals. Indeed, a new federal employment program announced at the conference was eventually stretched to include two community economic development projects as experimental demonstrations—one in the vicinity of Vancouver, British Columbia, and the other in rural Nova Scotia near Antigonish. Still later, some of the same civil service participants at Dalhousie helped design a five-year program of federal support specifically targeted for the community economic development efforts in small towns throughout Canada.

Interestingly enough, the Dalhousie conference paralleled a similar conference in the United States in 1969 that had brought together government and community representatives as well as church and foundation people. That conference also helped to institutionalize the community economics approach and led directly to the formation of a national association of CDCs, now the National Congress for Community Economic Development, which was to formalize and continue the interconsultation process and the government liaison or lobby efforts.

In each country, the participants at these conferences helped to make clear that a common process was taking place in many different settings. The wellsprings of community-based and locally controlled economic development arose from sources within the communities themselves. In each community, local action was preceded by an increasing awareness of deliberate or unconscious exploitation by outside interests, especially outside ownership of the productive institutions and assets of the community. It may not have been immediately clear or precisely formulated in every community, but somehow there was some recognition that absentee ownership means a constant stream of capital being exported in the form of such things as unreplaced depreciation allowances, rents, and profits which are never reinvested locally, so that a cycle of self-reinforcing deterioration takes over.

Mobilized by a sense of outrage at the exploitation, animated by a common identity in sharp contrast to the outside owners, armed with the guiding concept of community-based economics, and aroused to a common purpose, the local community can begin a search for a new beginning through self-determination. I will now illustrate this process by two examples of CDCs, one from the United States and one from Canada. The illustrations will demonstrate a social process but will also show the dependence of that process on real people, who represent the energy and the innovative thrust of their time.

Two Early
Social Inventions

THE HOUGH AREA DEVELOPMENT CORPORATION

MY first encounter with social innovation in a depleted community took place in 1968 when I and a colleague at OEO had the assignment of assessing possible initial grant recipients for the new CDC program. For this purpose we made a site visit to the Hough Area Development Corporation (HADC) in Cleveland, which in the end turned out to be the first grantee under the program. HADC is not the typical CDC, but it certainly represents CDCs that rose out of urban black neighborhoods in the mid-1960s. Because it was a direct response to a riot that had taken place in the Hough neighborhood in 1966, HADC is a dramatic version of what occurs in any depleted community where new resources are found, despite the appearance of disarray and depression.

HADC was formally incorporated in 1967. It arose out of a small district of about 45,000 or 50,000 residents on the black East Side of Cleveland, which was unbelievably dilapidated. In those days, one would want to drive through Hough as quickly as possible, not because of the many idlers standing around on the street corners, but because of the sheer depressive effect of rampant poverty, the crumbling houses, the seemingly uncared-for children, and the overall atmosphere of hopelessness. By 1966, postwar population shifts had changed Hough fundamentally from a stable middle-class or working-class, mostly white neighborhood.

When the riot occurred, Hough was probably about 90 percent black, mostly poor. Even as the poor blacks came to predominate, the overall population decreased in the postwar period by about 36 percent. In 1966 Hough still had some small businesses owned by whites, some of whose proprietors might live there close to their stores. Thus in that time of racial disorders, Hough was one of the earliest to suffer a rampage that targeted white stores but burnt dilapidated black homes as well.

The Reverend DeForest Brown, a local black community leader who had worked with young people as a Neighborhood Youth Corps supervisor, took the stimulus of that terrible time to energize a neighborhood planning council, a leftover of a citywide decentralization plan of some twenty-five years before: The Hough Community Council. The council had been a place for more talk than action, and it was unprepared to take any responsibility for looking to a future after the riot. But Brown had other plans; he was a minister with only a small storefront congregation, but he was a masterful organizer. In 1967 he was elected president of the council, and he set out immediately to revitalize the organization's planning function. He was backed by a wide spectrum of residents who had been informally talking with each other for several months about the need for the black neighborhood to take more responsibility for its own welfare and development. In fact, many had already been galvanized to take action by a voter registration campaign organized by the civil rights group, the Congress of Racial Equality (CORE), that had, in part, been the reason for the recent election of a new mayor, Carl Stokes, the first black mayor of a major American city.

Brown enlisted a broad informal group of local readers to pool their ideas and their energy, and he called the group the Machine, for which he was immediately dubbed the Machine Operator. Given their continuing consultations about the community, it was not surprising that, in the first full meeting of the Machine, members proposed the organization of a nonprofit development corporation that could take on the kind of project activities that the council could not. The council was viewed as a broad political base, with the new corporation as its action arm.

Crucial to this process was the technical assistance of Burt W. Griffin, an unassuming but vigorous and inventive white lawyer who at that time headed Cleveland's Legal Aid Society. On behalf of the Machine, Griffin incorporated HADC, but more important, he offered Brown a post at the Legal Aid Society as a tenant organizer. This post gave Brown both a direct mandate and a salary to continue his community organizing efforts so that he could give up his post at his church. While Brown did the basic job of gathering people together and getting them to share their ideas and visions for a new future, Griffin provided resources from his vantage at Legal Aid—recruiting a young law student from one of Cleveland's most prominent white families to be Brown's administrative assistant and arranging for the assignment to HADC of VISTA volunteer lawyers.

The first project that HADC took on was the planning of scattered-site housing for larger families, building on Brown's tenant organizing work. The plight of the larger families seemed to be most pressing in a district of rotting housing and the continuing outflow of population. The president of one of Cleveland's leading manufacturers privately offered substantial financial support for this project. Meanwhile, HADC also worked up a proposal for economic development planning, crafted by the VISTA volunteers, and submitted it to the federal Economic Development Administration (EDA) for modest funding. The EDA never even responded to their proposal, but our office at OEO learned about the group from a sympathetic low-level EDA staff member. HADC seemed to meet the criteria we had set for a potentially successful demonstration of the new program for CDCs. It was a self-initiated and independent group—not just established to take advantage of a new federal source of money, as so many groups were in those days and for years thereafter. It was broadly representative. Its large board (every member of HADC was then also a member of its board of trustees) included every local influential person in that neighborhood except one. (The hold-out was one minister who had resisted Brown's courting.) The three dozen or so black HADC trustees included a prominent architect, social agency directors, businessmen, and leaders of street gangs, as well as welfare activists. There were Republicans as well as Democrats, and there were political independents. The board was also not simply black; there were two white members—the Legal Aid chief and Brown's administrative assistant. The board thus ran the gamut of political and social representation of class, party, and social philosophy. Surely it could speak for "the community" of Hough. Not only was it clearly a coalition of the black residents, but it obviously had excellent working relationships with prominent white leaders of the city. It was also on good terms with city hall, which we considered to be a real need if a group was to engage in any definitive development projects. Moreover, it had already demonstrated a capacity to carry out its own programming—although, to be sure, its housing project was still early in the works. And finally, for our own agency purposes as well as the requirements of the relevant legislation, the organization operated in a distinctly defined neighborhood where focused efforts could have a visible effect.

During our site visit, my colleague and I discovered impressive leadership—not just the enormous talents of DeForest Brown, but the dedication of other members, such as the architect, the Legal Aid chief, a former numbers runner who was good at figures, and a steady businessman who had doubled as a fence in earlier days. There were others too, whom I came to recognize over time as crucial to the success of the group—although all ceded to Brown the special gift of getting diverse people to work together, and one or two told me that he had already changed their own lives for the better. Clearly, HADC had the internal resources to do the job for its neighborhood.

Within a few weeks, we were assisting HADC to prepare the kind of written proposal that would sail through the bureaucratic hurdles at our agency. But in those days of black-white suspicion, the task was not always easy. Once when my colleague and I had to admit that the agency would retain certain strings (that we personally did not agree with) over the expenditure of the investment capital to be awarded to HADC, we were warned that only our personal opposition to the unavoidable strings would get us out of the neighborhood safely that night. On another occasion, DeForest Brown informed us in the presence of HADC board members that we might as well go home because we were apparently without influence to change that rule—although moments later he privately admitted he had been grandstanding for the benefit of his own colleagues. Brown walked a thin line between public and truculent independence of the Washington bureaucrats and private diplomatic acceptance of our inability to deliver everything that he (and usually we) wanted to happen. He saw his role as the translator of "Black Power" into terms that the white world could accept and the black residents could feel proud about.

A couple months later, DeForest Brown's deputy, Franklin Roosevelt Anderson, who headed CORE at the time, the political group that had promoted voter registration in the Cleveland ghetto, took me to meet a young black nationalist whom DeForest had enlisted in HADC's behalf. This must have been a tough job for DeForest because the nationalist was dead set against the whole white world and saw no reason to collaborate with any arm of it. He was Ahmed Evans, who lived in the adjoining black district of Glenville but also had a base in Hough. Ahmed (as he preferred to be called, rejecting a last name that was too reminiscent to him of the white society) drilled a small band of his followers, young men who learned from him military tactics and avoidance of contacts with the white community. I spoke with him only briefly, and yet he seemed to me to be as mentally troubled as many of the young men whom I used to work with in hospital settings as a psychiatric technician in the army. We shook hands when I left. Later on, Anderson expressed surprise that Ahmed had shaken hands with a white man, but he pointed out that Brown had been "working on him." Then and many times over the years of my association with Hough, I had occasion to realize that DeForest and other leaders of HADC had a deep capacity to relate to people in trouble, as so many Hough residents were on one level or another. To the leaders of HADC, Hough was not just a place they were proud of, despite its depression—it was the home of friends and neighbors, and there had to be an allegiance to anyone who lived there or had a real commitment to the people of Hough, on any level. I think DeForest taught me that too.

The year I came to know HADC was a national election year, with Vice-President Hubert Humphrey running for the presidency against former Vice-President Richard Nixon; and Humphrey chose to announce the million-dollar grant to HADC as part of the kickoff to his campaign just before Independence Day, 1968, in Cleveland, a key city in a key state. HADC therefore formally received its grant as of July 1.

The keystone project in the HADC plan, at that stage, was a very ambitious housing and shopping center development to be called the Martin Luther King, Jr., Plaza. As distinguished from other similar and major projects in other cities trying to rehabilitate depressed areas, this project was to be exclusively an expression of the capacity of the black community. It was to be architecturally designed by blacks (the firm represented already on HADC's board), was to be constructed by black contractors, and was to provide a setting for black-owned businesses. The government funds would make this project possible, despite the reluctance of conventional financing sources to put money into Hough.

But scarcely had the group started to work that July of 1968, when suddenly one day the entire black population of Cleveland seemed ready to rise in rebellion. Ahmed had been drilling his little band of young men in the middle of the street, someone got nervous, the police came, and their action aroused the anger of Ahmed's group, who holed themselves up in a shoot-out with the police. News and rumors of killings on both sides electrified all the black neighborhoods, and fires and other sporadic disturbances began.

I happened to be in Cleveland that evening for interviews with some city officials on the next day—which of course never took place—and that night HADC people came by from time to time to my hotel room, which became a telephone communication point for the HADC people who were engaged in an ultimately successful effort to dampen the fears and disorders in their black community. Through the decision of Mayor Stokes, the HADC leaders were able to get the almost exclusively white police excluded from Hough and the other black districts that night, taking the responsibility themselves for roaming the streets all through the night, calming the young street men who might otherwise have started the fires, lootings, and battles of a major civil disorder. The fact of the matter is that when, in a few days, everything had settled down, it was clear that Hough had been virtually spared any of the usual destruction of that season of riots when, for example, white stores in black neighborhoods were torched and looted and when police trying to protect property were stoned by local residents and shot back at them. In the 1968 trouble, damage had been done in other neighborhoods, but Hough itself had been governed by its own people, and no life had been lost there and little damage was suffered. The trouble had basically been restricted to the Glenville area (separated from Hough by a long, broad finger of parkland), where the Ahmed Evans episode had begun.

It should have been recognized as a success story for local self-determination and self-governance by a community at grave risk. After all, it was well understood in the final report made by the President's Commission on Civil Disorders only a few months earlier that quite often the presence of white police in a racial disorder was more an exacerbation than a means of control. The legislation under which the OEO program for CDCs was authorized specifically sought action to counter "rising community tensions" in black urban settings, and the CDC approach had shown that supporting local black institutions was a valid way to counter those tensions. But in Cleveland, the mayor was pilloried from office by a resentful police force which mobilized others in the white community. Nevertheless, HADC had demonstrated its capacity for community building and moved on to the creation of the King Plaza and other development projects. Later on, when Ahmed came to trial, the metropolitan newspaper (under a pandering and racist editor) accused HADC of complicity and corruption—charges the group was cleared of in a federal investigation. The charges again used up time and resources, but HADC again moved on with its own agenda; and today the Martin Luther King, Jr., Plaza is a reality—an unusual shopping facility on top of which is a small townhouse development with its own green area.

HADC is a story of extremes in outside exploitation and derogation, together with internal disorder and desperation. It is a story that is particular to the times of racial confrontation that marked the 1960s, but the outlines of the same story can be discerned in times of a quieter desperation that nevertheless rumbles to the surface, leading a forgotten community to take on a new life of hope.

New Dawn Enterprises, Ltd.

The home base of New Dawn Enterprises at the northernmost tip of Nova Scotia had never endured the intensity of civil disorder that characterized Hough of the 1960s, but it too, like all CDCs, sprang out of chronic economic crisis that was made intolerably worse by new threats. In this remote Canadian setting, as in the inner city of Cleveland, informal community leaders joined together to find in themselves and in their setting new resources for revitalization. When I first met Greg MacLeod (the major founder of New Dawn) at the Dalhousie conference in 1975, he had such joy and pride in the place and people he came from that I found it hard to believe that he represented a district that was in such severe economic trouble, with chronic unemployment at about 25 percent. Greg was a coal miner's son, a priest, and a professor of philosophy, but most of all he was a community activist who revered his own cultural heritage as a Scotch Catholic and was fascinated by everyone else's background and ethnicity. Very quickly we became good friends and began a long association in which I worked for him and his group on the early stages of their CDC, as well as on issues of organization and project development as the years went on. I too have come to appreciate deeply the people and place that New Dawn works with.

Also in contrast to Hough, the area is one in which most residents, like MacLeod, have had a long history of family connection with the community, and that very history was fundamental to the creation of the CDC. New Dawn was founded in 1976, almost ten years after HADC, in the old industrial city of Sydney, Cape Breton Island, Nova Scotia. More than three hundred years before, Cape Breton had been settled as an outpost of France, but finally in 1763 the English managed to destroy French power, a victory that left behind a lingering bitterness among the French settlers who stayed on. Later, the Scots came as immigrants, leaving behind their own troubles with the English back home. At that time, the late 1700s, Cape Breton was seen by Great Britain as a very minor colony useful primarily as a commercial fishing base; but with the Industrial Revolution, Cape Breton's coal mines brought it to a prominence that was enhanced about the turn of the century by a huge steel plant. The plant profitably combined the ore of nearby Labrador with the coal of Cape Breton. With the steel plant at Sydney and the circle of little coal-mining towns around Sydney, the area came to rival Pittsburgh as the heavy industry center of North America.

However, the major resources were owned, lock, stock, and barrel, by English companies, which extracted rich profits and cared little for the islanders. Bloody industrial disputes in the 1920s solidified the local feelings of exploitation—feelings that today can still swing between a sense of helplessness and a strong urge for self-determination. Eventually, by the 1930s, the workers' demands could no longer be denied, and today Cape Breton is unshakably unionized, with the United Mine Workers and the United Steel Workers being preeminent.

The history and strength of the unions, which were sometimes backed by individual priests and ministers (although the churches were generally not out in front), offered a base during the Great Depression for new efforts at economic self-determination. Upon this base was built a further tradition of cooperatives and credit unions, which began as a weapon against company stores and against the wholesalers' price squeeze on the local fishermen. St. Francis Xavier University, on the Nova Scotia mainland just across the Strait of Canso from Cape Breton, established its extension services on the island, where the cooperative ideas took firm root under the charismatic leadership of Father Moses Coady. Although the structure of co-ops emphasizes benefits to individual members rather than community strength, the co-ops became an institutional tool for community unity.

Nevertheless, Cape Breton probably never really recovered from the Great Depression. The production demands of World War II were only a brief respite from imminent decline, and after the war the strength of industrial Cape Breton was spent. Coal could not compete with oil, and the steel mill was increasingly obsolete, with no reinvestment by the absentee owners. By the 1960s government had moved in to buy up private industry's ruins. Federal and provincial policy at first threw dollars at the problem and then determined that the coal mines, at least, should be phased out. The more profitable steel operations were moved to Halifax. The remainder of the steel industry was allowed to limp along—because no political leader could manage either to take the heat of closing it down completely (an incredibly disturbing prospect for residents even given vocational and other adjustment procedures and allowances) or to justify hundreds of millions of dollars of new government investment. In any event, at that time, with no longer a real industrial base, Cape Breton was apparently supposed to return to farming, forestry, and fishing, with an active tourist sector as a minor fillip. In 1967 the federal government established an agency in the region to deal with its special problems—the Cape Breton Development Corporation, or Devco. It lurched from one development policy to another, with changes in its administration, eventually holding that there was no more need for heavy industry in Cape Breton. Indeed, discriminatory freight rates for shipping had already siphoned off much trade from the deep harbor of Sydney to the interior centers of the Great Lakes and the St. Lawrence Seaway.

The area that is called Industrial Cape Breton—a nine-hundred-square-mile district of small mining towns and villages surrounding and including the core city of Sydney—has a population of about 130,000. The rest of the island (about four thousand square miles) is comprised of 45,000 more residents very sparsely settled on farms and in villages and towns located along the coast lines of the sea and of the great inland body of salt water, the Bras d'Or Lake. The French and Gaelic cultures still survive, but later immigrants have come from virtually every other part of the world, drawn originally of course by the industrial development and its spin-offs.

Cape Breton was an independent colony but in 1867 was joined to the Province of Nova Scotia, a move still challenged by Cape Bretoners, who will at times threaten to secede and join the

United States as another state. Not until the 1950s was the island also joined physically with the rest of the province by a fine causeway that bridges the Strait of Canso and links the island to the peninsula of Nova Scotia proper. However, that causeway, which opened up general access and thus specifically attracted tourists to come to drive the spectacular highway along the sea cliffs of the Cabot Trail, was sometimes looked upon as a mixed blessing. Once, long ago, someone had prayed to God, "Especially do we thank thee, O Lord, for the Gut [Strait] of Canso, Thine own body of water which separateth us from the Wickedness that lieth on the other side thereof. Amen." The prayer is still ruefully if humorously remembered. It is, for instance, framed and hung on the wall at the home of Greg MacLeod.

With such local feeling and history, it is no wonder that in the late 1960s the residents organized their answer to the outside in-itiatives and planning that seemed to be controlling their lives. The federal Department of Regional Economic Expansion had de-cided, in effect, that Cape Breton was a lost cause and that develop-ment efforts should be concentrated several hundred miles away at Halifax, selected as the nearest possible growth center. Devco seemed impotent in the face of this decision. Cape Bretoners needed their own planning group. Spurred especially by activist teachers at the local college—who took Moses Coady as their model—local citizens founded the Metropolitan Alliance for De-velopment, deliberately MAD, for short. They sought, at the least, compensating projects that would cushion the transition crisis of the closing mines. The local college itself was a symbol of demands for local autonomy and the support of local resources. It had been organized originally as a satellite campus of St. Francis Xavier, the church-related university located across the Canso Strait at An-tigonish, but residents, including many of the teachers who had received their undergraduate training at St. Francis Xavier, were insisting on an independent, secular community institution that would get its own funds from the Nova Scotia Department of Education. They did in fact gradually gain full independence; so it was natural for the MAD leaders within the college to spearhead the demand for a major local vocational institute that would sup-port the need for jobs. MAD was successful in this effort and also in reversing a planned federal action to close the national Coast Guard Academy located on the Sydney Harbor. (The academy was to have been moved inland to Ontario, far from the sea.)

These victories were significant, but they also served to focus local attention on the many other economic liabilities of the island, especially the depleted housing stock. It also seemed as if the long unhappy tradition of substandard company housing was somehow being carried forward by the deterioration of the housing stock. So it was that some of the MAD leaders, including MacLeod, ponied up a couple hundred dollars apiece in 1973 to form the Cape Breton Association for Co-op Development and began a range of housing and other real estate projects. Actually, however, preliminary plans in 1972 foresaw not just housing but a variety of cooperative enterprises for which the association would be an umbrella.

The first housing project exemplified the potential for mutually supporting and interlocking benefits in community economic development. It involved the rehabiliation of an old building on the edge of Sydney's commercial section. The first floor was designed for continued commercial use. A store would occupy part of this street-level space, and the Cape Breton School of Crafts would have the rest. The school, backed by association members, included a storefront shop to sell cooperatively the products of local artists and craftspeople. Small apartments, to be rented on the open market, were developed on the second floor. Friendly financing was arranged through the Nova Scotia Credit Union League, federal manpower grants provided wages for disadvantaged workers hired for the construction phase, and professinal design and legal services were contributed by board members, who also personally guaranteed a short-term construction loan that supplemented the mortgage terms. The result was a building that was self-sufficient in rents, even with free rent for the first five years for the crafts school, which was only very modestly financed and could afford little rent. So the community development group ended by owning a self-sustaining asset with an equity value substantially above its total financing; and the community at large had seen a dilapidated commercial structure rescued and put to broadly beneficial use.

To make for more flexible management and promotion of projects like this one, as well as social service programs, the association incorporated itself in 1976 as New Dawn Enterprises, Ltd., aiming at "Business for People." After learning of the U.S. experience at the Dalhousie conference in Halifax, the founders chose a nonprofit structure modeled as a CDC. Within four years,

New Dawn had established a senior citizens' home and three dental clinics—increasing the number of dentists on the island by 15 percent, a major impact when patients routinely waited for one year to get local appointments rather than have to travel to Halifax. It also added or upgraded about 150 units of housing, some at market rates, and some only for low-income families. Rehabilitating other property made it possible to establish and spin off a home for former mental patients. New Dawn also rehabilitated a home that it rented (and eventually sold) to a residential program for the mentally retarded. In the meantime, it also offered a variety of services, usually manned by volunteers, for senior citizens and others. In the course of all this work, New Dawn had drawn into Cape Breton about $4 million in government funds for its own or other projects that spurred local economic activity.

One special emphasis of New Dawn has been the promotion of cultural activities—in addition to the School of Crafts, which serves perhaps one thousand students a year. This New Dawn focus has included folk concerts (in the Gaelic *ceilidh* tradition of a musical party and celebration), the publication of a book of songs by a local musician, Allister MacGillivray, and the publication of another book of local folk songs and compositions by various local musicians. The cultural activities have been intentionally aimed at increasing local consciousness of Cape Breton's cultural traditions and thereby building a stronger community feeling.

THREE

Rethinking the Basic Problem

N EW Dawn Enterprises and the Hough Area Development Corporation are far apart in geography, local tradition, and population. Yet in each setting, in the face of local crises and a history of external exploitation, new resources were created by the residents themselves. And these resources in turn mobilized other resources that carried forward the process of revitalization. Each of these two groups faced what looked like a very different set of problems and chose different solutions. Yet in both instances (and elsewhere in both countries) it should be possible to discern a common pattern, both in the basic problems confronted and in the solutions attempted.

It is not hard to recognize massive economic distress, whether you encounter it in Hough or in Cape Breton or elsewhere. What is hard is to come to the kind of understanding that suggests a practical means of improvement or even prevention. Without that understanding, well-meaning efforts to combat the impoverishment of a community are wasted. I do not know precisely how the leaders of HADC or New Dawn first came to rethink the problems of their communities, but I know that they had to reject certain ideas first and come upon a different way of looking at what was wrong. In this chapter I explore the task of rethinking what the depleted community really is, and I focus on the mystery of the apparent absence or loss of money and capital, which seem so central to such a community. This exploration will more or less represent how community leaders conceptualize the basic problem that they face. It means sidestepping the usual economic ideas.

The outward signs of impoverishment in a community are obvious, whether that community is a rural village, an inner city, or a small town. The first thing that a visitor notices is the physical deterioration. Too many buildings are in poor repair, and so are streets and roads. The civic areas especially can telegraph a lack of care and resources; a public lawn looks mangy and forlorn or a swing in a playground dangles uselessly from one chain; the bench in front of the county courthouse is missing a board. Or retail businesses can be an accurate tip-off—stores are abandoned, with or without a "For Rent" notice, and even those still operating do not seem to keep their commercial signs painted or repaired. And trash seems to be everywhere.

But it is not the physical environment that seems most crucial to an atmosphere of depression. It is the impression that you get of what people's lives are like. Perhaps it is the sight of quite apparently able-bodied people sitting around doing nothing in particular, not because it is their leisure time but because there is nothing in particular to do. There are few jobs and less hope. Walk down the street and strike up a conversation with someone sitting on a front stoop. "Conditions are bad around here," a woman might tell you, and the man sitting next to her on the steps will solemnly nod agreement. In an inner-city area you may see commonplace signs of drug transactions and feel uneasy about footsteps behind you; in a more rural area, people may seem friendlier, but they are perhaps more passively depressed. In either setting, passersby ignore the prostrate alcoholic sleeping it off in a public space. The children often seem so lively and bright-eyed that you cannot believe that they will probably grow up to face the same "conditions around here" and become transformed into the slowed-down adults whom you have just talked to.

The physical and human picture can be unnerving. Either you shrug it off, like Spiro Agnew (Richard Nixon's first vice-president), who once commented blithely, "When you've seen one slum, you've seen them all," and so felt no need to explore the problem further. Or you are galvanized to take some kind of action. Similarly, if you are a local resident, either you take the misery for granted, or you know you have to do something. But if action is to be effective, it is necessary not only to recognize the outward symptoms of the trouble but also to find the key definitions or ideas that must guide any remedial effort. How the basic problem takes shape in your mind will suggest one set of actions and rule out others.

For example, if you call it all "being poor," you start down the well-beaten path of carefully describing the needs of a poor person and how money can change that person's life. That would bring you to such actions as food stamps, or guaranteed annual income, or welfare, disability, and dependency allowances, or other means of direct or indirect transfer payments, such as free (or low-cost) services in health care, housing, nursery schools, and so on. Such direct or indirect money transfers are, of course, absolutely essential for those without the current chance for sufficient work income. For those you think could work if they had a chance, you might also offer vocational training and job counseling and referrals—again on the assumption that the problem lies in the person, who in this case seems to be poor because he is unprepared for employment. All these actions are certainly meaningful ways, and usually required ways, to help those who lack some or all of the basic necessities.

Yet they ignore two facts that together point to an additional necessary set of actions. First, in many areas that you would clearly label as "impoverished"—for example, really poor rural districts in Appalachia, Northern New England, or the Atlantic provinces—many residents will deny their poverty. And there is a certain validity to their claim. After all, they are not much different from most of their neighbors, and that is the way things have always been—hard, not much money, but people have still managed to get along somehow. And so they may reject access to new money as a threat to their sense of themselves. In some instances, the observer must conclude that the residents are basically accepting of their situation, despite what seems to be unacceptable living conditions. In other cases, residents may express deep dissatisfaction but define their needs not in terms of money but in terms of the lack of opportunities within their community, opportunities that money, as such, cannot buy. These may include, for example, a chance for a rewarding job that does not take the person away from his or her community.

The second troubling fact that the personal poverty label ignores is the environment of the poor person. Subsidizing the costs of the basic necessities, including the costs of finding a job, does not change that environment, although it may encourage the person to leave for a better environment. Leaving may indeed be a good solution for any one particular person or family. But the slum remains a slum for those who stay behind, and jobs are scarce for those who remain in a poor area. Actually, people in general do not move easily, and lower-income people move even less easily, for a whole variety of reasons that can be wrapped up in everyone's aversion to breaking off the ties of place and personal relationships that define much of all of our lives. You know this because even when people do move, they are sometimes so bereft that they will take any opportunity to get back home. The most poignant example I know of involves Cape Breton, which has had to export so many of its people to find jobs in other parts of Canada. At one point when the OPEC oil embargo had gone on long enough to predict a fairly long-term rise in the market for coal, the operators of the Cape Breton mines advertised for a score of openings for miners. Now mining is probably the most dangerous of all occupations in terms of serious injuries per hour worked, not to speak of the other disadvantages of the job. Yet about two thousand responses to the advertisement came from all over Canada and even from the United States from former Cape Bretoners applying for a job that would take them back.

It should not be surprising, then, that most poor people naturally continue to live in the impoverishing environment because it is their home, and that fact makes the cost of assistance to them much higher. Higher costs can be due, for example, to the fact that in a poor district the supermarket margins are squeezed to the point of store closure, leaving only the smaller stores with higher prices. In poorer urban areas there are also costs associated with higher crime rates and less police protection. Housing costs are much higher and the quality lower; thus housing allowances do not buy much.

So it is not enough to conceptualize the problem as the person's being poor and therefore in need of one thing or another. In fact, as you wander through a distressed area, your feelings of concern and puzzlement at the recalcitrance of gross economic distress may turn to frustration; in some people, including residents, those feelings can turn to desperation and anger. Those feelings in themselves offer a clue to a crucial reconceptualization: it must not be so much the lack of money as the lack of the human tools— call them psychological, cultural, political, or social tools—to make a basic change in the local circumstances of life and to produce the economic and other opportunities that most residents despair of reaching. It is as if the local people had somewhere along the way lost a vital secret, the secret of how to make things happen the way they need them to happen. It is as if someone had long ago forgotten just where the tools were last laid down; and they have rusted away.

Yet not everyone even in the poorest community feels a lack of capacity to make things change. There are always some who know how to manage somehow, who have the knack of seeing what to do with limited resources, at least for themselves and their family. Some of these people can also communicate their own hope to others so that together they can accomplish something important —plow fields together, organize a block security patrol, even start a business, whatever makes sense to the situation and their joint talents. I think of a middle-aged black woman in southern rural Georgia whom I met because she had been recruited to promote a fledgling CDC I was trying to help. She was excited by the possibility of joint action; she had earlier been active in the civil rights campaign in the area, despite her poverty. I visited her once in her home off a back road. It was spotless but threadbare, and I could see the fields around it through the chinks in the walls. But she managed. She raised a few turkeys, and now and then she would give a baby turkey away to friends who were worse off than she so that they could start a flock themselves and make a little money— and she would teach them. Yet of course her efforts alone could not renew the whole community; others must join in. How much of such human resources a community has and how these fit with the other kinds of resources available can spell the difference in increased productivity and increased satisfaction for a whole community.

To produce change, then, one must promote and facilitate the use of the human and other resources that are already available in the community. However, what makes definitive change so enormously difficult for the community as a whole is the fact that each community, from the richest to the poorest, is constructed out of networks of interlocking forces and institutions that maintain it, that keep it in its recognizable form as that particular community. A community of any economic level may be changing, but it almost always changes slowly enough year to year that it remains recognizable and identifiable to its residents as the same old community. A poor community is thus steadily maintained in its impoverished form by a net of self-reinforcing processes and practices of impoverishment, both in its internal functioning and in its relationships with the surrounding society. Any attempt to change one part of the net is opposed by the other forces shaping the community, keeping it the way it is and neutralizing the attempted improvement.

A strategy for change that selects just one part of the community as a focus for improvement labors under that disadvantage —it is likely to be neutered in the long run by the rest of the community influences. For example, a school administrator or group of parents may focus on increasing expenditures for a shamefully underfinanced school in a very poor community, but their efforts will have limited results when too many students do not have enough breakfast to concentrate on their morning classes. A broader point of view might include a breakfast program in the school, but even that does not deal with the disinterest in school itself when students and their families do not value what the school offers, when in fact what it offers is often irrelevant to their lives. If schooling does not in itself predict a better life, then simply improving the schools will not fundamentally change the poverty of the community and its residents. Some individuals will benefit and will reward their teachers for working with them in an otherwise dispiriting environment, but most pupils will simply slip away into aimlessness.

Somehow, then, any effective strategy has to consider many parts of the net of interlocking community influences and deal with them more or less simultaneously or at least in interconnected phases so that the different parts no longer neutralize improvements but actually reinforce the change. Where does a strategy for change begin to enter in and break up the vicious circle of mutually reinstating forces of impoverishment? The first step, in any case, is to reconceive the basic problem, to recognize that it is not a matter of individual or family poverty but the poverty of a way of life, the way of the community. The second step is to recognize that it is not a lack of money that makes people and their community impoverished, but a lack of the human tools to make the changes that people want. A third step is to recognize that there are many people in the community who represent a relatively underused human resource. And a fourth step is to recognize that trying to make changes has to take into account the community as a system of mutually reinforcing influences—which would mean working for change on many different levels concurrently. Only then can residents and their allies seek and find the best points of leverage within the community that offer opportunities for effective action. At that juncture, it is essential to get a handle on the various kinds of resources that the community has to begin with.

Each community, of course, has a different pattern of available resources, and these resources can be inventoried, so to speak. Conventionally, an inventory produces a local review of what the economist calls the "factors of production": land (including all other natural resources, such as coal, standing forests, and so on); labor (including not only numbers of potential workers, but categories of skills); capital (including both the dollars that are accessible for new investment purposes and the usable results of previous investments, such as buildings, highways, manufacturing equipment, and so on); and the managerial and entrepreneurial resources (that is, the people who can put the other factors together, facilitating the creation and exchange of goods and services). A useful inventory will include a classified list of the major local businesses and industries (including, of course, agricultural and other productive activities not usually thought of as industries). Possibly that list would even contain some major businesses that had been closed in the recent past.

To have a grasp on all this information about a local area is to have a powerhouse ready to be put to use in making decisions about local development, but such an inventory has omitted a critical category of resources. It ignores the category of social, cultural, and psychological tools that residents of a community already have or must have in order to make things happen. A locality may, for example, have significant coal resources, people to mine the coal, access to capital and managerial resources, a ready market, and so on, but still not be prepared to exploit all those factors simply because the social and psychological tools of the community do not include those that permit or promote putting all the factors together.

For example, both the Navaho and the Cheyenne, on reservations in the United States a thousand miles apart, have resisted the exploitation of coal resources on their lands. Another instructive example concerns a band of the Micmac Indians, whose reserve, located on the Bras d'Or, a huge inland salt water lake in the center of Cape Breton, includes an uninhabited island in the lake. Canadian federal officials once offered the band large sums of money for them to develop the island themselves as a marina and an Indian village attraction for tourists. This project could have brought desperately needed jobs and income to a band that exists almost solely on welfare payments. The economic development officials could not understand when the band representatives refused the aid, saying that they wanted the beauty of the island left in its original state. The island was, in fact, an annual gathering place of all Micmacs for traditional and religious ceremonies. Of course, not all the Micmacs felt that the aid should be rejected, and that had encouraged the government officials to press their proposal, but to no avail.

The case of the Micmacs illustrates some crucial issues. It certainly points up the potential for critical differences in perspectives on what is presumed to be usable but unused in the resources of the community. Outsiders may argue that coal should be mined, forests harvested, or whatever, but local residents may feel that the resources are being properly used for what they are—to them. And each side may have internal opposition and external allies. Ignoring the cultural tools by which the community lives can be critical because those tools define what "economic" resources are and how they will be used.

The ideas, attitudes, preferences, and values embodied in the local perspective are expressed in the institutions of the community that produce the decisions on development—that is, decisions on changes that are crucial to reversing the impoverishment of the community. Thus for Native American communities, attitudes toward land and its use and the institution of a tribal council as a way of making decisions to give voice to and implement those attitudes are essential parts of the inventory. The residents' consideration of their own priorities and the deliberate evolution of a program and of local institutional equipment for achieving and protecting those priorities are an essential part of the process of local change. This is true not only because it should be, from the democratic point of view, but because change will not last or even occur at all without it.

I do not want to give the impression that the category of social, cultural, and psychological tools is important only for the unusual situation, such as a Native American community. The Micmacs of Cape Breton are not the only ones there who are ambivalent about opening up their communities to tourists. I have heard other Cape Bretoners, non-Indians, complain, even if partly in humor, about any pressure to attract tourists, though that would mean jobs and income for the residents. "No, indeed," they will say, "the summertime is so beautiful here; that's when our relatives come back to visit; we want to enjoy ourselves then, not be running around taking care of tourists." Again, of course, not everyone thinks that, but there is enough of that perspective so that the possibilities of the tourist sector are not exploited.

To repeat, the existing array of institutional tools—the organizations and accepted practices by which the community carries on its life and looks to its future—offers the opportunities for change as well as the likelihood for stability; in that array are also the community's despair and its uncertainty. It behooves one, therefore, to recognize the wide range and influence of that array of local cultural, psychological, and social tools. The significant practices include such matters as the accumulation of capital, which will vary enormously. In some communities, it is most usual to accumulate capital in the form of race horses; in others it is dairy cattle or savings deposits or burial insurance policies. Other critical practices will include the techniques for local decision making, even if the local technique is to default and leave things to outside decision makers. One would want to include the ways that education and other training are regarded and carried out at or outside the home. Of course, there are also all the provisions for the basic necessities of food, clothing, and shelter. Such provisions may mean importing both the money and the materials for food, as occurs in a so-called welfare-check economy in an area where people do not raise their own food, there are no farms, and no one has a garden. Or the provisions for the basic necessities may depend upon earning money and food imports by exporting labor, having residents migrate or commute for work with the expectation that they will send or personally bring money back home.

Organizations exist for carrying out these practices—organizations like racetracks, church schools, farmers' Saturday markets, employment agencies, courthouses, the local branch of an international bank, bed and breakfast tourist homes, technical institutes, shopping centers, and so on. All these organizations express the priorities and preferences of the local community with more or less accuracy and with more or less satisfaction for all concerned. They also embody the effective or creaky mechanisms by which the community can be mobilized. On the one hand, depressed communities will exhibit a set of social tools for self-maintenance and stability even if that stability means a status quo of impoverishment. On the other hand, such communities may nevertheless manifest some potentially important resources for change in their institutional equipment. Yet for all such communities, poverty resides in the impoverishment of their social equipment as well as their economy. Thus one cannot take for granted that given some new resource—say, an offer of government funds—a community will have the tools to use it.

A careful and self-conscious review of the institutional practices of the community often redefines what seems to be an economic problem as really being a problem in some other aspect of the community—say, the pattern of decision making embodied in local institutions. For example, it is ordinarily assumed by outsiders and humbly accepted by residents of low-income areas that the forgotten community has an economic problem in that it has little or no capital for investment and that somehow the essential capital must be brought in. This idea, of course, puts the community at the mercy of the demands of the suppliers of outside capital—the requirements attached to a government grant or to a multinational's investment. Thus, the definition of the local problem as economic—lack of capital—helps to reinforce the depletion of the community. It even depletes the community's sense of its own capacity. Yet reviewing the situation in the light of institutional patterns of decision making could reveal the problem as something quite different, when one examines, for instance, the decision patterns that govern making a loan in that locality. Research can make it abundantly clear that the so-called low-income area generates considerable savings (that is, available capital), but that these savings are often being deposited in institutions whose decisions do not include local investment. In short, there is available capital, but it is conventionally exported to other localities.

A prime example of the export of capital is the bank practice of redlining for home mortgages. This practice takes its name from banks or other lenders drawing a symbolically red line around a district to indicate that no mortgages should be made for structures within that district because presumably money can only be lost on such loans. The bank will have a branch in the district to collect savings but will not channel any money back for local mortgages. Naturally, when no mortgages are available to buy and fix up a home in that district, properties decline further, making them a worse risk for investment. The redlining practice is one of those very effective reinforcements of the impoverished community. A government policy of pumping more cash into the pockets of residents of that district would not make a change in the housing of the area if the improved savings continued to go to the same banks with the same practices. The solution to redlining is either to set up a new savings institution that will reinvest locally or else somehow to bring about new institutional practices in the existing banks. Low-income communities have successfully (and unsuccessfully) used both techniques. Establishing a community development credit union is one example of the technique of creating an effective new institution; in the United States, using the force of the federal Home Mortgage Disclosure Act and the Community Reinvestment Act against offending banks is an example of forcing improvement in existing institutions.

Redlining is a fairly dramatic example of how an economic problem can be recognized as a social and political problem, an institutional problem. But there is a whole class of similar and less visible institutional practices that inhibit the local use of local capital resources, and these can vary from one setting to another.

In Canada, for example, in contrast to the United States, bank branch managers typically do not have authority to make substantial loans; they must refer decisions to their central office. Even if the district is not subject to some kind of redlining, consider the impact on the forgotten communities of, say, Kent County in the Province of New Brunswick when loan requests there are referred a thousand miles or more away to the headquarters of the Bank of Montreal or the Toronto-Dominion Bank. The impact of this institutional pattern is widespread, because five large national banks dominate the whole of Canada; they are represented by branches in every fair-sized community, low-income or otherwise; and it is not legally feasible to establish a competing commercial bank. It should be no surprise, then, that community-based credit unions as a counterinstitution play a much more important role in Canadian communities than in the United States, even though Canadian credit unions are legally restricted from some of the essential activities in which commercial banks can engage.

Again, however, decentralization of decision making to a bank branch office is not necessarily a solution to making local capital available locally. When the branch is in a district with a high proportion of some ethnic or racial minority of which the branch officers are not members and have little understanding, loan practices can restrict the flow of capital simply on that basis. Black loan applicants dealing with loan officers in a black ghetto face that problem. In an examination of capital in U.S. black ghettos, Theodore L. Cross recalls a Hartford, Connecticut, banker's comment "that he had never known a Negro in whom he had confidence for more than a three-hundred-dollar loan." That sentiment is probably extreme today. But if the problem is not strictly prejudice against the minority, it may be simply a lack of familiarity with a particular way of life that does not fit the bank manager's idea of a good loan customer. This is a matter of psychological and cultural perspectives.

In Western Canada in the central city of Winnipeg, the population is increasingly low-income and heavily minority—especially Native American. The inner city there is today a public sector economy: that is, private sector activities have shrunk to a minimum. There are more than one hundred service organizations, supported by public funds, that are targeted to the inner-city population and its problems. The economy is built upon transfer payments to individuals. How will the branch manager from Toronto (much less the Toronto office itself) judge the propensity for good loan behavior among such potential customers? It is simply much easier to reject or discourage the local residents. And yet welfare recipients, as such, can be excellent and dependable borrowers. Low-income credit unions have demonstrated that fact. The task for the loan officer with low-income applicants, as with others, is to assess each applicant individually and to make a judgment based upon the criteria that are applicable. However, for those without knowledge and experience of the ethnic or social group involved, applying the criteria may be either impossible or potentially so time-consuming that the applicant is swiftly rejected. The problem is not the loan worthiness of the applicant, but the patterns of relationships between the lending institution and the population it would serve.

Up to this point I have ignored the usual concepts of economic development—the measures of gross national product, average family income, and so on—and have emphasized instead social and psychological elements. The process and assessment of economic development at the community level are in fact not so much matters of hard economic data and statistics than of the psychological, cultural, and institutional characteristics of the community. For practical purposes, economic development is not the promotion of increases in gross national product or median family income or average per capita income or savings rates and investment capital or any of these usual indicators that people are accustomed to think about when they consider this idea. Instead, economic development is the creating and strengthening of new and available social tools in a community.

This very different formulation of economic development arises when one is forced to look into the issues and problems of a local economy, the economy of a small rural district or of an inner-city neighborhood, a community economy. Suddenly the abstract ideas of conventional economic goals—cast as they are in terms like *average family income* or *gross national product*—shrink in meaning. Confronting the tasks of local economic development discloses that the terms do not mean enough in practical activity.

It is true that the conventional terms and goals do describe some possible positive results of development, but even as ways to describe some useful results they leave much to be desired. For example, you could raise the average family income quite a bit in a small neighborhood by importing a few millionaires and some other wealthy people and putting them in expensive, high-rise, multiunit condominiums on the choicest and most scenic site in the neighborhood. Indeed, that solution has been pursued in the past—most notably in the disastrous West End urban renewal project in Boston in the mid-1950s. It finally produced nice, tall, new, expensive buildings looking out on the Charles River, but there was a lot of psychiatric debris from that tear-it-all-down-and-then-build-it-up-again project. The people who were uprooted from the business and family flats that were destroyed to make room for the high-rises suffered from the resulting emotional disorders. Another example of misconstrued measures would be improved revenues from a county's main agricultural product upon the introduction of a new seed strain. The new revenues can increase the local GNP ("gross neighborhood product") and yet make no particular impact upon the incomes of the families working on the corporate farms in the county, for the revenues would redound only to the corporations. Clearly these results are not what the local leaders have in mind when they talk about community economic development.

Fortunately, most local leaders who are trying to mobilize their neighbors do not have to unlearn a misleading vocabulary and set of presuppositions. They come to the problems and eventually to their own definitions from their immediate experience, so it is easier to formulate the definitions in ways that fit real life. For the professionals in the field of economic development, it is a different matter; and the technical and professional evolution of economic development as a general field and of community economic development in particular depends upon jettisoning the conventional perspective. The experience, both successful and unsuccessful, of local community economic development programs will be helpful for building up a foundation of new conceptualizations and strategies; but it will also be necessary to take a good hard look at the usual and conventional ideas and strategies to see what is lacking in them.

FOUR

Some Mistaken Strategies

I N the past the conventional practice of local economic development has been based upon certain ideas about proper strategy—which, upon careful examination, turn out to be wasteful, illusory, or worse. They are, however, so well ensconced in the field that it is difficult to avoid them. I want to review some of these strategic ideas to sensitize the reader to the dangers they pose. I will also describe the efforts of community groups that have gone counter to the conventional view, because their stories can encourage others who might otherwise worry about bypassing the established ideas.

The most discouraging of all the conventional policies of economic development is a concept that can be called "economic triage." The term *triage* in its original use denotes a policy for battlefield medicine by which limited supplies of drugs or other medical treatment resources are channeled to a specific class of the wounded who are, for military purposes, the most important to conserve. The primary criterion is who will be most likely to survive to go back to battle. However, there can be variations on that criterion. For example, as a trainee in the U.S. Army Medical Corps in 1951, I was instructed that medical assistance should go first to officers and then to enlisted men. Depending on the particular military situation, there can be other categories of priority, such as scarce technical specialists. Thus, for example, I understood from an army nurse in the Vietnam war that helicopter pilots were a priority category.

Analogously, in both Canada and the United States the federal governments have in the past staggered along under a so-called development growth policy that has channeled limited economic development funds to "growth centers," that is, to areas considered more promising than other nearby areas. In Canada the policy was so extreme that rural residents of a district or village defined as a lost cause by federal and provincial standards were asked to move to the nearest growth center—to give up their communities and, with relocation grants, choose a more viable place to live.

Quebec, New Brunswick, and Newfoundland were the scenes of perhaps the most egregious instances. In the 1960s, the fisherfolk of Newfoundland, for instance, were exhorted by their premier to "burn your boats." The government offered to buy up coastal village homes, lands, and the fishing boats as an impetus for residents to move to a growth center like St. John's. The Quebec case had a long history. In the 1930s the Quebec provincial government had urged settlement in the backlands of eastern Quebec by the unemployed of the larger cities; and in fact thousands of people settled, built cabins, and carved small farms out of the wilderness. Then, in the 1960s, the settlements were told that they should be abandoned. The provincial government decreed that the villagers would get $10 to $15 an acre for their farms so long as they burned their homes (or moved them to an approved location near a growth center), never to return. Those who did not take up the option found that they were refused participation in Quebec's standard farm loan progam—which they had used in the past. The doomed areas were not to be given any further resources.

Of course, not all the villagers accepted the government planners' verdict on their lives, but it was not until 1970 that organized resistance began, after ten villages had disappeared and many others had been decimated. In two years one arm of the resistance grew into a development cooperative under the initials J.A.L., derived from the names of the participating villages, St. Juste, Auclair, Lejeune, and Lots Renverses. Galvanized by the pressures from the provincial government, J.A.L. began starting new businesses in forestry and agriculture to provide a future for residents who did not want to move. Other villages began their own groups. Eventually a confederation of such local development groups was established to provide mutual support and technical assistance for the new businesses that they were founding. Today the provincial and federal governments gingerly accept the local initiative and provide support for these projects.

In the United States, by contrast, the economic triage idea did not focus on rural removal; instead it has been epitomized in urban removal projects. In such instances, effective resistance was impossible. Thus, in the mid-1950s, in Boston's West End, for example, the whole neighborhood was simply leveled; the experts thought it was too difficult and too poor to rehabilitate. Instead it was rebuilt for a wealthy class. The previous residents might or might not get relocation allowances; in any case, the allowances could not compensate for the disruption of their lives and neighborhood relationships. Simply from the financial standpoint, according to research cited by Herbert Gans in his study of the West End, the average uncompensated dollar loss for displacement in the U.S. urban removal practice was the equivalent of from 20 to 30 percent of a year's income. Moreover, in the West End, interviews at the time of relocation documented "an extensive amount of grief and depression shortly after moving," and two years later, repeat interviews showed that a "majority had suffered emotionally... and almost everyone was... paying considerably more rent."

Whether the policy makers in these situations were oblivious of the human and financial costs for uprooted residents or simply calculated that they were worth it for the benefits to be achieved elsewhere is a moot point. In any case, as one U.S.-government-sponsored project put it, "Although the natural preference is to orchestrate vigorous growth, a concurrent and essential function [of government economic development programs] is to supervise an orderly decline, especially of those areas lacking the necessary human and physical resources." "Necessary" in whose eyes? And for what purposes? As the J.A.L. group demonstrated, local people will have a different perspective on what is needed, and of course they do not want to be supervised into an orderly decline.

In 1965 the U.S. government specifically "embraced a concept of growth centers [embodying] ... a trickle-down approach" for surrounding distressed communities, as Levitan and Zickler report. By 1972, surveys showed that there was no spillover effect on the depressed areas, but the same policy continued to be maintained by Congress and the Economic Development Administration. Paradoxically, there was a concurrent political pressure to extend the eligibility for economic development assistance to the vast majority of *all* U.S. counties, with the result that federal funds were as dissipated as they were dispersed.

The problem with economic triage is not that there has to be some priority (heartless or otherwise) in the distribution of limited resources. The problem is that such priorities ignore the fundamental technical lack in the distressed community: the lack of internal tools for revitalization and for increased productivity. The organizations or institutions that allow residents to concentrate their energies and focus their efforts in the use of financial capital resources, for example, may have disappeared, or they are simply weak; or perhaps they were never there in the first place because their functions were not needed before or because the functions were handled by outside organizations and institutions that no longer operate in the community's interest or perhaps no longer even exist. From a policy standpoint, the issue is not how to disperse the population, disband the community, and destroy the tools that do exist, but how to encourage the creation and evolution of new tools. How can new organizations and institutions be established? That is, how can new tools be designed that are appropriate to the changed conditions and to the particular pattern and set of resources already in place—meager as those may seem in the eyes of some outsider?

A second misguided idea holds that economic development is primarily and even solely business development. On the basis of this misapprehension, popular but wasteful local strategies have been designed. These strategies have received so much support from outside the struggling communities themselves that the communities are lulled into believing they are efficacious. The strategies might be called the "beggar-your-neighbor policy," the "boost-your-city campaign," the "big-bang theory," and the "high-tech gamble."

If the *basic* solution to the problem of economic development is mistakenly assumed to be new businesses, then it is understandable that some communities and state or provincial officials will promote the *beggar-your-neighbor policy*. The game here is to help your own area by stealing an industry or facility from another area—or at least by persuading the target company to start a new facility in your locale rather than in someone else's town. Everything is assumed to depend upon getting new business to locate in the community, and almost anything is acceptable as a way of making this happen.

A poignant example of this strategy was well publicized in 1982, when Muncie, Indiana, and Springfield, Illinois, competed for a new truck-manufacturing facility. Each city courted the company with a string of financial incentives, including tax reductions and customized factory sites, as well as with brochures, dinners, trips, consultants, and so on, touting all its possible advantages and denigrating the attractions of the competing site. And, of course, in the end only one of them could win the campaign. The other had spent its treasure to no avail.

The usual location-incentive techniques fly in the face of strong evidence that has been around for many years that, in fact, outside companies generally do not make decisions on the basis of free factory sites, tax reductions, and so on. On the economic dimension, labor costs are probably most important, and they account for the export of jobs from the United States and Canada to places like Taiwan and Hong Kong. Harrison and Kanter thoroughly reviewed the location-incentive picture in terms of both economic theory and the available empirical evidence from studies of tax and other concessions. They conclude "that there is neither theoretical nor empirical support for the belief that interstate business incentive differentials make an important difference to the decisions of firms with respect to relocation, expansion, or start-up of new facilities." They continue: "Yet the policies continue to be used—even when officials admit that they are unlikely to create jobs. What can explain this apparent inconsistency? Is it just a stubbornly irrational attachment to an outworn conventional wisdom? Or [is it something] . . . which conventional economic analysis cannot grasp?" In the end they speculate that, since it appears that the concessions are urged by industry leaders who avail themselves of them only for an occasional mere windfall advantage, the location incentive is simply an income transfer plan for major corporate businesses after they have already made their location decision.

The *boost-your-city approach* is the hype variety of the location-incentive strategy. Talking up local advantages and feeling good about them is supposed to make a difference. Certainly, local pride is an ingredient of economic development, but putting "I Love New York" on bumper stickers and book bags, for example, is not what got New York City back from the verge of bankruptcy.

Boosterism was an enthusiasm especially popular during the Great Depression. As a child in those days, when my own father was out of work for some time, I remember when people came by our house begging not just for money but for a sandwich or anything to eat. At about this time, we children were being taught in school to sing a new song praising our city. Getting someone to write that song and then getting everybody to sing it was supposed to get our depressed city going again. But local economic development does not and cannot depend upon a business location strategy with a hype dimension. Companies looking for a new location will be glad to know that the potential new community base has a sense of self-esteem, but again that is not in itself how the location decision is made.

Interestingly enough, there is good evidence that the location decisions of manufacturing industries are influenced especially by the quality-of-life concerns of the managers and their families, those who will be making the decision about relocating. I was once told of a dramatic case in which a Canadian community did not get a certain new facility when the wife of the chief manager-to-be complained that there would be no ballet instruction for their daughter. The facility was thereupon located where ballet was more accessible.

Another recent example of such considerations is the choice of the small coastal town of Salisbury, Maryland, as a site for a new facility for the world's largest aerospace company, Grumman Corporation. "Quality of life" was the prime concern, and the company received no special concessions or incentives. *Expansion Management,* a magazine for expansion-minded companies, reported: "In addition to considering where it thought [about three dozen transferring] employees would want to move, Grumman sought to locate near quality educational facilities for the employees' children and for technical personnel to further their training. It also looked at state taxes, trends of those taxes, available housing at reasonable costs, competitive wages, and where pools of labor were located." In addition, the company received assistance from the state of Maryland: 50 percent of the cost of eighty hours of training for some of its three hundred production employees. Since this state aid (routinely available to all expanding or new companies) probably amounted to less than $4000, it was obviously not a significant incentive. Clearly the main attraction was the community—"a striking resemblance to the Long Island of 30 years ago [where the company had originally been located] was the deciding factor."

The salience of such attitudes in corporate decision makers should alert a community to the broader and more sophisticated view of local development, which involves much more than financial incentives for new outside businesses. In short, it raises the question of the kind of community in all its features that will have to be developed in order for it to be a more productive and satisfying place to live—in accordance with local priorities and preferences.

By contrast, another approach, the *big-bang theory*, ignores all the mysteries of location choice and assumes merely that an extra large new facility of some kind is the basic solution to a distressed area's needs. The superindustry is supposed to encourage the creation or growth of other businesses for its support and its supplies and for satisfying the shopping needs of the work force employed at the facility. Unfortunately, the explosive local expansion from a big-bang project—a huge refinery, a high dam, a pipeline, a military installation, or whatever—all too often spells disaster for the unprepared community, and no community can be prepared for the abrupt change of the massive development project. Whatever the indices of social pathology were before, they now increase with the sudden influx of population attracted by the facility. Crime, alcoholism, and family disintegration are some of the results; others include a strained municipal budget that cannot rise fast enough to accommodate the need to construct new public services and facilities such as sewers, schools, or water systems. A recent example is what happened to Aberdeen, Scotland, when North Sea oil offered it the opportunity to install big refineries. The city expanded swiftly in population and local sales, but it also expanded swiftly in crowded housing, crime, and violence. In a more general case, Santa Barbara, California, discovered by a careful study that any new industrial facility would cost it more in necessary new services than would be offset by the improved tax base represented by the facility.

Such examples do not describe the other destructive results of big-bang projects—for example, when a new power-generating dam must obliterate whole villages as the resulting reservoir builds up. There is also the vulnerable dependency of the locale on the major facility, spelling another kind of disaster if the facility closes down or must be saved from closure only at great cost. Such is the history of two heavy water plants, government-sponsored facilities, on Cape Breton Island. They were maintained for years only at a huge loss during a severe decline in the demand for the special nuclear fuel they produced; finally they were shut down in a sudden surgical cut that devastated the two home communities.

In general, dependence upon government installations, such as a military camp, makes the community vulnerable to a government economy drive, especially when the installation probably was not necessary in the first place but was built as a political measure. But neither is a major private enterprise any insurance against closure. A corporate facility will also be shut down as an economy measure, not because it is not profitable but because it is not making a large enough profit and by corporate calculations thereby exceeds target opportunity costs. This is a good illustration of how little importance is placed on the marginal benefits of tax incentives. In Cape Breton, the private owners of the Sydney steel facility pulled out because their disinvestment had finally made the facility unprofitable and the offer of massive tax incentives was no inducement to stay. But even when a corporation tries to hold on, dependency can be dangerous. Take the case of Peoria, Illinois, and its mainstay, the Caterpillar company. The decline of that company over the past few years has meant catastrophic unemployment in Peoria.

The tiny township of Sebastopol, Ontario, has the dubious distinction of having to withstand first a government close-out and then a private pull-out from the same installation. With a total population of about 550, in a seven-township area of about 3000, Sebastopol was the site of an army radar base, housing several hundred military personnel. The base made an annual subsidy payment in lieu of taxes to the municipality, as well as offering many employment opportunities to the surrounding civilian population. Moreover, the military's own recreational facilities were open to local residents. But in 1975 the base was suddenly shut down, and its facilities were sold off to an outside private developer. The local residents thought the sale meant a new beginning for the area because the developer envisioned a four-season tourist facility and started building retirement homes. However, within a couple of years the developer disappeared, leaving a tangle of debts and unpaid taxes that virtually bankrupted the area. A CDC was organized eventually by the local residents, but it proved to be overwhelmed by the enormity of the rescue task.

In all these cases, by placing reliance upon major outside resources, the community diminishes itself in the sense that such dependency downgrades what the community can do for itself. In a depleted community, residents experience a greater sense of their own helplessness, a defensiveness and hopelessness which is a crucial part of the problem.

In another strategic misadventure, communities place bets on high tech—that is, on creating locally a new Silicon Valley. All the problems inherent in locating and attracting major new industry are compounded by focusing local business development goals on a single industrial sector. The *high-tech gamble* begins with the unwarranted assumption that society is moving in one particular direction and that the community must also ride that way if it is to succeed. This misguided theory of local economic development depends upon the basic fallacy that the economic future is a direct result of new kinds of industry, especially manufacturing industry.

Actually, placing bets on high tech is as risky in the local economy as it is in the stock market. To begin with, high tech equals high risk, because the shakeout stage after fast growth is usually associated with some pretty fast retreats. The volatility of new technologies is demonstrated in the spectacular failures of some early success stories in the computer industry. For a distressed locality to choose this means for development is foolhardy, especially since the critical mass that makes a Silicon Valley is not something that can be planned in a replicable pattern. The high-tech strategy is probably best suited to an area that already has significant high-technology resources. That fact immediately cuts out the kind of distressed community that must plan a strenuous economic development program. And as an addendum, I would point out that many of the jobs created by the electronics and computer industry are low in mobility and pay, scarcely better than that of the fast-food employee.

All these strategic illusions are based upon the preconception that vigorous growth of new or expanded businesses is the immediate solution to a lagging economy, because the businesses will create jobs for local residents. That idea can be so totally wrong that it can be potentially disastrous. An illustration comes from a consultant, Avrom Bendavid-Val, who was asked to aid a small New England town in its local economic development effort. He reports his experience in his monograph on planning:

> The principal goal of the [local economic development] effort was "to reduce unemployment substantially." To this end, the town leaders proposed to create an industrial park on municipally owned acreage. They planned to launch an industrial attraction

campaign based on the inducements of nominal rents, financing benefits, the natural beauties of the area, and a nearby Interstate Highway interchange soon to be completed. The result, they hoped, would be the location of new industry in the park that would create jobs for their jobless. On closer examination, however, it turned out that the core of the unemployment problem was associated with an unprecedented immigration into the area over the past decade. It had become fashionable among urban young people to move to rural communities like this one, and many did so figuring that in due course they would find a means of support. Many eventually did settle in. Many eventually left the area. But many lingered on, receiving "transfer payments" from relatives, finding odd jobs, availing themselves of various forms of social assistance, and somehow making ends meet while maintaining the registered status of "unemployed." The population of the area was small enough that these people had a significant impact on local unemployment statistics.

The strategy that the community was contemplating represented a large investment. It would alter the community environment dramatically and would preclude other uses for the community-owned property for all time. The major part of the unemployment problem, however, was likely to be passed over by such a strategy. The people who constituted the problem were not likely to accept factory jobs in great numbers in any event; not for that had they chosen a rural life style. On the contrary, new factory jobs in the area were likely to attract significant numbers of job seekers from elsewhere; and should one or a number of the factories founder in a few years, a much more serious local unemployment problem would be created. Yet, as a means of achieving the stated goal, the [industrial mall] strategy made sense on the face of it. [However,] had the goal been stated as "Accomplish the rapid economic assimilation of jobless immigrants," a very different strategy—perhaps emphasizing job-skill matching, counseling, small business assistance, training, and so on—might have suggested itself.

If the idea of economic development as some kind of business development proves to be a misguided oversimplification, then just as misguided is the idea that local economic development will depend upon macroeconomic statistics of population growth, the supply of raw materials, and so on, which generate per capita income, gross national product, and the like. That idea generates what might be called the "larger view," another strategic perspective that can mislead local economic development. That view sees economic development primarily as a product of major uncontrolled forces at loose in the nation and in the world. Thus it suggests the importance of studying birth control factors, budget deficits, world interest rates, balance of payments, the demand for major commodities such as wheat, coffee beans, pork bellies, or oil, and so on. Intellectually, there are very good reasons, of course, to recognize the influence of such factors, but focusing on them offers few clues for local action.

No one should deny that the health of the national (or international) economic environment will to some extent constrain a community's own economic health. Good citizens of any community should concern themselves with the macroeconomic forces of the world for that reason alone—and offer their own views and demands to the policy makers in the wider arenas of economic life. However, even in the face of discouraging economic environments, local communities must and do find local means to improve and stabilize their own condition. They cannot wait for the effects of population controls, International Monetary Fund conferences, deficit reduction, and the like. They need to mobilize their own resources in ways that fit the opportunities accessible to them.

Point St. Charles, squeezed between the St. Lawrence River and the Lachine Canal, is one of the most depressed areas of Montreal. Over 40 percent of its fourteen thousand population, mixed Francophones and Anglophones, are on welfare or other transfer payments, and even the official unemployment rate is 15 percent. Abandoned industrial sites, relics of a long-gone railroad center, epitomize both the problem and a potential resource of this neighborhood. A coalition of neighborhood organizations, Programme Economique de Pointe St. Charles (PEP), decided in 1984 that they must take their destiny in their own hands because neither the city nor the province nor the federal authorities had any ideas on programs that would create the permanent jobs and the opportunities for local improvement that are desperately needed. Yet PEP had to begin a revitalization program within a national economy that was faltering badly and within an international recession that would only get worse before it could get better.

Residents of Point St. Charles had no quick solutions to their dilemma; they knew only that they had to begin a search for their own way. The first opportunity they made use of was the leverage offered by an upcoming provincial election; in this context their request for funds for an inventory study from the provincial government met a swift and favorable reception. With this grant they set out to establish a program for revitalization that would build on what resources they could recognize in accordance with the prime goals of the community, as these would come to be formulated along the way. The impending provincial elections might be called the "trigger opportunity" that launched the Point St. Charles Program, now already into small business technical assistance and loans, among other activities.

The trigger opportunity need not be the accessibility of a government grant. It may be a change in attitude or leadership in an outside private institution affecting the community. That was the beginning history of Boston's Roxbury Action Program (RAP). RAP began in 1969 with a few thousand dollars diverted from a regional church group that felt it ought to encourage black self-reliance instead of just administering programs for needy black people. With this seed money, RAP went on over the years to lever private investment capital for a multimillion-dollar housing rehabilitation and construction program for its mostly low-income black neighborhood. Even during hard times, RAP was able to generate the necessary financial backing in the private sector to carry out its work—although that success did not prevent it from also seeking and obtaining state government money as well.

Local efforts, as I have mentioned, will inevitably be constrained by the larger economic environment of the country, and RAP's experience was no exception. For example, in 1975 the threat of New York City's bankruptcy started a chain of events that for years delayed RAP's largest housing construction project. RAP was on the verge of obtaining a low-interest mortgage commitment for its project from the Massachusetts state housing finance authority when the repercussions of New York City's troubles hit the financial markets all over the country. Interest rates on state and municipal bonds responded with sharp increases, and the Massachusetts state housing finance agency was not immune to the tidal wave. It too began to have to pay more interest on the bonds it issued; and as a consequence it required a higher interest from its own borrowers. RAP simply could not make its low-income housing project work financially on the higher interest. Thus the project had to be put on hold for many months while architectural design changes and other cost-cutting measures were considered. In the meantime, other local problems intervened, so that it was years before the centerpiece of RAP's neighborhood revitalization plans could be built. Nevertheless, the initial problem certainly stemmed from economic environment events over which RAP had no control whatsoever.

At the same time, whatever the complications from outside economic forces, a community economic development program cannot and need not await improvement in the national economy. One part of the program might be delayed or even lost, but no local revitalization program is made up of a single project. In RAP's case, the organization moved on a wide range of other issues and projects in its overall program, including a pharmacy, a grocery store, a food stamp distribution center, and social programs both for the elderly and for the young people of the neighborhood. Only years later was RAP's major housing project finally completed, a tribute to their persistence in the face of many obstacles.

The genius of local efforts, as I try to document throughout this book, is to find ways to get around the constraints of an unfriendly environment, both internal and external to the community. When the resources arise out of the local people, the community-based approach to economic development is a working alternative to the dubious practices of the past in local renewal.

In sum, all of the misconceptions about economic development founder by ignoring the importance and the reality of community. The strategy of economic triage is a prescription for community destruction because it destroys the very texture of what is important to people—their relationships to each other in their own setting. The various ideas about business location incentives misdefine development as new businesses and mistake business location as a purely economic choice, disregarding what a company and its staff are looking for—a rewarding environment of rich opportunities for living, the kind of things a diversified community can offer. The big-bang theory is another technique for the destruction of community, while the high-tech gamble and the "larger view" in national policies have no practical relevance for the distressed community.

These distortions of what economic development means at the local level probably begin with the definition of economic development as essentially a growth in gross national (provincial, municipal) *product*. That idea and its associates—such as an increase in median family income or other purely financial measures—do not grasp the inner reality of economic development, which involves a social, psychological, and cultural dimension as well as an economic one. A working alternative view of economic development at the local level has to be recast in different terms. Initially, these will be rather general and simple. Economic development becomes a set of programs and activities that are appropriate to the particular community concerned, designed to improve conditions of life in that setting, and carried out under local control. These terms, however, carry deep within them some specific implications that make the difference between the effective use of local efforts and the further prolonged waste of the resources within the forgotten community. Implied in these terms are changes in the organizations and institutions with which people live together. It is these changes that will lead to improvements in income or improvements in production statistics.

It should be possible to start, then, where economic development actually starts—that is, with the creation of the institutional or organizational tools by which production and income are generated and supported, the *whole* range of tools. Conceptualizing the necessary effort in this fashion, one can avoid the wasteful strategies that I have described.

FIVE

Compass Points for Action

W RITING this book about community economic development requires a presentation that makes the field seem at least
somewhat orderly, but in fact it is no such thing: there is little consensus on what the basic terms and concepts mean. A term like
community, for instance, may seem readily understood or understandable, but any presumed consensus crumbles into a number
of different ideas as soon as real settings become the focus for
economic development activity. That has been my own experience
in moving from one setting to another, and the task of trying to get
one's bearings—the same compass points—in different neighborhoods or rural areas is considerable.

This was a problem from the very beginning for the Office of
Economic Opportunity program for community economic development groups. What is the community, the base for the
economic development activity? Contrasting the Hough district in
Cleveland with the Bedford-Stuyvesant district in Brooklyn, for example, raises puzzling questions about calling either or both of
them a "community." Both of these inner-city districts are over-
whelmingly poor and black in population and presumably can be
mobilized by a common sense of identity, and in both districts, a
locally based organization has projected a comprehensive program of resident-controlled renewal. Yet it stretches the imagination to consider the three hundred thousand or more residents of
"Bed-Stuy" as a community in the sense that they see themselves
as sharing some significant common identity by virtue of their
residence in that section of Brooklyn. It is somewhat easier to con-

cede the potential of that feeling in a district, like Hough, of less than fifty thousand.

Or take a far-flung rural district, like the entire area of Hancock County, Georgia, which was served by a CDC called ECCO (East Central Committee for Opportunity). Compare that to the even larger home territory of Impact Seven, a CDC serving seven counties in northern Wisconsin. What does *community* signify in these cases? Does it make a difference that ECCO represents the majority black population and Impact Seven a white population as well as a small Native American minority living on two reservations? Is it significant that the target areas of both these groups are delimited by legal county boundaries? What about the so-called Northern Kingdom that spans the White River bounding Vermont and New Hampshire? Somehow or another in this spread-out rural area there was a tradition of living together that the river did not quench and the boundary of state government could not bar; the Northern Kingdom generated a CDC—the Northern Community Investment Corporation—that operates in both states. So neither legal boundaries nor geographic barriers seemed to make a difference in that case.

Issues such as these have forced me to recognize the different dimensions in the term *community* as it can be applied to the targets for community economic development. The most obvious dimension combines the geography and the people. In effect, one draws an imaginary line around a territory and the residents of that territory. A community in this sense is a circumscribed locality with a more or less identifiable number of specific residents. In terms of this geographic-demographic dimension, the community is visibly embodied, relatively stable, and rather definite. For instance, Point St. Charles will probably always be defined by the bodies of water surrounding it. The Northern Kingdom may span state borders, but it does not reach across to Canada nor to the southern areas of Vermont and New Hampshire.

The geographic-demographic dimension has practical implications that a community group may need to consider. Drawing boundaries in one way may exclude the population from some resources, while drawing them in another fashion may bring resources in. Canada's LEAD (Local Employment Assistance and Development) program of aid for local development groups is restricted to "communities" (not otherwise defined) of less than 50,000. To get a LEAD grant, New Dawn drew a special subboundary of less than 50,000 within its general purview of industrial Cape Breton—population 130,000.

The importance of the geographic-demographic dimension is also documented by the fact that there are a variety of ways in which a community so defined might be undone by changes in that dimension. When the geographic barrier of a six-lane highway is erected across a previously well-defined inner-city community, the community may not stay united. In the reverse situation, taking down an elevated railbed may cause the adjoining areas to meld as never before. The population of any area may also change. Consider the effect of in- and out-migration by forced removal, as in Boston's West End, or by natural ethnic succession, as in East Boston, over several decades. East Boston at one time was mainly Irish, but it has always been a stepchild of the greater city, isolated geographically by a deep cut of harbor that even a major bridge and two tunnels have not redefined. In the 1950s Italian Americans began taking over the neighborhood that John F. Kennedy's father and his Irish compatriots once dominated but never managed to use as a local power base. And it also was not easy for their Italian American successors to establish the neighborhood as theirs. The geographic isolation from the central city and especially the enlargement of the adjacent Logan Airport interfered with the realization of their own priorities. Finally, in 1971, they organized the East Boston Community Development Corporation (EBCDC) to fight the airport expansion, to improve the economic opportunities of the neighborhood, and to protect and improve housing. EBCDC became a strong advocate for local improvement and a local voice in city affairs affecting the neighborhood. But, more recently, Hispanics have moved in in increasing numbers; and there is now a new stream of Southeast Asians. The needs of these people are not easily accommodated in the older patterns of EBCDC. Fifteen years ago I was peripherally involved in the early stages of EBCDC, and for many years I followed its evolution closely. In the past few months, however, I have found myself involved in developing financing for the housing needs of a constituency in East Boston that EBCDC does not serve and that has begun its own development organization.

However, a change in the population of the locality does not necessarily mean that community organizations built on the previous base are outmoded. Even a CDC may adjust to new needs. In contrast to the East Boston situation, the Spanish Speaking Unity

Council (SSUC) in Oakland, California, now serves the entire racial mosaic of its selected territory. As its name implies, SSUC started off working with Hispanic residents as a federation of the various Hispanic civic groups. But, as SSUC evolved, the whole poor population of the community became its constituency; now the SSUC federation includes organizations like a black professional women's group and a Filipino citizens' organization. SSUC has some kind of special commitment that has made it one of the most innovative and effective of all community economic development groups.

So *community* must mean something more than geography and a specified population. It is especially more than that if the community can generate its own comprehensive economic development program. To recognize what else is involved in *community* is critical, not for the purposes of mere abstract definition, but specifically for purposes of action and development programs that are geared to using each of the dimensions of what is, after all, the *base* of a local economic development program.

If one visits a CDC and attends a public meeting in the neighborhood, one immediately gets an impression that there is a sense of shared destiny and common identity: "We are all in this together," the residents seem to be saying, "and we have to work together to make things change." Community, then, has a *psychological* dimension. That dimension, in a perception of common destiny, common identity, offers the residents an essential mechanism for mobilizing themselves in a joint endeavor. An economic development program would include activities that can build and strengthen that sense of "we-ness."

Contrary to what might be thought—that poor people are too much concerned with the problems of survival—a sense of common identity can be fostered successfully in a low-income area partly because such communities, as I have mentioned before, have a strong sense of commitment to place, a strong localism. Low-income residents usually feel a basic identity with a neighborhood which is intensified because more of their lives are lived out locally. They do not have the ready and easy resources to move out either temporarily or permanently; this inability naturally reduces the capacity to think of one's self in another setting. Thus there is a greater personal investment in the immediate environment and in making it the source of life satisfactions. That sort of local commitment can be mobilized and built upon in a depressed area. By contrast, in more fortunate areas people are more likely to be open to opportunities for better living by moving to another setting. In that sense, there is likely to be less perception of community in a higher-income neighborhood, even though such neighborhoods may be more easily mobilized on, say, the immediate issue of home property values threatened by some local change.

Place helps to create and mobilize identity, but place is not the only element that builds identity in a community. At OEO, as I have reported, a heightened consciousness of black identity was considered an essential part of a black community that was ready to undertake a local development program. An interesting example of this influence is a group that never applied for or wanted OEO support for its development projects, the Roxbury Action Program (RAP). Serving a low-income black population, RAP has made a special effort to heighten awareness of a common black heritage. It instituted a set of alternative or counterinstitutional holidays which were observed by its own staff and for which community celebrations were organized—for example, the African-motif harvest and gift exchange festival of Kwanza in late December, W.E.B. DuBois' birthday on February 23, and Sojourner Truth's birthday on October 30. These dates were chosen to offer a special alternative to the more or less concurrent holidays of the majority society. Celebrating its own holidays was, for RAP, a way of strengthening local identity but in a way that helped to underline shared standards, values, and ideas by which the residents could recognize and articulate their destiny and identity and by which they could choose goals for a common future.

A *cultural* dimension, then, inheres in any community and is expressed in common ways of judging, believing, and valuing. Thus, if someone says, "Conditions around hear are bad," someone else knows what the fellow resident is talking about, feels much the same way, and makes the same judgments about those conditions. Of course, a concentration of people with one ethnic and racial heritage heightens the degree of consensus within the community boundaries, but even so the extent to which standards, values, and ideas are shared varies from person to person in the community, and so a local development program will often carry out activities that help to strengthen and articulate the cultural foundations of the community, to build a consensus of perceptions and expectations. Public meetings are the most obvious technique and one used by all sorts of organizations, of course. Other direct techniques might include adult education programs, a community newspaper, and special projects in the local schools. Indirect forms for building the cultural dimension are such things as stage plays, art exhibits, and music celebrations. New Dawn has always emphasized this sort of activity.

Carrying out these activities requires the more or less coherent organization of expectations and standards and so on for activities requiring dependable repeated or extended performance. In this sense, a community has an *institutional* dimension— that is, it has a network of interrelated organizations and patterned practices within which the residents do in actuality live out their destinies and pursue the aims they share or reciprocate. When people in a community see their fates as somehow bound together, this is not just a psychological perception. Their destinies *are* truly bound together because they share membership and participate in the institutions that make up the community. There is no meaningful life or identity outside those participations, and when the array of valued or desired participations is restricted, life in the community is itself restricted. Viewing this dimension, one can see how a community is impoverished by a lack of institutions (organizations and practices) by which it can develop. Furthermore, a development program based in the community must nevertheless use what institutional resources there are to strengthen them and create others. Out of a community college and its teachers came the impetus for New Dawn, for example. The members of New Dawn, in turn, are concerned to make sure that the community college (the University College of Cape Breton) is strengthened and maintained to provide specialized services such as business technical assistance to reach out to businesses that may not otherwise consider the college accessible.

Involving people in institutions from which they have been excluded (or not attracted to) is a technique for joining the available resources in the community with what is already on hand. For example, in communities in which racial, religious, macho, or other prejudices exclude some otherwise potentially productive residents, a development program will try to redress that waste. Earlier I mentioned redlining as an institutionalized impoverishment of the community, and, to repeat, if such institutional practices cannot be directly changed, then an economic development program will try to create new competitive institutions for mortgage financing, such as credit unions. In either case, the conditions of life are enriched for local residents as they participate in the new—to them—practices of home ownership; at the same time, the social tools by which change can occur are strengthened or created.

The most general approach to enlisting the unused human resources of a locality is called "community organizing," but organizing is never an end in itself, of course. It is a means to the achievement of specific local aims. Nevertheless, community organizing is also an institution-building process, initially in the creation and enhancement of the local advocacy group, without which no economic development program can be launched.

The institutional dimension has other practical implications. A community might have to produce a specialized insitutional form to qualify for community economic development aid. For example, under Massachusetts law, equity or loan funds from the state's Community Development Finance Corporation can go to CDCs only if more than 50 percent of the CDC board of directors is made up of people with low incomes. This provision has disqualified some CDCs that are faithfully serving low-income areas. A more common example of an institutional requirement for aid in virtually any state is incorporation of the community. TELACU, a CDC oriented to an unincorporated part of the county of Los Angeles, the Mexican-American district of East Los Angeles, figured that if they incorporated their community of more than four hundred thousand, they could automatically receive a large amount of state money for local purposes, including improvment of local schools. Unfortunately, the campaign for incorporation foundered on fears by home owners that there would be higher local taxes. Incidentally, this episode illustrates the significance of divergent views on what the destiny of a community should be.

To sum up: A community is a more or less circumscribed geographic locality in which the residents tend to see their destinies as somehow bound together, and where their destinies are in fact linked together to the extent that the residents share a common view of life and share (or overlap in) membership in most of the institutions in which they participate.

This is the kind of definition that can be empirically applied to any particular local setting—not so much to ask, Is there a community here? as to raise questions about how to strengthen the elements that make up a community. Community is not a yes-or-no matter; it is a matter of degree. And the intensity of community is an indicator of the potential base for a successful local economic development program.

Getting a fix on what community means is *the* essential orientation point. It is like finding which direction is north, and then the other compass points follow. For example, it has been common to talk of development either as community development or as economic development. Community development is often taken to be the course of action that deals with improvements in the so-called human or social conditions, while economic development generally focuses on business, financial, or industrial activity. However, so long as the impoverished conditions characterizing a community are systemically related, it is not possible to separate business and industrial problems from the human and social problems of the area. In fact, if community (on the institutional dimension) includes the entire network of organizations in which the residents participate, then it would include the businesses and other organizations (government and private nonprofit organizations) from which residents gain income through the exchange of goods or services. In short, it would include all of those institutions that are recognizably part of the *economic* life of the locality. It follows that community development would include economic development, but economic development presumably would focus only on one set of the community-based institutions.

However, it is not easy and maybe not even worthwhile or possible to try to make a sharp distinction between those local institutions that have relevance to the exchange of goods and services and those that do not—because virtually any pattern of socially organized behavior will have some effect upon the exchange process of production, distribution, and consumption. The effect is merely more or less attenuated. At the local level, effects of any local institution are very visible and can be fairly readily determined. One could research the purchases and products of any institution and determine its impact on the local economy as well as on the community in general. For example, one could determine the dollars spent by a seemingly purely cultural institution like an art museum, and one could thereby discover an economic impact from printing brochures, from paying staff salaries, and so on, as well as from what it means in terms of "imported" outside gifts and grants versus "export" expenditures for accessions bought outside the community.

Thus, at the local level, the distinction between what is and is not economic probably does not make much difference anyway. The task is not to define what are economic institutions and concentrate on them but *to select which actions with respect to which community institutions* are likely to offer the best prospect of achieving the specific goals that the local development process has established. Depending on community priorities, a well-endowed museum might participate most in community economic development by using its endowment income for educational programs during some specified period of years rather than by improving its collection by purchases of works from distant sellers. Perhaps some part of the endowment could be invested in a new local enterprise. Or, if appropriate, the museum might develop its collection of local arts and crafts. Or it might market its attractions to bring in large numbers of patrons from outside the community, whose expenditures would benefit the local cash flow. Such decisions would be deliberate efforts to increase the multiplication of the local effect of the museum's assets and income.

Together with the idea of the systemic nature of impoverishment, the points of orientation presented so far provide a framework for considering the act of community economic development. Specific decisions, as in the case of the museum, imply an intentional process; that is, the act of community economic development is not something that happens automatically, even though it is quite reasonable to expect that there may be circumstances under which some one or another goal can occur without intentional action, more or less automatically as the result of actions taken for other purposes. For example, there was probably no expectation in the U.S. antipoverty programs that such activities as Head Start and the Youth Corps would produce a large number of mayors, legislators, and other political leaders who continue to be responsive to the low-income communities from which they arose. Nevertheless, when a community has been depleted or bypassed for many years, the question is not under what circumstances it could rise again spontaneously, but how some deliberate actions can be taken to make specific positive results happen—even if some other positive results occur that were not planned or expected. So community economic development is reasonably to be defined as *purposive action*.

I have already argued that the depressed community suffers centrally from an impoverishment of its social tools for change. Its institutions are lacking in type, strength, and number and therefore cannot overcome the vicious cycle of poverty directly. It follows that the purposive action of community economic development is first and foremost to build those social tools. Furthermore, the institution-building process cannot be undertaken by distant actors, but must be *under local control.* A community-based problem requires a community-based solution. Residents will have to initiate, plan, execute, change, monitor, and evaluate the actions in accordance with their own priorities. "Under local control" means that the residents have their own institutional tools to carry out all those functions. Such tools may include local government, but will always require the greater flexibility of private agencies, like the community development corporation. And what is appropriate to the setting or locality in the activities and programs undertaken is simply what those institutions so determine. It should be clear, therefore, how important local control is and also how important it is that certain sorts of institutional tools are used to translate competing priorities into what is appropriate to the setting.

At this juncture, community economic development can be carefully and precisely defined (that is, observed and measured) by the purposively stimulated expansion in the number, in the variety, and in the strength of locally valued, locally based institutional processes. Those processes are visibly embodied both in organizations (such as businesses, church schools, and credit unions) and in physical structures (such as sewers) that are maintained by organizations (by a public works department or a property owners' association or whatever). Compare, at two points in time, the kinds of organizations a community has, their numbers, what assets they have, how vigorous they are, and how valued they are by residents, and this comparison can measure the systemic changes that a local economic development program produces, Thus, a community will be less impoverished in general at the time in which, comparatively speaking, it is substantially less impoverished in its array of such institutions, if they and their strength comport with local aspirations.

I want to emphasize that the sheer number of institutions is not itself the indicator of community economic development. For example, additional financial institutions beyond the capacity of the target area to use them is no measure of economic development; thus, an increase in the number of credit unions would obviously decrease the strength and effectiveness of each credit union if there were not enough potential members who wanted to join. Similarly, sheer variety in institutions is not itself a measure. Expanding the range of types of financial institutions to serve specialized needs may extend the opportunities for financing beyond the accepted values and priorities of the area. For example, if gambling is an important economic activity, legally pursued as it is in Las Vegas, Nevada, and if loan sharks offer the gambler the only institutionalized financing source, should an economic development program for a low-income neighborhood in Las Vegas create alternative financing mechanisms that will make money off the visiting gamblers? To what extent would such mechanisms fit local priorities? Since prostitution is legalized in Nevada, are there economic development implications for new institutions in that sector also?

I choose gambling and prostitution as illustrations here in order to highlight as vividly as possible the fact that local priorities can differ from one community to another. Such cases can also illustrate the fundamentally systemic nature of the network of social and economic connections and the necessity in economic development programs to recognize that network so that community economic development can be undertaken in an informed fashion.

For instance, consider here the outcome of a police crackdown on gambling in a certain North American Chinatown district where I once worked with some low-income community groups. In this community, as in most Chinese communities, gambling is a culturally significant activity. For instance, practically everyone gambles on Chinese New Year's Day, partly as a means of insight into what the new year will bring. However, in this particular Chinatown, year-round gambling, especially at the mah-jongg tables, was also a standard entertainment and was built into the fabric of the community. The businesspeople who ran the mah-jongg tables were a major source of community welfare funds, contributing widely to the various local charitable activities. When (with some support from antagonistic groups within the Chinese community) the city police campaigned successfully to shut down all gambling in the district, a substantial stream of money that had gone into the welfare activities in the area dried up. The other businesses and industries of the community did not fill the gap, and since, as is usual in Chinese communities, public governmental support is accepted warily, if at all, there was a severe decline in certain services. This decline included a shocking deterioration in the physical condition of the main community center building, which had previously been a major symbol of community strength and pride.

Subsequently, that particular Chinatown has had to struggle to recover and steer a new course in financing community welfare activities. That faction of local leaders, perhaps holding more occidental values, who sought the end of gambling in their neighborhood has not yet found a way to substitute fully for mah-jongg within the fabric of the community. Perhaps the most ironic part of the story is that a few years later, on Chinese New Year's Day, the police swooped down into the Chinatown again and broke up the holiday games of some leading figures of the community. This event was reported ethnocentrically as a local scandal in the occidental city papers. Outsiders did not recognize the difference for these local leaders between the organized year-round gambling and the organized New Year's Day gaming.

Contrast this community and its gambling pattern with that of a black community more oriented to occidental values, and consider the economic development implications anew. From 1969 on, the Roxbury Action Program sought to rehabilitate its small neighborhood, Highland Park, Boston. This was a very deteriorated black district, which nevertheless boasted some beautiful and historic buildings endangered by arson and neglect. RAP soon bought a historic, columned mansion for its headquarters, and one of the organization's first steps in rehabilitating its own building was to get rid of the gambling and drug activity based in a record shop on the corner three doors away. There was no question that these illegal businesses provided some employment, as runners and so on, for local people, including youths who otherwise had little hope of jobs. Moreover, the traffic offered additional customers for a tiny mom-and-pop convenience store on the opposite corner. The convenience store's elderly proprietor nevertheless joined with RAP in mobilizing police to clean up the neighborhood. The effort was successful. The illegal activity moved away, and the crime-fronting record shop closed. Unfortunately the proprietor of the convenience store also went out of business, lacking that extra small margin of cigarette and soda and other minor purchases that the numbers and drug traffic occasioned. He was rueful about the unexpected result, but he was proud of his contribution and in any case took the opportunity to retire.

The priorities of the neighborhood, as represented in RAP's program, required removing the unlawful businesses and accepting the costs of that action. At the same time, RAP began to develop a commercial sector, rehabilitating structures that eventually included a drugstore and a grocery, as well as other enterprises. And RAP also mobilized funds for youth training and youth recreation, among other social programs. In short, the organization recognized and planned for activities that substituted for those it destroyed. The key property development projects that RAP undertook have also encouraged both residents and outsiders (including city hall) to improve neighborhood properties. Again, knowing that neighborhood improvement through upgraded housing and gentrification is costly to low-income residents, RAP has also sponsored a variety of low-income and public housing developments that help to maintain the integrity of the neighborhood as a community for those with constrained incomes.

The contrast in the two reactions to gambling that I have posed is perhaps not as simple as I may have implied. Certainly the role and type of gambling activity in two different neighborhoods or in two different cities is likely to be different and to have different meanings within each community. A Las Vegas CDC (Operation Life CDC), to my knowledge, has not directly confronted the meaning of gambling (and prostitution) in terms of its own community economic development programming. But in any case, there surely is no single community economic development mechanism for dealing with gambling as either a legal or illegal activity. What does seem clear is that whatever action is to be taken, whatever mechanism is chosen to build new institutional patterns, it must grow out of a broad consultation process that has involved the ideas and knowledge of a full range of leaders and other residents in the community. Only by that technique will it be possible to adjust for the systemic nature of the community institutional pattern. Only by that means can a consensus be formed that will make effective the process of building new institutional patterns or rebuilding the old ones.

A final illustration of the relationship of community economic development to ongoing illegal activities will document this process further. A CDC in St. Louis, serving the black, low-income, Union-Sarah neighborhood, had a commitment to rehabilitate housing in a style that would give a message that Union-Sarah was not a dangerous neighborhood to live in. The CDC refused to put visible antiburglary bars on the first floor windows of its apartment buildings, relying instead on the policy that unprotected windows would advertise the area as a good place to live. Their policy was very successful in the sense that their buildings did not seem to encourage break-ins and, furthermore, the privately owned properties around them were also upgraded without bars or grilles. However, the CDC did not rest at symbols; it also designed changes in traffic patterns for a certain street (in cooperation with the city street department) to discourage public prostitution. There was a long street that stretched in, through, and out of the district and contributed to the practice of cruising through to pick up prostitutes who stood on the curbs calling out to passing cars. The CDC's plan was to break the traffic pattern by cutting off the street at two or three points and by inserting miniparks in a manner that prevented cruising but still offered access to each block.

The CDC did not expect to end prostitution totally. Indeed, I was told that it knowingly accepted as tenants some people it believed might be working prostitutes, so long as they were quiet, reliable, rent-paying tenants and did not ply their trade in their own apartments. However, the CDC did want to discourage the most blatant prostitution, on the assumption that an active traffic for prostitution was also likely to increase the risk of other things like drug sales, muggings, or break-ins.

The CDC assumed that in the immediate area of the proposed changes, most of the neighborhood residents (a high proportion of whom were elderly) would be only too delighted to have the prostitution pattern broken up. Therefore they did not make any special efforts to gain support for the street changes, and this decision turned out to be a fatal error. At a city hearing that was presumed to have been perfunctory for approval of the changes, the CDC was aghast to discover that many elderly residents came to testify against the proposal. They had been mobilized by the policitally astute pimps who had suavely persuaded them that there were too many risks and inconveniences—perhaps fire engines would be dangerously delayed, and so on. The CDC lost that round because it had not done its homework in involving the immediately affected residents in the changes. The CDC director told me in chagrin that they would have to wait at least a year before coming back again wit the proposal; they had been beaten properly, he admitted, but the next time they would organize the necessary support.

The illustrations given of the work of the community economic development groups—even though I have limited them to reactions to illegal enterprises—already suggest the framework for programs and activities in economic development. It will be useful to present briefly the usual classification of such activities so that they offer a systematic view of the potential patterns of community economic development strategies.

The major distinction made in economic development activities divides two great sectors—business and infrastructure—with the implication that an active business sector will depend upon a firm foundation of infrastructure facilities. Business may supply food, clothing, shelter, computers, and other goods and services, but it can do so only if there are public facilities to rely upon. Thus the farmer or other food producers must rely upon highways to get vegetables and meat to markets; clothing stores must rely upon a school system to turn out clerks and managers who can handle the arithmetic of a sale and of sales projections; and so on.

The infrastructure is usually in the public sector and is financed by taxes. For example, garbage collection, police and fire protection, and educational facilities are all *social infrastructure* facilities, while streets and bridges, parks and playgrounds, seaports and airports, are *physical infrastructure*. However, any one of these activities sometimes occurs in the ordinary business world. There are, after all, private profit-making garbage collection firms, and also companies for crime prevention and detection, fire fighting, and schooling, as well as private toll roads, marinas, airports, parks, and the like. So the nonprofit or for-profit source, private or public sector, of goods and services does not distinguish between infrastructure and business sectors, nor the types of goods and services, nor the intended market or consumer.

However, it is usual in Canada and the United States for infrastructure activities to be carried out by public bodies, and therefore it is meaningful in community economic development programs to focus on the distinction between private business and public infrastructure because in the depleted community the latter may show wide gaps unfilled by the public or governmental sector. Thus, while new businesses may be required for the revitalization of the area, it would be a dubious strategy to promote new industry when the road system will not support it. Although a CDC may not be able to assume responsibility for road maintenance in its community, it must assume responsibility for somehow getting that maintenance tended to. If the appropriate government units seem reluctant or unable to support the physical infrastructure needs of the community, then the CDC must take up the problem. And that is exactly what one of the most successful American CDCs (Kentucky Highlands Investment Corporation, or KHIC) did for the backroads of its rural area, organizing residents to work on the roads and to get a rebate on their taxes. KHIC also took the initiative to improve water and sewage systems, while it fostered the usual economic development infrastructure of industrial parks.

Note that although KHIC was concerned about a part of the

physical infrastructure of its community, it did so by fostering a change in institutional practices—in this instance, the road maintenance and tax practices of the local government. Other changes sought in a community economic development program might involve the plans of a state or regional development agency for physical infrastructure, or the plans and activities of a multinational corporation for new facilities in the area.

Infrastructure, as mentioned before, can also be in social forms—as in the school system or medical services—and correcting for any weaknesses there can be another community economic development program or activity. Thus New Dawn Enterprises took on the responsibility of promoting three new dental clinics for its community. These were actually private clinics, but New Dawn engineered provincial subsidies for equipment, constructed or renovated the necessary buildings, and attracted the participating dentists from off the island to take up local residence. The close connections between New Dawn and the local college has also resulted in educational programs geared to the development of the necessary human capital of local knowledge and skills.

More specific detail will be provided later about the infrastructure activity of community economic development and about the central matters of business development and investment capital. For now, it need only be emphasized that whatever activities such a program might engage in with respect to infrastructure, it must also always concern itself with the other class of development activity—business development. A program that does not pay attention to the expansion and creation of businesses is not community economic development. I want to emphasize here the central importance of community economic development activities in the business sector in order to offset any previous impression to the contrary. Business is not, as I have already stressed, the only or perhaps the first significant activity to be launched in any specific community economic development strategy. But some activity in that sector is an *essential* element of any strategy in community-based economic development.

Up to this point, my review of the compass points has assumed that community economic development is simply a practical activity with some technical and business aspects. But so long as it hopes to change the local scene, there is something more involved —namely, ethical values and preconceptions about what changes are desirable. As a matter of fact, community economic development in recent history clearly implies the application of a broad moral tradition. It uses a change or reformist perspective and expresses dissatisfaction with the results of the status quo because those results include communities that are ghettos of despair. This perspective insists that an emphasis on individualistic rewards is not tolerable if that emphasis means that the wounds of the many go unassuaged.

There are potentially radical implications to this position, including community ownership, community control of unresponsive private industry, and community challenge of unresponsive outside decision makers, whether in government or the private sector. Community economic development is fundamentally a technique for redressing inequities and exploitation. One does not choose to embark with others on a community's comprehensive development project unless one is already convinced that intolerable inequities occur in the way in which that community (and others) participate in the meaning and materialities of the larger society.

However, the notion that the community should have a better chance for that participation assumes further that at least some of the values of the larger society are worth participating in. The aim of community economic development, then, includes ensuring that the community can be a part of a pluralistic mainstream, not a revolution against it. In this sense, community economic development takes on the hue of a conservative philosophy. And in fact it does not forswear at least some of the techniques of the very economic system that has brought it to the impoverished status it seeks to overcome. Yet of course it must in the end be counterconventional. If conventional institutions were adequately built and connected, the community would not have been forgotten. So some changes that look startling to those accustomed to old ways must break the old patterns.

Community economic development, then, involves an internal conflict or tension between that aspect of it which is conservative and that which is change-oriented or even radical. To seek to participate in the mainstream of commercial America, for example, and at the same time to hold that the mainstream has been organized against your participation and must therefore be changed is, to put it bluntly, contradictory. Yet a resolution of that contradiction can take place in the field of action that enhances the community's capacity for self-determination. As the institutions that shape the life of the community and its residents are made responsible to it, and as they are opened up to participation by the residents in the process of development, the local systemic change begins to affect its larger environment, the society as a whole. In short, a reconciliation takes place between the local setting and the surrounding society as the latter is affected by the local changes.

For community activists, it is not enough to conclude that if you can't beat the system, you must join it, or that the system is no good and must be brought down. Community economic development does not admit to such simplistic choices. A comprehensive vision of local development must stretch into spans of twenty to fifty years, and daily activity in that long-term time perspective has to be a visible and meaningful process of expanding local resources for self-determination. Thus, a political base is surely required to extract from the outside world the necessary return of resources that have been strip-mined from the locality. But no community group can afford to concentrate only on political action. Conversely, a group cannot expect to succeed merely by creating or building community-owned businesses when those businesses cannot exist if they are limited to the local market; it must build levers to influence its environment so that local businesses will have a chance.

The balances struck among the multiple aims of a comprehensive development program—between, for instance, building a political infrastructure, on the one hand, and, on the other, meeting local and outside needs for goods and services—will vary from one setting to another. There is no one plan for each community. The single commitment is to a process of democratic decision: the balances are struck locally because that is where the balances take effect most directly.

The commitment to local self-determination will of course have its costs. A depleted community will not be as efficient in making its choices as one in which more resources of technique and specialization are available. A learning curve implies and even ensures local mistakes that might have been avoided by outside authorities. However, it is also painfully true that many of the earliest or original errors were not made locally. As one community activist told me, "We will make plenty of mistakes on our own. We don't need anyone else to make them for us anymore."

I do not believe that the discouragements and immensities of the task of reversing the processes of disinvestment, of human degradation, and of sheer total dilapidation in the ways of life in a forgotten community can be approached without some form of personal energy that can be broadly termed "moral," as non-economic as that term may sound. Community leaders and those they inspire for the long haul almost always cast their visions in moral terms. These terms may be rather secularly ideological and political, but often they are founded in the religious traditions of the community. It is commonplace to find, as in East Boston, for example, that the beginnings of the CDC evolve from the leadership of a priest where the disadvantaged community is predominantly Catholic, or of a minister where the community is predominantly Protestant, as in north Philadelphia and its Zion Investment program.

Religion as such need not be the primary motivating force in mobilizing the community in moral terms. Political formulations have been the energizing force in the quite clearly Catholic Chicano community of San Antonio in previous years. There the Mexican American Unity Council grew out of a more broadly political movement of *la raza*, the Chicano cultural, moral, and ethnic sense of identity. In Washington, D.C., about fifteen years ago, the Peoples Involvement Corporation (PIC) was quite clearly an outgrowth of political organizing that low-income black people saw as a way of gaining the influence that their growing numbers in the nation's capital could bring them. Today, of course, the capital is predominantly black, and local government reflects that predominance. But in the late 1960s the blacks were less sure of obtaining their due in a white-controlled city where, after all, many public facilities had been tightly segregated in the 1950s.

Whether in religious terms or in political ideological terms, the foot soldiers as well as the leaders of the community economic development movements in local communities see their work as having moral implications in redressing the wrongs of their people. And the observer may see these in the daily activities of CDC staff.

The comprehensive work of community revitalization is not simply a series of technical tasks, nor is the moral vision discharged merely by engaging in technical tasks. I became convinced of this truth one day when a staff member at PIC, a local resident, spoke to me in her office about her work as a housing counselor. Although she had little training, she helped neighborhood people who were buying a house but were having trouble getting a mortgage, or were in arrears on their mortgage payments, or were afraid of buying a lemon and wondered how to avoid buying one, or had already bought a lemon and wanted help in getting out of the deal, and so on. She told me about how important good housing was, and then she mused, almost wonderingly:

> Of course, I can't buy a house myself. I don't have a good enough credit rating. My husband had a girl friend who charged things on my account, in my name, all over town. So my credit is bad. If I could just find a good place to rent . . . I just don't have enough space right now. Of course, one problem is that I have someone living with me and my daughter, so that takes up more space. A 19-year-old mother with an 8-year-old daughter. I just found her on the street one day. She had been living with someone who beat her. Welts all over her. So I took her in. She's getting along okay now. I helped her get a job. She's a nice girl. But I surely do need more space.

Her voice trailed off, and then she had to answer her phone. I left her there on the phone and knew that for her, counseling neighbors on housing problems was more than a job; it was a spontaneous moral way of life.

No social scientist or financial analyst or other specialist working on community economic development can escape the moral choices that inhere in this work. No matter how technical one's own field, one will not be immune to the moral issues that practical action in this activity implies. It is best to be clear on that compass point from the very start.

PART
TWO

SIX

Gathering Momentum

O RDINARILY, community economic development is the responsibility of the local government, which may establish a specialized arm devoted solely to economic development. This is the
usual means by which a locality ensures that its economic development needs will be met, and there is a limited but growing body of
knowledge and practices for local government action. Yet the
depth of depletion of the forgotten community is an index of the
failure of local government institutions, and so the question is
what to do when local government, for a number of possible
reasons, does not offer the essential first tool.

Action implications will arise from the particular reasons for
the abdication of local government. The failure may be because, in
the political pattern of the nation, local governments are usually
not delegated sufficient resources or authority to carry out meaningful programs. Yet the authority retained by the other governmental levels is not exercised or is poorly exercised on behalf of
the local communities. In this instance, the resources that would
have to come from higher levels of government never reach the depleted community, by policy (in economic triage) or by virtue of
the fact that local government is too ineffective to mobilize resources that would be available from federal, state, or provincial agencies. Thus, perhaps the most effective means of ensuring a more
adequate distribution of the federal, state, or provincial revenues
to local government would be a systematic educational program
for local elected officials and the top administrative officers of
local government—simply to acquaint them with the federal and
the provincial, state, and regional programs of assistance for
which their communities are eligible, and how to get that aid.

In other instances, the local government may be fully active and in command of financial and other resources, but does not send these resources to some parts of the district that the local authority is supposed to serve. This is specifically the case in many of the largest American cities, where the so-called downtown interests can mobilize what is needed but the slum areas stay what they are. Put in other terms, the local government is responsive to some constituencies but not to the forgotten neighborhoods. Sometimes that situation may be due in part to the excessive size of the population served; the city government simply cannot be efficient and effective. In other instances, the city (or county) is under the control of interests that see no purpose in serving the forgotten community. This is the case especially when the area includes a denigrated minority—such as Native Americans in either the United States or Canada.

Whether the local government is simply ineffective for any one of a number of reasons or is deliberately exploitative of a particular neighborhood, the forgotten community is often beleaguered also by a history of abdicating its own decisions to more or less distant authorities in what is analogous to the colonial model of administration. Faraway decisions affecting the community's economy are made in a frankly exploitative manner, or are merely undiscerning, or take place not at all. The general result, as I have noted before, is a sense of alienation, a lack of hope that any action by the community can have any effect.

A further result may be a kind of reverse exploitation. The members of the community, in concert or individually, find ways to make their exploiters pay dearly for the isolation that has been forced upon them. Unfortunately but not unexpectedly, reverse exploitation reinforces the weaknesses of the forgotten community even when it is also a means for survival. A striking illustration is the use and abuse of unemployment assistance. In some very depressed fishing communities in Canada, abuse of unemployment compensation is a major fact of local economic life, and in the local small fish-processing factory, a worker may stay on the job only long enough to qualify for unemployment. The unemployment allowance is close to what the worker's earnings have been anyway, and he can use the free time to fix up the house or go hunting or whatever. Someone else whose unemployment aid has run out will then take over the job at the factory long enough to requalify for aid, and he in turn will leave to allow for another new incumbent. Employers collaborate in the process because it permits them to pay low wages—without which the facility perhaps could not even exist. And the government unemployment officers wink at the process, not out of venality, but because it is a way of life for the community. Perhaps the officials who live there recognize the practicality of the ritual. Naturally, this means of drawing income into the community from outside does little to increase the community's capacity for improvement or self-determination. Yet there may be some sophisticated local observers who see the process as a reasonable work-sharing institution in a community where paying jobs are so limited. An outsider is apt to see this process as self-destructive on its face. It is my own experience that such situations (for example, in the welfare-dependent Native American setting) are usually felt by the residents themselves to be demeaning. They do not define the practice as a sophisticated accommodation technique, by any means.

In any event, the point is that when local government misfires so badly, private institutions must be created to do the coordinating, planning, and catalyzing that local government might otherwise do. Whether the distressed city neighborhood or rural district can in fact evolve new private organizations to do the necessary job is quite another story. If such innovations are created and operate successfully, local governmental institutions will themselves be reinvigorated, if previously weak; somehow decentralized, if previously too distant; or forced to include new leadership, if previously discriminating against the excluded community. In short, the local government may in time take over the functions that the private institution has performed. Such a process took place in Hancock County, Georgia, an area of about nine thousand in population. The East Central Committee for Opportunity (ECCO), the local CDC, based in the rural black population, was able to mobilize its black constituency to influence and change the county government. It elected a county sheriff and other officers and reversed economic and other policies that had benefited the dominant white population in the county seat. It accomplished this at the same time that it was also creating new employment opportunities, including one of the very earliest catfish farms in the southern United States. The renewal of local government thus began with the creation of private economic development institutions.

The history of community economic development in Canada and the United States suggests that local government institutions have a certain disability for *beginning* the revitalization process itself. Flexible financial and human resources are needed that traditional practices in local government do not bring forth and that can only be mobilized in the private sector. In the depleted community, it is a fair hypothesis that the initial impetus for renewal will come from new private sources, which will eventually mobilize the tools that the local government can appropriately provide for further stimulation of private initiatives, and so on, in an interactive process.

Earlier I suggested that a new type of institution, the CDC, was actually invented in the 1960s to express and carry out a coordinated program of local redevelopment. It arose more or less concurrently in a number of different communities, each of which independently arrived at an analogous solution to its local problems. While today the idea of the CDC is widespread and relatively accessible to the language and thought of a depressed community, the idea is probably still a matter of rediscovery each time. Community leaders must conduct their own review of the local setting and discover in the process that a CDC or something like that is required. Unless that discovery is more than merely an abstract acquaintance with the idea of local development institutions, the very demanding work of community economic development will falter. Suggestions or persuasion or, worse yet, requirements by outside authorities (government agencies, grant givers, consultants, and the like) may seem to start the process, but it cannot sustain itself without the internal energy of local commitment.

This caveat is specifically aimed at any readers of this book who might be misled by anything I say about the importance of the CDC or other first tool in a community economic development program. It is not the tool itself that is initially crucial, but the local commitment to finding, rediscovering, or reinventing some such tool. An outsider such as an economic development specialist in a government agency or a newly assigned parish priest may view the community as needing a comprehensive renewal program from within, but that outsider cannot help plan a CDC or other like organization unless a broad community leadership is already prepared by experience and by internal discussions and thought for a new and ambitious start. I would take strong issue with statements such as that made in one particular Canadian federal document—that a neighborhood development corporation "can be initiated in several ways: if the citizens themselves do not take the initiative, a university, college, or community-development worker could initiate formation of the group."

There are, of course, significant roles to be played by an outsider coming into a forgotten community, but these roles depend upon the current status of the community and its particular stage of development. If a community has been left so far behind that it is not even contemplating change until some so-called outside agitator appears, then there is nothing whatsoever that a nonresident can or should do to press the community directly into community economic development. Instead, the most reasonable role—one often played in the 1960s and 1970s by members of the Company of Young Canadians and by the comparable young VISTA volunteers—is that of first helping the community find its own voice by confronting the local history of depression and exploitation. This is the true function of the outside agitator—the community organizer (United States) or community animator (Canada). Outsiders *can* help the community discover a sense of itself and of its power, and later this discovery can evolve into a concern with economic development.

Once the rudiments of community identity have been welded together and local leadership has been developed to mobilize that identity to common purposes, the role of the outsider shifts. What was essential in the earliest stage when the community was without a sense of itself and of the possibility of change—namely, strong and active outside stimulation and guidance—becomes a handicap in the second stage. From then on the community leadership must take the initiative. The initiative may take the community to the next stage, to preliminary self-preparation for economic development—that is, to some experience in the general tasks of institution building, but without any immediate or direct connection with a development strategy.

The second stage is not marked merely by one-shot successes. It is the time for creating some resource in the community or at the very least reconstructing and radically changing something. Helping to elect a friendly official is important, I grant, but not what I mean here by the critical events of the second stage. Getting a new street light installed at a dangerous school crossing can be immensely rewarding to a neighborhood that has seen too many accidents at that crossing, but that also is not what I mean. One-shot successes can be invigorating to a community group, but the organization must move on from that sort of experience to building some more substantial resource. Or it may work on both sorts of tasks at the same time—building a long-term resource and also achieving an immediate, one-time goal.

In Cape Breton, getting the vocational institute established is an example of success in creating a long-term resource. That was a rather expensive and ambitious institution to initiate; and the new resource need not be that dramatic. For some neighborhoods, the success has been modest—such as a new kindergarten program at the local school, a bookmobile to substitute for a closed library branch, or a community advisory board for local clinics and hospitals to humanize the way low-income patients are dealt with by those facilities. Even though sometimes limited in broad community impact, the creation of the new resource will have built skills in working together to accomplish something, will have established a track record of accomplishment that can be pointed to within and outside the community, and will have engendered the idea that the group can achieve even more. And all these gains will be in addition to the actual community facility that has been added to the base of local resources.

Since the essential task is to build long-lasting institutionalized resources in the locality, this sort of prior experience is a warm-up—an introduction to the sorts of complexities and trade-offs that are involved, requiring compromises and decisions that only local residents have the credibility to make for their neighborhood. An outsider can be of assistance in this initial foray in two ways: by providing information about how other groups have handled the same sorts of problems, and by providing contacts for potential outside resources, especially money, if that is a crucial ingredient for creating the new facility.

The same two functions—providing, or facilitating the gathering of information and providing contacts to mobilize other resources—can also be performed by outsiders at the point when the local group is finally ready to consider a program of community economic development. The local leadership will need to hear about the ideas, concepts, possibilities, and examples of other forgotten communities who have also found their own voices and then have gone on to more ambitious strategies. Such information can fall on deaf ears, however, and will be useful *only* when local people have already begun to conceptualize "the problem" as somehow comprehensively economic, more general than the single issues that have theretofore absorbed them. Local thought must also have already moved beyond the simplistic formulations of antagonism against the historic exploiters. Whatever the understandable resentments against past and present antagonists, the community must be ready to reconceptualize their static "us-against-them" perspective into a dynamic "how-shall-we-do-something-different" perspective. This is, at last, the point at which specific consultation by outsiders on the techniques of community economic development will be appropriate.

In 1969, in the backwoods of southwest Georgia, a few hundred miles south of where rural blacks in the ECCO organization were beginning their transformation of Hancock County, another rural black organization had its own vision. Its hopes rested upon developing an old plantation, Featherfield Farm, into a haven for tenant farmers who had been thrown off their rented land and otherwise threatened and discriminated against, especially during attempts at voting and voter registration. By something like a miracle, Featherfield Farm, a 4,800-acre tract, had been sold to them (and their national backers in the church world), and it offered an opportunity for perpetual common ownership, nevermore to be thrown off the soil that they worked and that gave them the very sustenance of life. So they were now setting about the task of planning a whole new community of small farms, shops, and services to be built upon the plantation. At a planning meeting I attended in 1970 in a huge tent erected on the plantation grounds, I did not hear the usual anger at the white oppressors, who, after all, had beaten and jailed some of the men, women, and children present at this planning session. Instead, I heard visions of a new world.

One small discussion group of black countryfolk that I had the opportunity of observing had been assigned the task of thinking about the issues of internal governance of the created community, and they were considering how to handle community members who did not abide by the rules—who might steal from their neighbors, for example. One participant made a conventional remark about punishment and jail, but the others gravely considered the issue at more length and favored the suggestion by another participant that in the new community people who broke rules needed to be reeducated, made to feel a part of the whole, and understood as troubled people who needed help instead of being rejected and thrown out of the community. One middle-aged woman, a leader who had previously told me of hitching herself into the traces of a plow to ready her own plot of land for planting, spoke eloquently of building a new way of life.

It is this sort of perspective, though expressed in less dramatic ways perhaps, that must move community leaders before they can take the deep breath and plunge into a long revitalization of their neighborhood or rural locality. There must be a readiness for construction, not just for opposition to an unfriendly environment, in order for people to learn from information about other development activities in other locations. In the case of New Communities, Inc. (NCI), as the Georgia group became, information and ideas flowed into the local black community through church and civil rights organization channels, exciting the local people with new concepts for solving age-old problems. A group of the local leaders even traveled to Israel to visit kibbutzim and to see firsthand the operation of the Jewish Land Trust, one of the models that they were considering for Featherfield Farm. The vision and deliberate action of the NCI group promised to provide a major contribution to the whole idea of community economic development. In the end, disastrous accidents snuffed out the project, but until then the group made good use of the information that came to them from the outside.

A further function that outsiders can perform is to facilitate the importation of seed funds that will give the local organizers some resources with which to lay their groundwork. The seed money need not be very much at all—indeed, initially it should not be so much as to require a great deal of attention to bookkeeping and other financial administrative tasks. It is inherent in the role of the interested outsider that he or she has a network of contacts outside the community that can be tapped to generate this kind of money for local purposes. Volunteers from such organizations as the Company of Young Canadians or from national churches will often be familiar enough with the bureaucracies from which they come to write and properly direct proposals to the right sources for small grants. If such direct sources are not available, indirect or so-called bootleg subsidies can come from the ongoing regular budget of a social agency, a church, or even a business with which the outsider is connected. In the Hough case, Burt Griffin of the Cleveland Legal Aid Society found a means in his budget to provide DeForest Brown with a salary so that Brown could work fulltime on Hough problems. Small sums can offer just that extra support that local people may need to develop their own powers, including the capacity and status to obtain still more funding from outside the community.

In summary, at the stage in which the community, although already finding its way, is not fully prepared to confront what is involved in comprehensive revitalization, outsiders (especially those who take up residence locally) can help to prepare the community to climb to the point at which it *may* begin to evolve further. Even from the sidelines, the outsider can offer assistance in the crucial first institution-building project that is selected and undertaken by local people, can open up channels for the dissemination of information on the experience of similar communities, and can arrange for minor financial resources that can make a real difference.

This outside assistance can be a critical influence in aiding the community to reach the launch point for a community economic development perspective, the point when the community has developed a strong sense of its own identity and capacity; when it has experienced some success in limited institution building; when an organization has been established with credibility of accomplishment both in its own eyes and in the eyes of significant outside sources of support; when a group of local leaders are recognized as committed to local improvement rather than simply to their own advancement; and when there has been a demonstrated capacity to mobilize people and some financial resources, both inside and outside the community.

Of course, good information, strenuous efforts at organizing, seed funds, and an energizing image of a better future do not alone lead to success in launching a development program. For example, the new community of Featherfield Farm was never built. The failure was partly due to an automobile accident which took the life of the black real estate man and civil rights leader who had engineered the purchase of the land and another automobile accident two years later which took the lives of, or crippled, a number of the other leaders (including the woman I mentioned from the planning session).

An instructive illustration of the interaction between local organizations and outside assistance in establishing a community economic development program is provided by the case of the East Boston CDC. I want now to give an extended account of the complex history of the East Boston Community Development Corporation (EBCDC), its original sponsor, the East Boston Neighborhood Council, and the Roman Catholic Archdiocese of Boston. By the late 1960s, East Boston had become a hotbed of Italian American community organizations, some of them conventional in any Italian American neighborhood, some electrified into existence by a series of major assaults upon the physical integrity of the neighborhood. Most grievous to the residents was the continuing expansion of Boston's Logan Airport as a major international facility. The expansion of the airport was taking place at the expense of neighborhood parks and residences. Not only did the airport authority condemn, buy, and raze 5 acres of family residential properties (in addition to 20 acres of parkland, and many more of other properties, for a grand total of 140 acres), but the construction process itself went on in defiance of traffic and safety considerations.

The East Boston Neighborhood Council (EBNC) became the community tool to contest the desecration of the neighborhood. EBNC had been organized in the 1930s. Anyone fourteen or older who lived or worked in East Boston could become a member. But like the Hough Community Council in Cleveland, EBNC had languished into inactivity over the years until it was revived in 1967 by a local pastor, Monsignor Mimie Pitaro, to mobilize the community in its struggle against the airport. Pitaro, working with local Protestant pastors, encouraged action by the mothers of the area most threatened by the construction truck traffic. In 1968, the mothers held hands and stretched themselves across a local street to block the passing of trucks to and from the construction site. They won their fight, and the construction activity was rerouted. The council continued its activity regarding the airport's water, air, and noise pollution. Takeoffs and landings, for instance, were so noisy that typically the morning class work was temporarily suspended during the most active periods of airport traffic. The council gained additional concessions and became recognized as a mover and shaker in the neighborhood.

The most dramatic event regarding the airport was the street blockade. Traditionally, Italian American women are not active outside the home, church, and family. So the activism and success of the mothers was unexpected and heady. Indeed, it might not have occurred except for the general atmosphere of citizen action in those years, the 1960s. In 1967, the year before the blockade, the votes of East Boston had been critical to the election of a mayoral candidate who had responded, after his election, by establishing a neighborhood advisory group for the administration of city development policies, as well as a local branch office of the city hall. In addition, the neighborhood had an active unit of Boston's pioneering community action agency for antipoverty programs. Together these two groups (made up of overlapping memberships) began to exert efforts at gaining control of neighborhood affairs that had traditionally been directed from across the harbor in downtown Boston. What was especially noteworthy was that the neighborhood even managed to establish relationships with other neighborhoods in Boston, including Roxbury. Several Boston neighborhoods were simultaneously being threatened by the plans for the same new major expressway that would destroy literally thousands of homes and businesses. The neighborhoods formed a coalition, and in a coordinated and protracted struggle, they finally got both the Democratic mayor and the Republican governor to collaborate in a rejection of the expressway. It was never built, as shocking a jolt to conventional expectations as the mothers' blockade.

It was this sort of activity that caught the eye of the archdiocese's urban affairs director, Father Michael Groden. And he remembered it when he was asked in 1969 by Jeff Faux, the federal administrator of OEO's new CDC program, whether any ethnic neighborhood groups in Boston were prepared to undertake a comprehensive economic development program. In posing the question, Faux had shrewdly recognized two things. First, the new OEO program was already especially interesting to both U.S. senators from Massachusetts. Edward Brooke, a Republican and the only black in the Senate, had a special interest in black community development; and Edward Kennedy had a special interest because his late brother Robert had originally sponsored OEO's legislation to promote economic development in low-income communities. The continued support of Brooke and Kennedy would be strengthened, Faux felt, if they saw good local projects in their own state. Moreover, Congress was controlled by the Democratic party, but a Republican occupied the White House; so Massachusetts straddled the gap politically. Second, Faux knew that the federal program should not be identified simply as a response to black community activism but should reach out to other low-income neighborhoods. Therefore, he hoped to find an eligible group in a white Boston neighborhood as well as one in a black. Groden took the idea of a community economic development project to the EBNC and offered his support in gaining funds for them if they were interested. They were indeed, and established a committee to plan with him.

Groden's office provided a range of technical assistance for the local group, which had no staff resources. He assigned one of his own staff people to help with the research and writing necessary for a formal proposal for grant funds; when those funds were granted one year later, in 1970, Groden's office handled the bookkeeping and the legal tasks of incorporating the East Boston CDC. The CDC's board was initially elected by the neighborhood council in its annual membership meeting that year.

Groden also provided critical political support. Although the Boston contact had been initiated by Faux, he would not also be making the ultimate approving decision on the East Boston proposal. He would make only the critical positive staff recommendation, if a good proposal were submitted; but the final decision would be influenced by political considerations at the White House. So Groden was involved with community leaders in wheeling and dealing on that political level as well. This process went so far as to include a telephone call to Washington which, with the cardinal's implicit consent, impersonated Cardinal Richard Cushing (Groden's boss, of course) down to his very well-known and idiosyncratic intonations and accents; this elaborate maneuver was made to express the strong personal interest of this politically powerful figure, who had administered the presidential oath of office to John F. Kennedy on the inaugural platform almost ten years before.

Clearly, the Catholic church hierarchy played a critical role in the initiation of the East Boston CDC, taking on a variety of technical and political tasks. But the council emerged in its own right in the process, representing as it did a rich spectrum of local constituencies. The twenty-one board members in and of themselves represented, informally, almost thirty different community organizations, ranging from a women's sodality to the Chamber of Commerce and a tenants' organization, as well as other politically salient groups like the East Boston Democratic Ward Committee and the local antipoverty organizations. The relationship between the council and the church was particularly close, of course, since it was mediated by Pitaro, but when the CDC was finally established legally, neither Pitaro nor Groden had a formal role within it. The tradition of open membership established by the council continued within the CDC, in which anyone fourteen years old or older, who lived or worked in East Boston could become a member by purchasing a $5 pro forma share of stock. Those without $5 could contribute work for the share.

In the years since it was established, EBCDC has promoted dozens of businesses with its loan guarantee fund, renovated housing for the elderly, invested in its own ventures, established a day nursery, and carried out a variety of other community-building tasks. One might say that EBCDC got on the fast track (even without prior institution-building experience) because of its relationship to the outside resource of the local diocese—and because of the mothers' blockade.

SEVEN

The Core Institution

A wide variety of projects like that which the East Boston CDC eventually undertook can only be managed when coordinating and implementing functions are undertaken by a central guiding institution that adopts the whole spread of community problems as its own. The particular form of such an institution and how it evolves is the topic to be explored now.

The reader, having learned that the East Boston CDC sold $5 shares in a for-profit corporation to the residents of the community, might suppose that this feature is standard. As a matter of fact, very few CDCs or other such organizations are organized this way. Most are set up as nonprofit membership groups. This and other aspects of organizational structure will depend upon local circumstances, history, and preferences, as I shall describe. In fact, there are many different variations among which to choose, and the form in any one locality may vary over time, especially to suit different stages in the evolution of the local development process. However, in both the United States and Canada, the ultimate basic legal form will be some sort of corporation: In both nations, the legal system puts a premium upon the flexibility, strength, and protection that the corporate form provides.

A community economic development program may begin under the aegis of a loose association for mutual consultation, discussion, and planning—like the Machine and its Chief Operator in Hough. But eventually a more formal organization will have to emerge if the program is to be credibly received inside and outside the community. In the city of Boston there is a small informal group of top bankers, industrialists, and other leaders of commerce and finance known familiarly in the press as the Vault; they take as part of their responsibility monitoring and advising on local development questions, especially in the downtown area, which they tend to consider as their own turf, and they regularly invite candidates for mayor to present themselves and their campaign proposals for scrutiny at Vault meetings. But even the informal Vault has taken a formal name, the Coordinating Committee, and has a rotating chairperson and secretary, though it has no bylaws. So even the informal club of the most powerful leaders of a major city has found it convenient to organize somewhat formally. Low-income community leaders, with less influence, will discover even greater benefits from formal organization.

In the case of New Dawn, with the local tradition of cooperatives, it was natural that the first formal association was legally established as a cooperative, the Cape Breton Association for Cooperative Development. However, as the work evolved, legal counsel advised the group to establish themselves in the form of a nonprofit corporation. They retained the prior organization as a subsidiary to own the property that had already been bought and developed, but they incorporated New Dawn Enterprises, Ltd., as the active arm of their broader program. In Durham, North Carolina, a community economic development program began on the base of a group of black community improvement and civil rights associations and a food cooperative, and evolved into a broader agenda as a CDC called United Durham, Inc. (UDI). UDI developed an industrial mall and also went into housing as well as other business enterprises, including a supermarket that grew out of the interest of the food-buying cooperative.

Initially, then, a community economic development program is not bound to a particular form of legal organization. The critical question is whether the cooperative or whatever will begin to conceive of its role in the community as working for the general improvement of the local economy and not merely as a service to its particular members. This role implies that its relatively limited and specialized format will and can actually stretch further than its initial purpose. If its work begins to include more than its main specialized activity, then it can be identified as a core institution. Nevertheless, it seems likely that any such group will eventually come to the point of producing an additional institutional tool that can be more flexibly directed to the whole range of community improvement activities, as may be necessary from time to time. Credit unions, food cooperatives, and worker-owned firms are not easily adapted to engaging in a wide range of development activities. Indeed, the original charter of the group may have legally limited its scope, so that it can only temporarily and cautiously do anything more. For this reason, then, community economic development will eventually demand the creation of a separate corporate tool.

The East Boston Neighborhood Council decided to create the East Boston Community Development Corporation as a for-profit organization mainly to symbolize its businesslike intentions. Actually, the shares were priced at the level of dues for civic organizations; if you did not have the cash, you could work it out for the group; and only one voting share might be purchased by any one person. Thus, there was really no particular profit distribution or share appreciation assumptions in this sort of for-profit structure. But to the organizers, a standard for-profit corporation would have more credibility in the community. Actually, the basic assets were initially maintained under the control of the council, a nonprofit corporation. Later, when the council's interest waned in community economic development as such, having spun off its interest to EBCDC, EBCDC established its own nonprofit arm, a foundation that would receive grants and also make grants to other charitable organizations throughout the neighborhood. Under the requirements of the U.S. legal system, for-profit organizations like EBCDC need such an instrument to avoid tax liabilities for any grants made to it.

For-profit and nonprofit organizations are often established in tandem for community economic development. One of the most imaginative of all such programs in North America is the Human Resources Development Association (HRDA) in Halifax. This nonprofit group establishes small businesses (with supportive social services and counseling) that specifically hire persons otherwise dependent upon transfer payments such as welfare, disability, unemployment, or other such allowances. The initial financing of each new venture comes from diverting transfer payments from the various levels of government, and the persons who would otherwise receive such payments instead receive regular paychecks from the HRDA businesses where they are employed. The paychecks represent, of course, more dollars than the initial capital of transfer assistance funds because the HRDA businesses are operated as viable, revenue-generating ventures providing market-rate goods and services. These commercial ventures have included an auto rental franchise, a small appliances repair center, and a bookkeeping service.

HRDA was created as a nonprofit corporation, but it immediately established a wholly owned, for-profit subsidiary, HRDA Enterprises, Ltd., to act as a holding company for the various for-profit businesses. Some stock in each individual firm is available as an incentive for employees and managers of the ventures; the rest is retained by the holding company, HRDA Enterprises, Ltd. The ventures pay taxes like any other firm and undergo all the same vicissitudes of success or bankruptcy; thus some HRDA ventures have failed. A company may be initially capitalized by government money, but it more than pays back what it has received in taxes on the corporate incomes and on the salaries of the managers and employees. The main point that I want to make is that here, as in the case of EBCDC, a dual structure was created—one for-profit corporation and one nonprofit corporation. That sort of dual structure has eventually been evolved by most of the United States CDCs, and it may well turn out to be the most useful format in Canada as well.

There are several reasons for this dual structure choice. The specifics of the law vary between the two countries and from one provincial or state jurisdiction to another, but in all cases there are the tax exemption considerations. Because the nonprofit corporate form forbids the distribution of the financial benefits of its operation to any person and requires instead that they go for charitable, educational, and similar purposes, the income generated by community economic development activities has certain protections from taxation in all jurisdictions. Freedom from taxation is important if the proceeds of development are to be reinvested directly in the community rather than drained off to other purposes by the taxing authorities.

In addition, the nonprofit format can be useful for maintaining the organization's credibility in the community, for otherwise the organization may be seen as simply a way for selected people to enrich themselves. Given the history of exploitation in the depleted community, any business-related activity will be suspiciously viewed as just another way to extract dollars from the residents. It is essential, then, that residents know and be convinced that the program is for broad community benefit, not for the good of some favored few. The nonprofit form helps give that assurance. A further advantage is that a nonprofit, tax exempt group can attract grants from private sources seeking a tax deduction for a contribution to an eligible organization.

If the nonprofit form has some advantages, it also has some disadvantages. And it is to offset those disadvantages that the for-profit form can be concurrently used. It may be used, as in the case of East Boston, to counter the image of government grant sponsorship and of the inefficiency often associated with grant-supported groups. Thus EBCDC aimed to present the image of businesslike operations and to project the intent of generating real profits from productive ventures. The for-profit, tax-paying form can also blunt the frequent criticism that accompanies any government assistance of such ventures, that they take dollars from taxpayers but do not return any.

Quite apart from what might be called the "locally desired image" for public relations purposes, there are other advantages that the community economic development group can gain from instruments that are organized as for-profit corporations. Banks do not like to loan money to nonprofit organizations, especially because if the borrower defaults, it is difficult to move against the organization: who wants to foreclose on a church or a kindergarten? Banks feel more comfortable if the borrower is a for-profit corporation with mortgageable assets or a prior good credit reputation. Thus HRDA Enterprises, Ltd., finds it relatively easy to borrow for the credit needs of its ventures, but it has discovered that its parent organization must be kept in the background. Moreover, strangely enough, some government assistance may be available to a for-profit business that is refused to a nonprofit firm, or even a cooperative firm. In the United States, the Small Business Administration has had a history of adamantly rejecting even for-profit firms when they are wholly owned by nonprofit community development groups because they are somehow not considered real businesses. In a similar vein, I once read a rejection letter that opined that cooperatives per se were un-American. Thus a CDC organized legally as a for-profit corporation would have an easier time dealing with people and organizations holding rather conventional views as to how a business is supposed to look. The for-profit structures of a CDC holding company and its subsidiary ventures offer one means of allaying some conventional anxieties, although not all problems in that respect are solved.

Whether the core institution is organized as a nonprofit or for-profit organization, it will be vulnerable to complaints that in its businesses it is seeking profits subsidized by government funds. All community economic development programs will at one time or another use some government aid from one or another level of government, and this fact in itself can raise issues about the status of a CDC for-profit business. If the government aid moves into a business venture owned by a CDC, someone in the private business sector is apt to complain—whether or not the CDC represents a competitive threat.

In northern Wisconsin, Impact Seven, a CDC serving seven counties, tried to get a county board to issue a permit for a wood chip mill. The board turned down the request, with members expressing reservations about the use of government grants for the capitalization of the venture. The board was happy, at the same time, to provide an okay for a Fortune 500 company to set up the same kind of mill in a nearby property. In short, it was not the type of industry or the location that bothered the board, but the idea of a nonprofit CDC establishing a profit-making venture with federal money.

A similar problem confronted the Southwest Virginia Community Development Fund, a CDC based in Roanoke, Virginia. The CDC used a federal grant to capitalize a corrugated-box-manufacturing concern and soon found itself and the government funding agency sued by another firm that was making boxes. The other firm charged unfair competition because the CDC's venture was subsidized by government funds. By a technicality, the CDC was dropped as a defendant and was free to maintain its enterprise. But the litigation prevented the CDC from using further funds for its expansion plans, so it had to sell off the business to a major corporation, The Dixie Cup Company. Dixie Cup has continued the factory in the area, maintaining the employment that the CDC was seeking and providing the necessary expansion capital. The other company too is still in business, a testament to the fact that competition as such was not really the issue.

Canada has a tradition of giving direct grants for private enterprise, under the rationale of promoting public policy in economic development. The United States—despite some prominent exceptions, such as the land grants to railroads in the nineteenth century—manages to be more indirect in its subsidies. And so free enterprise ideologues are more apt to attack CDC ventures in the United States as operating against the rules of business, but even in Canada New Dawn has had to defend itself from the criticism that it competes unfairly with private business in sponsoring the construction of subsidized housing. Someday another CDC in the United States or Canada may have to defend itself in court. Yet the real issue is not the legal standing of the CDC businesses, but the perception of them within the business community. The local community economic development organization needs to present itself and its work to the business sector and explain both its non-profit, community benefit format and its tax-paying, for-profit activities that run by the same rules as any private enterprise. The CDC that gives careful attention to public knowledge about its practices and goals gets friendly support from the business sector and heads off misunderstanding and antagonism. It becomes recognized as a constructive actor in the local economy.

The internal structure of the core institution has three major and formal organizational features—members or shareholders, a board of directors, and a staff—which have significant implications for the role of the group in the community. There is some broad base of members (for a nonprofit organization) or shareholders (for a for-profit organization) who are usually individuals but in some cases may be organizations. Thus the community as such is not the public base of the core institution so much as the individuals or organizations which have taken the initiative to establish the community development group as a formal institution. In the East Boston CDC, a coalition of dozens of organizations was represented in the council, but when the CDC was incorporated, individuals eventually became shareholders. Today there are about two thousand stockholders, either residents or other people who work in East Boston. In this case, as in most cases where membership is individual, membership is open to anyone who lives or works in the area.

Where the organizational base of members is not individuals but organizations, the members are limited to specified organizations, but these are usually organizations with open membership for individual residents. The format of the Harlem Commonwealth Council and the Bedford-Stuyvesant Restoration Corporation—both in New York City—depends upon representation of organizations. The corporate members include neighborhood block associations or other community groups with open membership—for example, the local chapter of the NAACP. The same kind of structure is true of the Oakland, California, Spanish-Speaking Unity Council. A community economic development organization, therefore, can be a federation of local organizations.

In the case of New Dawn, corporate membership is not broadly based on a formal level; instead this CDC is a self-selected group that has made a particular effort to ensure that a range of constituencies in the community are represented. For example, the local senior citizens group is asked to select a representative, as is the council of local churches; businesses, the major credit union, and other commercially oriented groups are sought out. The organizers of New Dawn chose a different path for membership and directors than that of the Hough Area Development Corporation. HADC recruited many dozens of organizational leaders, all of whom originally were directors, but New Dawn limits its membership to around twenty, a number that can also actively participate as board members. However, New Dawn also organizes committees of any other residents who want to deal with some single specific community project or problem. Thus, New Dawn's base is spread out through informal committee membership rather than formal corporate membership. Those who become active in the committees routinely find their way onto the governing board, which, by virtue of New Dawn bylaws, requires a regular turnover and limited terms for the governing directors (members).

It will be apparent that every community economic development group has some sort of collective formal leadership, usually a board of directors or a board of trustees. These boards are selected by the membership but not necessarily from the membership; that is, the members may choose a board that includes people from outside the organization in order to broaden the organization's technical or political grasp.

In both the United States and Canada, great emphasis is placed upon the democratic control of an organization if it is to engender widespread support. Open membership, general elections to a board, and other standard forms of democratic control are given a premium. However, in such groups, as elsewhere, such conventional control devices do not necessarily tag the actual level of community responsibility and accountability. The forms can be perverted to serve the ends of a venal group or individual. Therefore, to an outsider trying to assess the true relationship of a purported development group to its community, the history of the group's operation is often more significant than the particular internal rules of procedures that are formally called for in its bylaws.

A more or less self-selected group of leaders may in fact have a documentable history of rectitude and broad community representation as well as responsibility, responsiveness, and accountability. For instance, in New Dawn one finds a history of careful board consideration of potential conflicts of interest and resignations offered and accepted in a carefully evaluated fashion. In other organizations, where broadly based elections and electioneering are a part of the apparatus of community control, there may or may not be the same observant caution. I know one case in which an election suddenly turned out to be a maneuver by one faction to gain board control and to thereby reverse previous actions that had prevented the diversion of the CDC's resources to private benefit. The upshot of that election was that the staff director was fired to permit the hiring of someone who would be more complaisant. I am happy to report that the succeeding election returned things to normal and resulted in some procedural changes that would make it difficult for a similar coup to take place again. Yet because of that history and certain compromises that came out of it, I would still be cautious about the operations of that group.

A board cannot operate always as a single unit; a division of labor will be represented in organizational subunits within the board. Since the whole group ordinarily cannot act together more than once a month, an executive committee must be established to handle business between the full board meetings. When the whole board meets, the committee can report its activities and obtain formal approval of the actions it has taken. A long-standing organization with many different projects either under way or in the planning stage will also have a special committee for each big project or area of program activity so that more detailed supervision and policy development can be delegated efficiently and only major decisions need be brought back to the full board for review and approval.

Whether long-standing or newly organized or in between, the board usefully delegates responsibilities to various other *functional* committees (as contrasted to project or program committees) to focus on specific tasks that would not be efficiently handled in detail by an entire board. Most common and most important is the finance committee, which must have the capacity and will to demand, receive, review, and report to the full board on monthly statements of the financial condition of the organization. These statements may have been generated by the staff or by a contracted accounting firm and previously reviewed by the chief staff officer; but the finance committee has final responsibility to assure the board that everything is in good shape or to warn the board of impending problems and make suggestions about how to handle them. Such reports will include not only the overall budget activity of the organization but also that of individual projects when these have substantial budgets—even if there is a project or program area committee that also reviews the finances of its special concern.

Another possible subunit of the board is a committee charged with the function of long-range planning, including the kinds of arrangements that need to be made quarterly to accomplish progress reviews and consequent changes in plans, as well as annual exercises to generate one-, two-, and five-year projections. This committee would see that working papers are produced for board consideration, and it would also make sure that the board has a leisurely opportunity in a conducive setting to concentrate on the very important tasks of periodically settling on the new goals of the organization and the plans for their achievement.

Still another functional committee may be set up to deal with the board's own self-development—and by extension organizational self-renewal. This committee may be combined with the long-range planning committee, but it involves a real difference in function which can be usefully separated off and delegated to a different subgroup of the board. The self-development committee will concern itself with two highly charged tasks. It will seek out, recruit, develop, carefully screen, and otherwise discover and nominate formally or informally other potential board members, especially in the light of the gaps in experience and skills currently represented on the board. It will also respond to the need to increase the skills of current board members for discharging their heavy responsibilities. This function is particularly important in the case of new board members who must be brought up to speed for working with those who have been around longer. So there needs to be group orientation sessions (or, alternatively, a kind of individual tutoring) to alert the new board members (usually brought on to the board annually) to the continuing key issues of the organization and to the history of the organization as it expresses current issues and current goals.

Even long-term board members can benefit from an annual workshop focusing on a single important operational issue. Among such issues are the legal responsibilities of a board member, conflict of interest problems, how to ask questions about a financial statement, problems in the division of labor between board and staff, how to get the most out of a meeting, and so forth. Such workshops are designed and executed by outside specialists selected by the self-development committee. The self-development committee will have the responsibiity of sponsoring skill enhancement opportunities for all the board members in whatever form that may be appropriate to their particular situation. Since some board members may feel that they are perfectly capable already or may fear the interference of outsiders who are styled as experts, this task is a delicate one, but still necessary for a productive organization. In a larger organization, the board committee might also take on responsibilities for devising similar self-renewal opportunities on the staff level, though this probably ought to be the responsibility of the chief staff officer.

I now turn briefly to the final major organizational feature of a completely developed community economic development group —a functioning full-time staff. The volunteer efforts of committees and board members are absolutely essential to any successful program, but volunteers can do only so much; eventually the group will build a salaried staff, even if that means beginning only with one part-time person. Continuity of management on a day-to-day basis requires ongoing attention that volunteers ordinarily cannot offer. The creation of staff positions signals a sustained and broader effort, including board commitment to generate the resources to pay the staff to do the daily work. Without such a board commitment, an organization will find that too much of its staff energy and anxiety is bound up in finding money to pay their own salaries.

The three major internal differentiations—members or shareholders, board, and staff—imply the evolution of working relationships by which each group carries out its particular function in the total picture. The members or shareholders must represent the different affected constituencies within the community, select a board that will take responsibility and authority for economic development in the name of the community, and monitor the policies and operations of that board. For its part, the board will establish and reassess detailed policies, locate the resources in money and in technical knowledge to carry out those policies, monitor operations to see that the policies are appropriately executed, and take the lead in the community and outside it for articulating and promoting local goals. The staff provides the ongoing execution of the program, carrying out the board policies; it generates information and reports for the board so that the directors can make decisions; and it supports board members in the task of articulating and promoting the goals of the organization.

All this is quite naturally standard and also quite naturally a source of complex problems. Especially delicate is drawing the line among the groups for the responsibilities and authorities implied, a task that is never completed and that is an existential aspect of the core institutional tool. Simply because community economic development requires this tool, sophisticated interpersonal and organizational skills will make an enormous difference in the performance of the central corporation and its subsidiary or related units. At this juncture the quality of local and staff leadership, not the details of internal structure, becomes the critical element of success.

Let me continue, however, with some further details of the structural options that such groups will face. Because a community economic development program will include a variety of quite differentiated activities, the internal organization will reflect the different requirements of those activities. Quite apart from the dual structure option of having *both* a nonprofit and a for-profit administrative structure, the CDC (I will hereafter use this term to stand generically for all forms of the core organizations) will exhibit differentiated parts or even separately incorporated entities that specialize in one or more identifiable activities. Thus, it is likely that each CDC business venture will be separately incorporated so as to limit the spread of any liabilities that the operation of that business may engender. Initially, however, a new business activity may begin simply as an unincorporated division of the central organization, to be separately incorporated at a later point. In fact, all activities, including social services or medical services, for example, may follow that line of evolution. A senior citizens resource center can be organizationally internal to the CDC until it is smoothly operating, at which point it may be spun off as a more or less independent nonprofit corporation whose membership and board perhaps only partially overlap with the parent CDC.

In the early stages of the initiation of any program activity, it is not easy to differentiate the efforts going into it from much of the other work going on in the CDC, but after the developmental period, a separate corporation is apt to be established for psychological identity, accounting, tax, and liability purposes. At that time the CDC will confront the decision as to what degree of independence should be given to the new unit—whether, for example, an interlocking board relationship will be maintained.

For monitoring and management purposes, board and staff organization will mirror the corporate divisions and subsidiaries. The more complex and varied the program, the more board committees and staff specialization will be required. These, again, will raise nitty-gritty questions of how the whole operation is to be integrated into a reasonably interdependent and mutually supportive framework. In the largest and most complex programs, like that of TELACU, The East Los Angeles CDC now operating on a multimillion-dollar annual budget, board committees must cover major segments of the program and yet are more and more dependent upon adequate staff support to carry out their own function of monitoring the operations. It then becomes a major challenge to ensure that staff members are performing properly.

A final comment on structure is that there needs to be some specialized organizational attention to the matter of business development. No community economic development organization operates without some business development or investment activity, and the specialized tasks in that activity usually have to be located in a specific person or committee. As has been made clear before, community economic development is not simply business development, but no such program is complete without continuing efforts to create new business resources in the community. Because this activity is so central, business development issues suffuse much of the organization's work and thus may not be focused in one person or subgroup but will be a generally shared concern. At the same time, the organization has probably not fully matured until it has developed an internal specialized structure for business development tasks.

Stepping back from the details of organizational structure, one will discern a pattern in the evolution and format of the core organization, a pattern within which those details are subsumed. For example, how the group begins varies widely, but the core insitution is always initiated by local residents; it is not organized by an outside agency, even though such agencies may have critical influence at one time or another. It arises from specific local conditions, history, and problems and will be shaped by those local factors. It is not born once and for all in a final form; the structure will grow and evolve as it clarifies and chooses its major goals. It will always be somehow representative of the various subgroups or constituencies that are influential in the community, but there is no set format for that representation. The variations in structure and evolution will reflect the roles played by such constituencies; and whatever the structure and its representative nature, it will be both responsive and accountable to the varying constituencies. This responsiveness may mean ongoing compromises between conflicting claims for setting the priorities and using the resources of the organization. Overall, however, the structure will articulate the specific purpose (usually with strong moral or ideological overtones) of broadly and comprehensively improving the local economy for local benefit. And eventually the organization will evolve into some sort of corporate format with specialized structures for different tasks, most particularly for business development activities.

EIGHT

The Place of Business Development

B UILDING businesses is not necessarily the centerpiece of
every community economic development strategy, but it is always
an essential part. Even when other facets of local life seem more
important, the role of business will require attention.

A recent case in point is the Millers River CDC, a group established only in 1985 to serve an area of small towns and villages
in rural central Massachusetts. Residents are worried that the
whole way of life of that area will be changed because of an increasing influx of fairly well-to-do people who are willing to commute an hour or two to Boston or other large cities to the east. The
central concern is that housing is starting to be priced out of reach
for local people, especially for the coming generation of younger
families of very modest incomes for whom renting or even buying
had not been problematic before. The Millers River district thus is
no longer faced with the prospect of isolation and depression, like
much of small-town Massachusetts where the ancient industries
have moved away or just disappeared; but it does face the prospect
that the long-time residents will be squeezed out of their community. The community will be taken away from them, as surely as
the West End in Boston was taken away from its residents. So the
CDC has been exploring and experimenting with different forms
of housing development and land control in order to maintain a
base of affordable shelter.

The Millers River area, from the economic point of view, could
presumably specialize in being a bedroom community, especially
of spacious exurban estates. It would not need much local industry

or business because it could depend upon the business of other communities to provide the commuter jobs. However, if it is to retain the lower-income, noncommuting, long-term residents, it must consider how they will be earning a living in such a changed community. Building affordable housing offers a base for those of modest incomes only if they can continue to earn at least that level of income. That is one reason why the Millers River CDC is struggling to create a business development strategy as one dimension in its overall planning for inevitable change.

As they have studied the situation, they have concluded that they might promote the type of business that will support or participate in the projected construction upsurge. The task would be to strengthen local capacity to handle the kinds of construction activity that will be necessary, both for so-called affordable housing and for homes for the middle-income or other more affluent newcomers. At least then the supply of local electricians, plumbers, drywall specialists, carpenters, and other tradespeople and their less trained helpers can expand rather than be frozen out by outside architects or contractors. Moreover, the CDC is considering how workshop space can be included in planning for their new rural village project. In this manner, provision might be made for self-employment in the construction trades and other small businesses. The scale of such businesses will fit the CDC's vision of maintaining, insofar as is practical, the way of life and the ecological balances of the rural setting. In the meantime, the CDC is pressing on with its first project—the self-help construction of houses for those who are of very limited means but are too well off to qualify for low-income subsidies. Actually, that had been the CDC's top priority before it began considering any involvement in business issues.

It is indeed rare for any CDC to be truly prepared in its initial months to engage in any business development activity at all, even in those CDCs that begin with some idea of doing business development. Usually most of the initial leaders will not have had business as their own occupational background; the local impetus for thinking about community economic development ordinarily comes from people with organizational talents bent toward social activism and human services, not bent toward business ventures. So they are apt to be a bit wary of extending themselves into a new field. In the Millers River case, in fact, none of the initial prime movers came from the business world. They included such people as a community worker, a teacher, a librarian, a lawyer, a low-income rural housing specialist, and a town treasurer—mainly people of modest incomes and long local residence. As they began formulating their policies, they reached out for other board members who had business experience. That is just as common a pattern as starting off with some representatives from the business sector, as did New Dawn and Hough.

Although business sector representatives may become key movers in the early stages of the CDC, they are not, interestingly enough, the usual source of pressure for an early start in business development activity. It is often the nonbusiness leaders who generally emphasize from the very beginning the need to work business development into the community development program. The business people tend to hold themselves back to see what the others mean by this new perspective on what business ventures are supposed to do. The upshot is that even if the CDC has some key business and financial people on its governing board, all the members of the group are charting new ground with each other and tend to be very tentative about what they can do in the way of stimulating the business sector.

This tentativeness arises partly from what the group might recognize as a built-in tension or opposition between business and human or community development goals. If the group spans a wide enough range of local leaders, it will not take lightly the task of somehow melding this set of very disparate perspectives and procedures. It will have to struggle to integrate the different ideas and worries that each brings to the common enterprise. Those who are respectful of the difficulty of making a business profitable will wonder how the constraints of other concurrent nonbusiness goals can be handled, while those who look back at the history of the exploitation of people by profit-seeking businesses worry about how the local people can be protected in the course of the CDC's own business activity. In fact, the same person may simultaneously articulate both anxieties in the group's early discussions —and from time to time thereafter.

The place of a business development program within the overall strategy of the CDC is only one of the tough issues that the organizers will immediately face; other issues competing for attention delay quick movement into business development. Since members will be poised to pursue other local problems—to carry out other (nonbusiness) projects—these too have somehow to be fitted into the strategy. Suddenly the CDC directors find themselves confronted with the necessity of planning how they are going to do all that they have been thinking about. So the first major project for the CDC often turns out not to be a business project at all; it is a plan. And to make a plan, the group has to become quite explicit and precise about what it wants to accomplish. Only rarely have any members had experience in systematic planning; it will be a major challenge. In the process of struggling through the task, many issues come clear, and presumably some of them are resolved as the group bites the bullet in making its choices of what it can do and how it will seek the scarce resources (in people, time, and money) to do what it has decided upon.

This sequence of events will occur spontaneously in neighborhood organizations that are truly self-initiated, although the degree of sophistication in detailing plans will vary. In settings in which some outside source of help (a government program or a church grant or whatever) seems quite accessible to the group, the group learns that the outside aid entails other pressures to produce what, on its own, the group would eventually discover is needed for its own internal purposes. The CDC is thereby started on the long learning process of *corporate management,* the piecing together of internal and external resources directed toward a set of goals at different levels of abstraction and different probabilities of achievement. To some members it will be an exhilarating experience to confront this future; to others, the planning process will be too frustrating and too dull.

At this point, the body of people involved in the CDC may well undergo important changes, and the turnover in membership becomes still another problem to transcend. Let us not underestimate the trauma of losing some of the originators. The turnover in people who have become used to working together and seeing things together and accomplishing important things together is something that will periodically threaten the stability and future of any community group. The challenge is to change the relationships without destroying what was good in them.

Since there are plenty of published guides to planning (including planning especially in nonprofit institutions), I will not dwell on this general process for the CDC except to emphasize that, as with all plans, a CDC plan is not supposed to be set in concrete. It is only a tool that must periodically be reshaped to achieve its purpose as a guide to clarifying choices and helping to measure progress on those choices. As such, it is an essential tool, and CDCs that are successful learn how to use and update plans, both for the CDC itself and for each business development and other project.

Within the context of community economic development defined as an institution-building process, business development becomes defined as the subprocess of creating and strengthening community-based institutions in the local business sector. It is then helpful to conceptualize that particular type of institution—business—as simply a means *in the first instance* for producing goods or services for sale and thereby generating revenue for community purposes. Once this is clear, then the CDC board can clarify for itself and decide upon two successive questions that will shape its business development plans. What purpose is this revenue to be generated for? And how much revenue are we talking about anyway (that is, how big will the business or businesses be)? Logically, a board should proceed in that manner, but usually it does not do so right away. Instead, the CDC leaders tend to begin (naturally enough) with some a priori ideas of the kind of business development activity that they assume is needed. Recall Bendavid-Val's New England community where the consultant discovered that the proposed project (an industrial park) would have exacerbated the community's problems. In that instance, the community had not adequately analyzed its employment needs and would have created jobs that did not fit the local needs.

However, let us assume that the CDC has carefully built its plan from a systematic analysis of the local setting and its problems and has specified the exact purposes of its aim to generate revenues from the increased production and sale of goods and services in the local community. What purposes might they be pursuing? *Employment creation* (of carefully defined job opportunities) is only one of the possible purposes of business development by the CDC. In fact, some business development activities may not pursue increased local employment as a prime goal at all. Other purposes, as sought by CDCs in various localities, have included the following.

Profits. Surplus revenues from the business are expected to help support other program expenses of the CDC. For example, profitable rents from an office building project may be designed to support the CDC day-care center.

Neighborhood shopping convenience. Revenues will offset the full costs of providing (selling) the good or service that had not previously been readily available to local residents. For example, the CDC may establish a taxi company successful enough to offer reliable service to a neighborhood that has been discriminated against by existing taxi companies.

Employment training. Revenues from the business where the training takes place will be sufficient to tolerate and subsidize the costs of on-the-job training. For example, a light manufacturing plant might hire otherwise unemployable youths for electronic assembly work with the expectation that such employees can be taught enough to be promoted internally or helped to find better-paying jobs in other industrial settings.

Visibility. Revenues will be self-sustaining so that the business can provide continuing public evidence of the work of the CDC just by being there. A CDC may find such evidence important as a way of recruiting some constituencies to its banner who are not particularly motivated by human services goals; or the business project may be designed to have a significant impact in underpinning the group's political influence. An example of a very visible project is an assistance program for new microbusinesses (mom-and-pop ventures) by which the CDC can get a widespread and favorable reputation for its concern with a struggling but potentially very productive constituency.

Multiplier effects. The business will produce revenues that will recirculate in the community to generate more economic activity, including spin-off ventures. For example, establishing a local shopping center will attract residents to spend locally for goods and services rather than go to some other shopping plaza and will encourage local people to start businesses that will be tenants in the center.

Some types of business institutions are designed to accomplish one of these purposes better than other types, depending upon the local setting. In addition, some businesses will be more likely to include a number of payoffs, while others will not easily fulfill more than one CDC purpose. In any case, the CDC must decide on what community aim is to be achieved by the business development activity. It thereby answers the first question that will shape its business development plans: What are the revenues generated for?

When the CDC confronts the second question—how much revenue is to be generated—it answers the question of scale, predicting how many jobs are to be created, how much profit can be expected for supporting CDC programs, how much job training can be provided, and so on. In setting a goal of how much revenue should be produced, the CDC willy-nilly sets the direction of the type of business development strategy to be pursued. For example, if very large revenues are to be achieved in order to create a substantial number of jobs in a relatively short time, that goal would more or less suggest one particular strategy—namely, recruiting one or more large outside firms to establish a large local facility with many jobs to match the skills of the local unemployed labor force. In short, the CDC has pretty much ruled out starting a new company itself. In fact, by settling on the need for a swift major job impact, it has decided against any new company. New companies cannot be expected to produce a large number of jobs in a short time; or if so, the company would have to be started on a capital scale that is not really feasible for a CDC and its likely partners. So recruiting an outside corporation is, by default, the strategic choice for swift major job impact.

As I have indicated earlier, the company-chasing strategy is quite risky, but sometimes a CDC may feel that it has the necessary clout or package of incentives that can make this an appropriate approach. For example, the Bedford-Stuyvesant Restoration Corporation in its beginnings in 1967 had the necessary influence to pursue such a project. For a brief period in the late 1960s, major corporations considered it both feasible and good public relations to assist in the improvement of America's black slums, and Restoration stood out as an attractive opportunity for exercising this sense of corporate responsibility. Restoration had access to many top corporate leaders, including the chairman of IBM, who was on the board of the D&S Corporation, organized to work beside Restoration. Through this connection, the CDC persuaded IBM to establish a cable-manufacturing facility in the Bedford-Stuyvesant neighborhood. This was Restoration's first major business development project, and when the plant was set up in a local abandoned industrial building, it paid off swiftly in about three hundred new jobs.

On the one hand, even that impressive result did not make a significant dent in local unemployment (then measuring in the many thousands in that huge Brooklyn district); the district was not attractive enough to IBM for a really major installation (at about the same time it established a similar facility employing three thousand in a sunny, attractive, small city, Boca Raton, Florida); and neither IBM nor any other major outside corporation tried to duplicate IBM's contribution to the Bedford-Stuyvesant economy. On the other hand, Restoration can point with pride to a significant coup in enlisting IBM; the facility was certainly a very visible recycling of unused industrial space; it created good-paying real jobs; the local work force (contrary to pessimistic fears about the quality of workers from this deteriorated neighborhood) turned out to make this facility one of IBM's most productive; and the productivity encouraged IBM to later double the facility's size (expanding on another site) and to maintain it to this day.

Certainly Restoration would not have gained so swiftly the number of local jobs that IBM provided if, for example, it had chosen to promote smaller local ventures generating smaller revenues. Yet it is also evident that choosing to seek out the major revenue-producing project was possible for that CDC only because of the special circumstances of its access to the IBM chairman and the historical setting of that time.

Incidentally, with its special access to the New York City corporate world, Restoration also successfully pursued at that time the creation of a high-powered consortium of banks and insurance companies which committed funds to a major mortgage pool for the community, then suffering badly from redlining. And again, contrary to conventional pessimism, the mortgage pool made a good return to the lenders. Restoration thus illustrates how a CDC can achieve a major impact with major business development activities; but its special capacity to mobilize resources was (and continues to be) much different from that of most CDCs in a depleted community.

The two issues—purpose and scale—in business development planning ordinarily make it clear to the community group that what it seeks to do in its first business project will have a long lead time. Perhaps it will not be accomplished in a few months or even a few years. This extended time perspective may be intolerable to some of the early activists in the community group and to residents who expect something quick from the CDC. Business development activities usually cannot satisfy the urge for something to show early on for a CDC's efforts. Thus, in the overall plan of the CDC, other activities may be laid out that will have an earlier visibility than the long-term business development project. In fact, it is usually necessary for a CDC to have this sort of capacity for phased results so that there can be some rewarding feedback to the staff, to the board, and to the residents watching the work. The larger the intended scale of business efforts, the more important it will be to pay attention to the shorter-term benefits that can also be achieved along the way.

The Hough Area Development Corporation obtained a grant of over a million dollars from the U.S. government to begin its program, partly because its first and showpiece project was to be the development of an ambitious one-floor shopping mall with a garden above and townhouses for middle- and low-income families. The Martin Luther King, Jr., Plaza was to be a symbol of black pride in that architects, builders, commercial tenants, and families were all expected to be (and eventually were) drawn primarily from the black community of Cleveland. Of course, it was an exciting project, but assembling the land, drawing up the plans, getting the zoning approvals, arranging financing for subsidized housing, finding the right tenants, and so on, was to be a long process, and HADC knew that it had to do something else along the way to show concern with other community issues. Therefore, it also planned for the creation of a Handyman's Maintenance Service which would hire low-skilled, unemployed residents for janitorial, landscaping, and other similar contracts with major Cleveland facilities. That project addressed direct job creation needs. Another project, also pursued at this time, aimed at promoting local black construction firms. A loan fund was established to offer financing for operating capital for small contractors. With these projects HADC demonstrated that it was actually creating a range of new resources for residents while the agonizingly slow and virtually invisible progress on the plaza went on.

Aside from recruiting an established firm to set up a local branch as Restoration did, there are two basic choices in CDC business development strategy. Either the CDC engages in some sort of *technical support and assistance* for local business people (or others who can be attracted to move into the locality), or it gets involved in *direct investments* (as HADC did with Handyman's Maintenance and with the contractor loans). Let us first examine the opportunities offered by the first choice.

In choosing the route of assistance to business people, the CDC in effect will be deciding to act primarily as a *catalyst* for the efforts of others. Instead of directly creating or expanding a local business, the CDC offers aid to those who are building their own businesses. This approach will engage entrepreneurial energies and resources that the CDC all by itself would find it hard to deploy. Moreover, such assistance is a good deal less expensive than trying to start or finance new businesses.

One might suppose that there are plenty of technical support resources sponsored by government agencies (such as Canada's Federal Business Development Bank or the U.S. Small Business Administration), by universities, or by other established institutions, and that these resources could serve all the needs of the CDC's neighborhood entrepreneurs or would-be entrepreneurs. But often those services are not well designed for local needs. The format or settings discourage local residents, many of whom tend to believe that the service is not really for them. Thus the CDC on its own or in association with established programs can fill an unmet local need—for example, by sponsoring low-key seminars for aspiring business people that will introduce them to the resources available through the CDC or others for training, financing, marketing, and other technical assistance.

It is not only the smaller or new businesses that can use the CDC's help and thus contribute more to the economic health of the community. Recognizing this fact, Brooklyn's big CDC, Restoration, does an annual survey of all industries in Bedford-Stuyvesant to keep track of their problems and plans, especially regarding decisions about, or consideration of, expansion or relocation. In one instance they discovered that a company had outgrown its quarters but could not find any local space that would fit its needs and so was planning a move from the neighborhood. Restoration put a parcel of land together that they had been planning to use for other purposes in business development, sold it to the company, and thus held that major employer in the area. Since that company's average wage was almost 50 percent more than the average family income in the neighborhood, retaining those jobs locally was a significant achievement. An active CDC that is really sensitive to the place that local business plays in its community will keep itself informed and ready to play a critical part in promoting local private business institutions, big or small.

Helping others start, expand, or maintain their businesses is an alternative to the CDC's creating its own new businesses, but the assistance activity itself can be organized as a business venture which is financed by fees paid by the client businesses that use the services. This arrangement is particularly likely if the CDC offers *support services* like bookkeeping and legal counsel, for which a business would expect to pay appropriately.

A more comprehensive support service is involved in the so-called *incubator* concept, which has been used by the Richmond County Development Corporation of Nova Scotia and a number of other community-based development groups in Canada but not, interestingly enough, to any great extent by CDCs in the United States. In this approach, the CDC builds or renovates a structure that is designed to accommodate perhaps ten to twenty beginning small businesses that require only a small amount of space and cannot afford the usual available rentals. Included in the incubator project may be secretarial, telephone-answering, bookkeeping, and other services for which each new venture can contract on the scale necessary to meet its needs. There will also usually be ready access to technical counsel on the problems of beginning businesses as well as ongoing advice in the general areas of marketing, financial controls, personnel, and so on. Incidentally, the incubator setting offers a valuable side benefit that the budding entrepreneur can appreciate—namely, association with others who are also struggling to start up their businesses.

Opportunity for peer group interaction is a significant free side benefit in the incubator project, but of course the costs of space and other services must be defrayed, and the CDC, if not subsidized to provide this comprehensive aid, will have to offer it on a businesslike basis that will meet expenses. The incubator concept has, in fact, been used as a profit-generating venture by private industry—most specifically by Control Data, Inc., of Minnesota—and there is no reason why a CDC might not also contemplate a profit stream from its foray into this sort of economic development project. However, its concern with the local economic environment would ordinarily reduce its profit expectations and increase its readiness to support local new ventures at less cost to them.

The incubator approach, involving, as it does, investment in property development, is a kind of conceptual bridge between the technical assistance strategy and the direct investment strategy. In the latter, the CDC with access to investment capital makes an *equity or debt investment* in a new or expanding venture; that is, the CDC takes an ownership stake by an equity financing or it can stay at some distance from ownership by offering a loan to the business or its owners. The conventional investment world has ingeniously devised a veritable cornucopia of different types of equity and debt investment forms. Some indication of the various forms of capital that have been turned to use by community-based economic development groups will be provided later on in this book in a discussion of financing.

Whatever the type of investment, the CDC is taking some very definite degree of risk of loss of its scarce financial resources. For that reason, like conventional investors, CDCs often want to see others at risk in the same venture, partly to spread the risk and partly to involve the expertise and efforts of others in making sure the venture will go. Therefore, very few CDCs go the route, like Bronx Venture Corporation (BVC) of New York City, of choosing to hold the entire equity of its businesses. Although BVC has relied upon bank financing and other credit, it can boast of wholly owning (or virtually wholly owning) all the local businesses it has started or bought out and expanded. (Its venture managers have access to some stock.) Moreover, this CDC can also claim to have succeeded, so far, in making large profits from its business development activity.

With a model like BVC to emulate, one might suppose that most CDCs are the sole owners of those ventures in which each has made direct investments. Actually, that is probably true for equity stakes, but that ownership picture does not take into account the many other direct investments of debt capital (especially through CDC revolving loan funds or revolving loan guarantee funds) by which CDCs help finance local businesses without any CDC ownership participation whatsoever.

For equity investments, however, the Kentucky Highlands Investment Corporation (KHIC) offers a successful countermodel to BVC. Early in its history, KHIC determined that the management problems of its first venture, its wholly owned toy-manufacturing firm, took too much of its staff and board time. So the CDC decided to take a different tack and to operate in much the same way as a traditional venture capital firm: that is, it would back an entrepreneur for a local facility, taking an investment position of varying degrees and types of ownership but leaving majority stock to the entrepreneur, who would make the firm his or her full-time concern. KHIC's philosophy was that if it could make wise choices of whom to back, it could rely upon the entrepreneur and his or her management team to make the business a success—because it would be truly the entrepreneur's business and not the CDC's. In this manner, the CDC would achieve its job creation and financial aims without having to involve itself in the day-to-day details of management.

Such *joint ventures* are a frequent tactic of many CDCs in the United States. However, the joint venture approach in direct equity investment often appears to board members and other CDC supporters to risk more than the dollars invested. To many community activists, the CDC ought to insure the interests of the community by holding at least majority stock ownership, if not full ownership. The reasoning is that only with such massive ownership can the CDC control the business enough to make sure that it will provide the community benefits for which the investment was made. The fear of exploitation is so severe, especially in the earliest stages of a CDC, that the typical group often does not like to even contemplate offering investment funds to a business that it cannot control.

Yet many CDCs have devised appropriate tools, based on conventional venture capital controls, which can ensure that joint ventures will be operated to the benefit of the community, even when the CDC has only a small percentage of stock. The tools are in the provisions of the *investment agreement* between the entrepreneur and the CDC. The investment agreement can effectively address the natural concerns of community groups that any business they aid financially will aid the community. For example, if the CDC aims to create jobs for local residents, the agreement can contain a provision for local hiring of candidates referred by the CDC, for the types of jobs to be made available, for regular reporting to the CDC of the composition of the work force, and for financial and other disciplines when the company does not live up to its agreement. If the CDC is especially concerned that the facility stays in the neighborhood, the investment agreement can contain a provision that prohibits moving the facility and even a provision that would prohibit the company from establishing any additional facilities outside the community except by approval of the CDC.

In short, if the CDC offers capital to the venture, it has the right to exact performance on the goals that the CDC is seeking. These requirements may include, in fact, target performances in sales, revenues, and profits, as well as monthly financial reports and annual audits to confirm the performance. And the disciplines for not meeting the performance targets can include such drastic measures as a takeover of the company by the CDC. After all, that is precisely the sort of requirements in the conventional corporate world that venture capital firms exact from the companies in which they invest. Even the barracudas of the venture capital field are tolerated because they will offer what the entrepreneur has not been able to get elsewhere—the necessary money to get the business started or expanded. A CDC does not have to take on the devouring image of some denizens of the venture capital field in order to defend the interests of its community, but there is no reason why it cannot make a reasonable investment agreement that gives the entrepreneur enough freedom to make the business a success and the CDC enough assurance that success will pay off for the community.

Recognizing that a community is more than a disparate collection of businesses, the CDC will also recognize that its relationship and contribution to the joint venture are not expressed solely in the investment agreement. The words of contracts are only one visible element in the relationship. What also happens, even when the CDC's partner is an outsider who comes to the community to start the business, is that all the social and psychological ties that involve a business in its local setting begin to grow informally and formally around the venture and its managers. A whole network of relationships is established which reinforces the local economic development perspective that the CDC is promoting. Generally speaking, the ousider becomes integrated more or less swiftly and surely into a network with other local businesses, local banks, local suppliers or clients, and all the meaningful ties of human interaction of neighbors, employees, favorite restaurants, new friends, and so on. Thus, a new small business can become inextricably a functioning contributor to the round of life that the community offers, and in these circumstances, the possibilities of negligent or deliberate flouting of community values are decreased far beyond what is represented in the investment agreement. The partner in the agreement becomes the partner in the community's future.

The first joint venture of KHIC strikingly illustrates what this investment approach can offer in wide community benefits. In 1972 two young men from Tennessee learned that the CDC was seeking new ventures for its target area, and they believed that their background (MBAs and relevant experience) would predict success in producing camping tents. With the assistance of consultants, the CDC evaluated their plans and helped to formulate them in the necessary detail to launch Outdoor Venture Corporation (OVC). KHIC's investment was $100,000 in stock and $120,-000 in a loan to the company. The entrepreneurs raised an additional $440,000 in credit and equity (including their own money).

OVC settled in a deteriorated, rural Kentucky coal-mining county in which the majority of the population lived below the official U.S. poverty line. By 1980 over 220 people were employed by OVC, more than 75 percent of whom were previously unemployed and untrained. Now many of these people occupy supervisory positions. Within two years OVC expanded into new facilities—the first industrial construction in the county for a good many years. In a nearby town, a small manufacturer of farm gates diversified into tent poles for OVC and other tent producers, and a local trucking company with contracts from OVC qualified for an interstate license and thereby reached out-of-state customers too. OVC uses a line of credit from a regional bank that anually pumps $8,000,000 or more into the county to finance OVC's needs. OVC itself has established a sheltered workshop for the handicapped, and the company president spearheaded a successful campaign for the county's first public library.

The entrepreneurs were somewhat hesitant about committing themselves indefinitely to living in such an isolated area, and KHIC's investment agreement did in fact bind OVC to stay. Today the contract restriction is unimportant. The reception by the rest of the community was so welcoming that the newcomers have settled in for good. Local people went out of their way to help them. One company lent OVC complete plant facilities at a nominal rent for the first two critical years of the business. Employee turnover rate is among the lowest in the industry, and local suppliers (like the trucking company) take special pains to provide service to their primary customer. This is not to say that all has been easy. The company underwent a union-organizing strike, and everyone had to learn the hard way to accommodate to each other. However, since 1977, when OVC signed its first union contract with the Amalgamated Clothing and Textile Workers, union-management relations have been fully harmonious.

KHIC's loan has long since been paid off, and its equity is worth a good deal more today than its original value. Thus financially the project was a success, but it also achieved the CDC's job creation goals, and the unplanned ripple effects in community building exemplify what a meaningful joint venture can accomplish in spin-off benefits. A CDC need not maintain ownership control in its direct investment program in order to integrate a business into the values and aims of the local community.

Finding grants and other funds for direct investments in its own or in joint ventures is a major accomplishment for a CDC. Today it is probably easier to get grants for the business assistance strategy. Whatever the challenges, the CDC's choice of one or the other of the two major business development strategies will grow out of its initial decisions about the purposes of its activities and the degree of impact it wishes to achieve in business development. In turn, those choices of goals and aims will have grown out of the basic historical and cultural setting, as well as chance occurrences (or resources) that the CDC may seize upon. Two contrasting examples will demonstrate the play of such circumstances.

In a cultural setting like a Chinese American neighborhood, entrepreneurship is an especially strong element. Therefore, assisting prospective businesses would be a natural choice for the initial business development activity of a local CDC. This in fact was the initial program of the Chinese Economic Development Council in Boston, which established a service to help would-be entrepreneurs develop their business plans and make loan applications to a sympathetic local bank. But entrepreneurship is not as prominent an aspect of American Negro communities, and so CDCs there are more likely to emphasize the second strategy, which will involve direct investment in the CDC's own venture or in selected joint ventures with potential partners.

The Hough Area Development Corporation offers a good example of the usual pattern in a black neighborhood. HADC began its first manufacturing business by investing in a wholly owned venture in the field of rubber injection molding. Selecting that venture was almost totally accidental. In 1968, as HADC was starting up, a major Cleveland firm, McDowell-Wellman, had some surplus industrial real estate, equipment, and trucks that it wanted to give to a community group. As it turned out, the proferred gifts did not seem appropriate to any sort of business that HADC then envisioned, but in discussing the prospects with McDowell-Wellman, HADC became interested in a new industrial machine that the company had designed, which, though sophisticated, could be operated by relatively low-skilled workers. The upshot was that HADC began planning a venture that was based on this machinery. It became Community Products, Inc., which employs primarily former welfare mothers who turn out specialized small rubber parts for the automobile and major home appliance industries. The particular choice of business field was accidental, but the direct investment strategy and the creation of jobs for lesser skilled workers was deliberate.

So the early business development activity of a CDC is likely to grow rather directly out of its initial setting and circumstances, in which it makes a choice between one of the two most likely major strategies. However, almost no CDC remains wedded to the initial choice. Almost all will move on to add some effort under each major strategic rubric. For example, although the Chicano culture typically emphasizes the small business or microbusiness, particularly the bodega or tiny retail outlet, the business development work of TELACU in the Mexican American barrio of East Los Angeles has ranged from technical assistance to minority businesses, to a major industrial park for outside firms, to the purchase of a small savings and loan bank. It has also created a consulting company that found a ready market for urban planning and development contracts with the Los Angeles city and county governments.

TELACU offers an interesting illustration of the problems of integrating the business culture with the community services culture. It began under the sponsorship of the United Automobile Workers union and concentrated much effort on strengthening the social, cultural, and political resources of the Chicano community. An elderly housing project, for example, was designed with special input from the prospective tenants on their (culturally shaped) needs, and the construction itself involved delicate negotiations for the cooperation of Mexican youth gangs living in the site area. An art museum, including art courses, an atelier, and a commercial shop for art sales, is another TELACU project, as are a variety of social services.

However, when TELACU first determined to gain the support of government agencies concerned with business development, they set up an independent suite (across the street from the main office) with carpeted floors and quiet conventional offices that breathed a business atmosphere. Their counseling services to minority businesses operated out of that setting, which was expected to be more reassuring to the business world (and the relevant government agencies) than the community-organizing offices. Today, TELACU is so successful in its whole range of ambitious business development projects that some people feel that it can and needs to use more resources that will reemphasize its activist beginnings, that it should open up more of the storefront-type service operations to accommodate the great remaining needs and aspirations of the people of its poor neighborhood. Even a tremendously successful CDC with a multimillion-dollar budget, like TELACU, will always have to juggle the priorities of its program to deal comprehensively with other community-building activities besides business development.

NINE

Building the Community Infrastructure

I N recent years the word *infrastructure* has become an indispensable term to describe the entire complement of community facilities that the particular locality has or may require for the encouragement of business. The term encompasses such disparate community equipment as water systems, waste disposal sites, bridges, recreational areas, roads, schools, churches, medical and dental services, housing, and government services. *Infra* itself means "below," and the term *infrastrucure* was originally used in a military context to refer to military fortifications or installations "below" the fighting forces—or more generally, the underpinnings of the capacity of an army to defend itself or to launch an attack. So in the economic development context, the infrastructure is the underpinning for the economic activity of the community, and it is usually understood as referring more specifically to the underpinnings for business activity—and thus necessary for programs for business development.

Which infrastructure equipment is available or projected to underpin business activity will vary from community to community, depending upon the vision of itself that the community may have. Just because some businesses must have access to hazardous waste disposal sites does not mean that the community necessarily considers how to provide that service so as to have it available for potential new firms. Or, to take a less extreme case, not every community may feel the need to divert its resources to build a major sports stadium, even though sports are a recognized attraction in business development.

Infrastructure is most often conceived of in physical terms, like the provision of waste sites or sports stadiums. But the term has been generalized to refer to nonphysical assets, the social infrastructure, the institutionalized arrangements for basic services —medical, educational, entertainment, governmental, fire protection, and so on. Even the social infrastructure may require physical facilities like the buildings for schools and hospitals, but as well-financed and *well-organized* basic services, it underlies local vitality quite apart from the physical facilities involved. Generalized to this extent, the term *infrastructure* spreads to everything in a community that business may use. However, just as with the physical infrastructure, each community may have a different sense of what it wants and needs in the way of social infrastructure. Thus one locality will feel the need to establish its own institution of higher education, like Cape Breton and its campaign for its own college, but another community may be content with relying on a university in some other locality.

In healthy communities, businesses themselves sometimes create physical infrastructure equipment, but they can do so only within the context of existing community facilities. Sometimes an industrial concern constructs its own septic tanks and other waste disposal facilities, its own water tank and drainage system, and roads connecting the various buildings on its property; and all this it may share (at a price, of course) with other businesses. But it and those other businesses will still depend upon public bridges and highways, for example.

The range of possible business contributions along social dimensions is much greater, but again, these contributions are possible only within the context of other community resources. For example, in the field of education, a thriving business may provide some specialized training program for potential employees and others. Wang, a computer firm, has established in its home town of Lowell, Massachusetts, a graduate institute with a master's degree program in computer sciences. But no firm can readily establish and maintain the schools to teach the basic reading, writing, and mathematical skills which it expects all its employees to have upon hiring them; the basic educational infrastructure must be in place already. Similarly, a company like Stride-Rite, makers of shoes, pioneered in setting up day-care facilities for the children of its workers, but most businesses will have to depend upon such institutions in the local community. Or a firm may offer wide health plan benefits; for instance, a large factory may even include an in-factory emergency clinic and perhaps continuing services for certain health risks like alcoholism. But for the most part, a firm cannot be expected to establish and maintain a general hospital for its employees and their families. Basic medical facilities need to be available already.

Businesses contribute to community infrastructure also by providing essential services to each other. A commercial bank provides financial services to other businesses, even to other banks. And there must be businesses to serve the employees of other businesses. A manufacturing firm may have a cafeteria for its workers, a loan guarantee program for employee home mortgages, and a set of especially satisfactory pay scales; but the community surrounding it has to provide other necessities and amenities of life so that the firm's employees can find the goods and services that their pay can buy. In this sense, perhaps all business is the infrastructure for some other business. In short, then, the subterm *social infrastructure,* when it includes all the arrangements for service to business and its workers, would appear to include the entire set of institutions that a community may have. Amorphous as that may seem, it helps to recognize that the creation of businesses (or promoting their creation) is dependent upon the local institutions with which the business will stand.

As I have emphasized before, some major parts of the physical or social underpinnings for business development are usually lacking in the forgotten community or in poor condition, unattractive either to established companies or to new entrepreneurs. Accordingly, a community beginning its own organized development must confront the task of building resources that are ordinarily taken for granted in more affluent settings. A CDC must always have some element of business development as a part of its program, but it will also always discover that it must work to strengthen and improve the community's infrastructure equipment.

Infrastructure projects, however, are not necessarily undertaken for the direct purpose of encouraging new or established business. To improve a neighborhood school may be useful indirectly in preparing a local work force for the industries and commercial establishments of the area, but a CDC may be more directly concerned with the meaning of an improved school to students and parents. Other infrastructure projects may be planned to directly serve both business and individual residents. For example, the Union-Sarah CDC in St. Louis has jointly planned a vocational training institute with local industries to fill their recruitment needs, but the institute concurrently fulfilled the CDC's aim to upgrade skills for residents of the neighborhood.

In fact, for a CDC, its infrastructure projects usually have the special characteristic of promoting multiple community goals concurrently—intentionally or not. A CDC in a depressed rural area of southern Virginia, the Southwest Virginia Community Development Fund, was instrumental in developing and financing a private water system for small farms owned by low-income families. This well-chosen project improved the livability of the farm area, but it also contributed very directly to the income-earning potential of the farmers by providing irrigation possibilities. Or take the idea of a CDC establishing a day-care center for very young children, as has the Spanish-Speaking Unity Council, a CDC in Oakland, California. Research has demonstrated that a first-rate day-care program will pay off in improved school performance for the enrollees later on when they go to school, and it will reduce their risks of illness and delinquency. At the same time, it reduces the stress on parents, improving their health status over the years and of course permitting them to take on more regular jobs at better pay. Local employers are benefited by reduced employee absenteeism and turnover among the parents hired. Moreover, new jobs are created in the day-care center itself. The center can also be a source of other benefits. For example, the CDC may improve its financial asset base by purchasing the property at which the center is located—not so difficult in some cases when the program has a solid contract with the local public assistance agency or other third party for day-care services so that its mortgage payments are secure.

In general, infrastructure projects can achieve so much in so many different dimensions that they deserve high priority in CDC planning and analysis; in comparison to business investment projects, infrastructure projects tend to have more possibilities for inventive payoffs. Moreover, direct investment in infrastructure can underpin the CDC's own longevity with perhaps less risk than direct investment in businesses; that is, most infrastructure projects respond to more general, basic needs of the community than the single business and so have a greater chance of staying in operation. For example, a CDC industrial park project is apt to have greater stability than an individual business located in the park.

The appropriate local mix of infrastructure and business projects depends upon the survey of local problems that the CDC initially conducts in order to plan its program. And for any sector of infrastructure activity, the CDC may choose, as in its business development work, to take a catalytic or direct role; that is, it may stimulate other organizations (including local government) to take action, or it may engage in developing the new resource itself. Or, of course, it may combine the roles. For example, CDCs in Boston have encouraged the city government to establish a housing loan guarantee fund out of the federal Community Development Block Grant that the city receives, and with that support the CDCs expect that they can directly develop low-income housing themselves.

Setting specific infrastructure development goals must be preceded by a careful review of what the community already has at its disposal. Often a very depleted community will have failed for many years to recognize that it includes unutilized or underutilized infrastructure facilities, both social and physical. In inner cities it is common to find that a church or neighborhood agency has not adapted its activities to the changed and poorer population of the neighborhood. The lagging church or other agency is a prime target for revitalization. Getting such an organization to redirect its work to meet local needs may not be easy, but it could represent a substantial resource. Physical infrastructure— especially real estate with underlying good utilities, electricity, water, sewer, and so on—is literally buried treasure to be discovered. Of course, that discovery is precisely what happens in the process of gentrification, when outsiders begin to recognize the previously disregarded housing values in a depleted neighborhood. The challenge to a CDC is to recognize the treasure first.

This was the task for the Roxbury Action Program (RAP) in 1969 in the hilltop neighborhood called Highland Park. Here was a dilapidated neighborhood that outsiders called a "slum"; but it had breathtaking views over the city of Boston, historic buildings, gently curving human-scale streets, and vest pocket parks, even though they were nothing but junkyards then. RAP recognized that gentrification was just over the horizon but still far enough away to get a headstart on key parcels of housing. It aimed not just to do some critical projects itself but also to get the city of Boston committed to rehabilitating selected structures for public housing; and RAP also encouraged and assisted moderate-income black families to buy the valuable homes that would go out of their price range once the gentrification process began. Looking back, RAP can see today that it had only five crucial years before it could no longer have enough influence to maintain Highland Park as an affordable place to live. But that was enough time to become designated by the city renewal agency as the prime developer for the neighborhood, to put some model projects of its own in place, to see that the city bought and renovated a block of old and attractive stone structures for its public housing agency, and to get the city to rehabilitate the parks and repair the streets so that the local residents could benefit from improved values before gentrification began in earnest.

The underutilized physical resource in a neighborhood may not be housing stock; it may be a disused, dangerous waterfront area begging to be redeveloped for recreational, residential, or commercial purposes; it may be industrial property long abandoned, or weedy, junk-filled vacant lots scattered throughout the neighborhood. All these things on first glance make the neighborhood unattractive but with imagination and effort are transformed into major assets. But, it may be asked, why would a CDC recognize the potential of such eyesores and be able to develop them before more experienced and wealthier developers do?

Basically, the CDC has the advantage of being a developer already on the scene. It will have earlier knowledge of the dormant resource—assuming that it has made a proper survey of its area. The local people involved in the CDC will be familiar with the property; they are, after all, the most intimately bothered by its dereliction and can envision being benefited by its development. Properly organized, the CDC will also have built the political connections and influence to protect an early decision to develop the project. Moreover, a CDC can contemplate the project without the key distraction that a conventional developer must face: the calculation of so-called financial opportunity costs, the costs of having to pass up opportunities to make good money elsewhere.

A conventional developer (or financier) asks himself if he might make more money on another project in another city or another neighborhood; a two percent additional projected rate of return on the development investment might turn that decision. For the CDC there is no location choice: the only choice is to do something for and in the community. The issue is not whether this project would make two percent more on the CDC's investment, but whether this project, rather than another, will provide a more attractive range of other community benefits. For the comunity group, financial opportunity costs are rarely important in the way they are for the conventional developer.

Because the community group is not bound by the same profit and time targets that conventional developers (or venture capital firms) set for themselves, it can undertake projects (both in business and property development) at an earlier point and at lesser projected rates of return. That advantage allowed the East Boston CDC to start its first project, which was small but had an early payoff. The CDC learned that a small vacant lot was for sale because the subsoil would not support a major building. The CDC snapped up the parcel to preserve it for recreational purposes and later sold it to the city for development as a park. In the meantime, it was maintained in a tidy fashion for local children; the CDC gained prominent status as a real estate actor; and the CDC rather than a later speculator garnered the ultimate financial benefit. Yet no one else would have gone into the deal at that time and under those conditions for the small financial return it would have promised.

Of all physical infrastructure projects in which a CDC might engage, housing usually remains the most attractive. Housing development is, in fact, one of the most common CDC activities— either the construction of new housing or the rehabilitation of existing structures. In both Canada and the United States, there are various direct and indirect subsidy programs sponsored by authorities at different levels of government, and such programs are usually less attractive to conventional developers than they are to neighborhood groups because the immediate financial benefits tend to be modest. So a CDC has a good chance of getting the necessary financing. It has an even better chance when it teams up with private sector actors in the housing field, whom it can often attract as partners, since the CDC is apt to be less interested in possible profits than in the housing itself. In the United States, the prime example of this arrangement has been the special technique of limited partnerships for housing development projects. The so-called limited partnership makes use of federal tax credits and tax deductions that are of no interest to a nonprofit, tax-exempt organization like a CDC but are valuable to high-income investors. The CDC as "general partner" builds and controls the housing, passing through the tax benefits to its passive limited partner investors. For several years, with the decline of other housing subsidy programs on the federal level, the limited partnership has been the crucial means for creating new housing resources for low-income residents. Even some state and local government programs of financial support to local developers, including CDCs, have been geared to fit this tax law and to thereby lever more housing with the same state or local dollar. Since the summer of 1986, a new federal tax law has modified this situation, but CDCs apparently will still benefit by the limited partnership technique.

In Canada, the federal support program has depended upon the provision of low-cost mortgages, and even 100 percent mortgages have been available. Again, up until recent changes in Ottawa, a CDC with adequate staff resources and connections could readily qualify for and obtain the mortgage money to make a housing project feasible. In the face of changes in law and policy, it cannot be stressed too strongly that in neither country is it possible to produce so-called affordable housing without some sort of subsidy or subvention. The grants or low-cost financing may come from government or private sources, but they must be present. The economics of housing construction and rehabilitation is such that housing units built today have to rent or sell for more than low- or moderate-income residents can afford—just to pay off the mortgage-financing costs. Since of course the residents of a depleted community are almost exclusively low- and moderate-income people, creating decent housing for them turns out to be as challenging as it is basic to the livability of the community. Just because it is so basic, it is a prime goal for most CDCs.

In the process of creating adequate housing resources that are affordable in the context of the kinds of jobs that the CDC hopes to create or encourage in its business development activities, several concurrent benefits are achievable. As with most physical infrastructure projects, housing development contributes to the CDC's long-term asset base. Even if the CDC develops the housing with the specific purpose of selling it off—say, to a cooperative of tenants that the CDC expects to organize—it can increase its capital; at the same time, ownership, properly managed, can throw off a modest income stream. Moreover, under a careful plan of remortgaging over time, the CDC can take advantage of appreciation of its housing to generate capital for new projects, and appreciation is a likely prospect in a community that is revitalizing itself.

It is also true that a CDC, as it increases its property holdings, gains the stature and influence that property conventionally implies in our society. So a CDC will have more chance to throw its weight around in the private sector—for example, with banks from whom it may seek financial backing for an entrepreneur it is trying to sponsor—or in the public sector. Local government appreciates an organization that improves the tax base, and so the CDC will have an added dimension to the political influence of the voters it can organize in its neighborhood. I should note here, parenthetically, that the prospect of an increased tax base is, naturally, a two-edged sword. The CDC must plan for the resulting tax increases on its own property, as well as the increase that is associated with revitalization and consequent gentrification. Specifically, as in the RAP case, the CDC will need to make provision for long-term affordability of housing. The prospect of an increased tax base can also be used for CDC financing purposes with local government in the technique of so-called tax increment financing. Tax increment financing, in effect, uses the expected return over time in additional taxes as local government capital to invest in the property that will eventually produce the added taxes; the government agency borrows on that future and uses the proceeds for the project that will produce the new taxes.

Focusing as I have on the physical and financial aspects of infrastructure development, I have slighted a critical institutional element in all such projects. It cannot be stressed enough that merely constructing or improving a physical asset of the community will not answer the needs of the community unless, simultaneously, the CDC constructs the institutional arrangements for properly maintaining the physical structure. In a deteriorated inner city, for example, a newly renovated apartment house can fall back into the disfigurement of graffiti, the stench of urine, the despair of drugs, and ultimately the finanical failure of the building unless tenants and management together are integrated in a social relationship that will properly maintain the property. A cautionary tale comes form the experience of the Greater Roxbury Development Corporation (GRDC), a Boston CDC based near RAP. GRDC was forced to declare bankruptcy of a 325-unit housing development which had deteriorated physically and socially. Leaks, falling plaster, inoperative utilities, and generally uninhabitable and uninhabited units existed along with a destructive drug culture. Under new management and with police assistance, GRDC has just instituted a major drive to eliminate the drug sellers who for all too long had terrorized the other tenants; court action has freed up funds for the rehabilitation of deteriorated units and systems; and GRDC must now go about the task of strengthening the capacity of tenants to make the place livable again.

Exactly how tenant and management relations should be organized will vary from one locale to another. In some settings, management and tenants may be combined in a self-managed cooperative, but in these cases the CDC must have ensured that tenants have the necessary training in cooperatives and in property management—and that they have available to them adequate technical assistance over the long haul. Perhaps the most common arrangement is for the CDC to maintain the landlord role, but it will still have to enlist tenants in a common perspective on property maintenance. This arrangement requires reasonably supportive policies that recognize the financial problems and culture of the tenants, combined with unflinching demands for adherence to the policies; it requires that the CDC keep adequate management skills on its central staff, people who know how to screen and keep good tenants; and it requires provision for an adequate management budget within the whole financial plan of the housing development project. A CDC may run its property directly in this manner. Or it may set up a housing management company, a subsidiary, to insulate itself partially from what will have to be tough decisions. The same management requirements will apply to the subsidiary, but the CDC management company will be able to more clearly account for the costs of management and will offer a vehicle to attract contracts for housing management from other owners, thus promoting new jobs within the CDC complex—and some income for the CDC.

The same requirement for a properly organized program of maintenance and administration inheres in other physical development projects. If an industrial park is to be successful or a water system or shopping plaza is to support itself, the CDC must attend to the social organization of a financial management structure just as carefully as it attends to the engineering of the physical structure. If the CDC does not intend to maintain an ongoing responsibility for the new physical asset, then it must be sure that the new (or existing) organization to which the asset is turned over will be able to discharge that responsibility. Thus, for example, it is not enough to just turn over a piece of parkland to the county government; the CDC will have to assure itself that the county government agency concerned is committed to proper management, and perhaps it may even want to set up a citizens advisory group to monitor the park on a continuing basis. A CDC can be rightfully proud of its accomplishments in improving physical resources in the neighborhood; they are usually visible and invite public satisfaction and support. But the CDC has done only part of its job if it has not followed through on the institution building that is the basic process of economic development.

An inspiring example of a community working at various levels in the physical infrastructure activity of housing redevelopment is provided by a community group and its network in the North of Howard neighborhood of Chicago. North of Howard is a polyglot, dozen-square-block deteriorated area on the Evanston edge of Chicago. It is separated from the rest of the city by the elevated and from Lake Michigan by a ridge of expensive, high-rise condominiums, which taper back into a furrow of middle-income units, which in turn swiftly descend into this low-income neighborhood. An ecumenical network of urban ministries ("Good News North of Howard") has established a CDC (Peoples Housing, Inc.), some small businesses, low-income housing, a Catholic Worker shelter, an alternative kindergarten and school, and, most notably, the cooperative redevelopment and sweat–equity ownership of a dilapidated hotel known as The Jonquil. The last project most epitomizes the marrying of social and physical redevelopment. By rehabilitating the physical resources of the neighborhood, the community group has joined local people in the rehabilitation of themselves, for the old Jonquil Hotel had become a drug and prostitution center with many single rooms occupied by whole families who could afford nothing better. Good News Partners, a cooperative formed of residents of the Jonquil, bought and rehabilitated the hotel, step by step, themselves. The co-op members were not experts in construction techniques—to an interested observer the pointing of the exterior bricks is a bit rough— but they did it all. Then some of these same residents (including former convicts) organized a cooperative construction firm that has gone on to do subcontracting work for the rehabilitation of a nearby twenty-one-unit abandoned apartment house developed by the CDC for a low-income family cooperative. The newest rehabbed apartment house was intended to answer the needs of the families for whom the small quarters at the Jonquil are unsuited. These families and others joining them have decent new quarters, but they are also developing their skills in managing the apartment house, backed up by the management staff (and consultants) of the CDC.

It is clear from this example how investment in the physical infrastructure will (or should) always involve the social arrangements of meaningful institutional structures that link people into new patterns of behavior that more immediately respond to the needs of the neighborhood and its residents. However, addressing community infrastructure needs does not have to begin from physical infrastructure projects; the CDC can also approach the needs of the neighborhood directly by *social infrastructure* projects. Social infrastructure requires investment in people rather than property or business enterprise and builds the *human capital* of the community.

In direct comparison to the financial or physical capital of the neighborhood, represented in dollars available for investment or physical structures and equipment on which investment has already been made, human capital is also an investment that is ready to use and that is represented in the residents themselves. Specifically, it is the productive energies and skills, or capacity for learning new skills, that exist in the people who make up the CDC and its neighborhood.

As I have pointed out earlier, an outstanding resource in human capital in the depleted community becomes visible in the process of setting up and governing a CDC. Suddenly, if it were not recognized before, it becomes clear that there are exceptional talents for organizing and directing a development program. At the same time, it has to be emphasized that the CDC experience is and must be used as an opportunity for developing new leaders, especially since it is inevitable that successful CDC leaders will be attracted to other challenges, other jobs, and that a second line of leadership must be prepared to take over.

Arabella Martinez and David Carlson, in their 1983 report, *Developing Leadership in Minority Communities,* focused on the CDC experience and find that "CDCs have generated significant and responsible leadership." But they and others have not seen enough attention given to the development of second-level personnel and feel that CDCs need a "conscious human resource development strategy." It seems quite likely that the kind of entrepreneurial personality of the usual successful CDC leader does not easily find the time and energy needed for bringing along junior staff. Martinez and Carlson also believe that today's new wave of CDC officers may be less activist and more technically attuned to financial and economic issues, but without enough exposure to the ideas that "undergird the original conception of the community economic development program and strategy."

Thus, just because the depleted community does indeed have resources for leadership does not mean it can safely ignore the tasks of infrastructure development in the realm of human capital. And, of course, human resource development extends far beyond the requirements of leadership to include all sorts of skills. When organized well to work together, all the skills of the community become the *social capital* or social infrastructure of the community, which will create additional human and social capital.

Social infrastructure programming in a community economic development strategy focuses on one or more of four possible activities: political development, human services, cultural enhancement, and education or training. Meeting needs in any of these arenas will require initiating organizations or changing existing organizations—in short, institutional development.

Political development means, of course, the activation and organization of residents for gaining influence in the decisions made by the government agencies (or the outside private sector institutions) that impinge upon the neighborhood. *Human services* is the term for all those activities that respond to the problems of living that arise most virulently in low-income areas, even though they also appear elsewhere: illness, drug addiction, child and spouse abuse, nutritional disorders, delinquency, lonely social isolation, and so on. All these problems clamor for attention by a community organization because they threaten the stability of life for all in a depleted neighborhood. Human services projects address these needs.

Education and training in infrastructure programming includes more than what might immediately come to mind; it can include board orientation sessions for the CDC's own directors, career opportunity workshops for young people, infant care sessions for teenage parents, improvement of local public schools, and employment or employment readiness training for different age groups.

Cultural enhancement projects may seem to overlap to a large extent with education, but they can be more specifically defined as those activities that sensitize and deepen the local residents' appreciation of the values of their own cultural background. The aim is not to educate so much as it is to enable the residents to take pride in what is native to their own cultural equipment and to make use of it. As a community-building activity, this can have a major impact in those neighborhoods or rural areas which have special ethnic characteristics, such as Native American enclaves.

Virtually all areas of social infrastructure are potential targets for CDC action in most depleted communities. Again, because time and resources are limited and because successful work will require a broad consensus within the community, the CDC will have to develop and periodically redevelop a set of priorities and plans for its social infrastructure activity. Wherever separate organizations are to be established by the CDC and are expected to be self-sufficient, the projects might be called "social ventures." The creation of social ventures, as with business ventures, implies careful planning for survivability. Thus New Dawn systematically established a halfway house for the formerly mentally ill by drawing up a financial feasibility plan, renovating the property, negotiating rates with the government disability officials, and finally spinning off the service to an independent group under a board of directors and a manager who were particularly devoted to the field of mental health.

Or the activity might be catalytic rather than direct, encouraging other organizations to take a more active or broader role in some social need of the community. In this instance the infrastructure activity might be termed "social activation." For example, Impact Seven, a seven-county CDC in northern Wisconsin, has provided support for alcoholism projects initiated by local Native American groups for their reservations.

Federal, state, provincial, or local funds are typically available to community groups for enlarging or starting human service, educational, and cultural enhancement projects—much more available than the more substantial sums usually needed for business or physical infrastructure development. This availability has two implications for CDCs programming in social infrastructure. On the one hand, the CDC may be distracted by the government's golden apples and take up a project that is actually low in its own priorities, just because the money is accessible. Since the CDC's most valuable resource is the energy and commitment of its people, that resource should not be diffused by projects that do not have a critical salience in the CDC's program. The proliferation of social projects and the attention and emotional commitment that they require can shift the CDC perspective from long-term development to short-term immediate service. For example, the board of a CDC in Columbus, Ohio, found it so much easier to accept money for counseling and social services that it gave up all other development work, including business development, which seemed to compete too much for its attention. The act of giving immediate help became more immediately rewarding, and the long-term needs of the residents unfortunately fell by the wayside. On the other hand, social infrastructure projects can create many new jobs and should always be reviewed in terms of that benefit as well as for the potential for direct social results. Unfortunately, funding sources for many types of social projects tend to be somewhat fickle, especially since government priorities shift from year to year. This instability threatens long-term support of the project and thus the potential for long-term jobs. The human disappointments and a certain reinforcement of poor job attitudes caused by the sudden loss of external funds and the consequent disappearance of jobs, no matter how well performed, should be considered when weighing whether or not to take up proffered social grants.

Insistence by the CDC on a commitment for multiyear funding can do much to reduce these risks. The design of the project can also ensure at least some continuing program income. For example, a senior citizens center sponsored by a CDC might take out insurance, so to speak, against the loss of grant funding, by contracting with a local hospital to provide senior citizen services for hospital patients, using the same skills that the grant supports. Developing a reputation for competent services to seniors might offer the project access to other ongoing private contracts and some income stability even if parallel government grant funding is arbitrarily withdrawn.

In effect, then, social infrastructure projects ought to be reviewed for their potential as long-term institutional resources in the community. Although it is also true that for any number of reasons a CDC might be willing to take on the expense and risks of a short-term social project, surely the development perspective requires that the survivability of the project should be taken into account in making decisions about launching it, just as one would take the same account of the survivability of a potential new business. The social market for social projects requires careful market research.

As to multiyear funding, even though initially the CDC may be informed that such funding is not possible in a particular case, it is interesting how much leverage the CDC may possess for changing bureau rules. Once a CDC has developed a reputation for competence, it may be approached by a government agency to accept a grant to provide services. At that point, the agency may be susceptible to all sorts of rule bending if the CDC stands firm on its principles. After all, the CDC has something valuable to offer to the grant makers—namely, a chance for a successful project, which grant makers recognize is all too rare. Of course, not only multiyear funding but other grant conditions may be insisted upon by a grantee who has a good reputation.

In this respect, it has been my experience that U.S. groups are apt to be daring and assertive, while Canadian groups seem to assume that the government bodies are too strong. I once attended a Canadian national conference of community development groups that were meeting with some of the federal and provincial government officials who ran the grant programs that funded such groups. It was a marvelous opportunity for the groups to instruct the government officials about the inventiveness and energies released by local initiative in the wide variety of innovative projects they represented; but instead the groups tended to seek guidance, to ask what they should do, and to request the government officials to take the initiative in thinking up ways to help them. It was no wonder that one provincial government officer suggested that the federal grant program ought to be closed out and that any remaining funds should be shifted for internal use by provincial human services departments; the independent local groups acted as if they had little to offer.

I contrast this occurrence with a meeting of CDCs in the United States when they confronted federal government officials in President Nixon's administration who planned to divert certain community economic development funds to a new purpose. The officials had organized the meeting to promote their own new direction—in which the local development groups would have little participation. Actually, the new program had already been presented to a cabinet meeting as an innovative policy initiative and had received the blessing of the president, and a special national advisory council had been organized by the officials to give it credibility among low-income communities. The community development groups were outraged because the new program would siphon off dollars from "*our*" program. They confronted the officials vociferously. And in preparation for the meeting, they had even arranged (by a sophisticated campaign of contacting friends of the advisory council members) to get key advisory council members to back off from supporting the new initiative.

In the course of the stormy meeting, the civil service officials called in reinforcements. A politically appointed and presumably more politically sophisticated agency official was called in to head off a disaster and to mollify the community groups. On the way to the meeting, he accidentally encountered one CDC leader. The official anxiously asked, "Tell me what I should do to correct all this." The CDC leader at first hesitated and then, in mock solemnity, said only, "Well, repeat after me: 'Our Father, which art in Heaven. . . . '"

The self-confidence of the CDCs was justified. The end of the story is that the new project was redesigned to take about 50 percent less funds from the general community economic development appropriation and to accept on its board a preponderance of those representing the forces that had opposed the plan in its original form. Thus was established an independent national institution that to this day directly supports community economic development projects—the Opportunity Funding Corporation (OFC). OFC operates as a financial intermediary to lever capital for CDC ventures and for minority and other disadvantaged entrepreneurs.

This story is a good introduction to the political infrastructure activity of those involved in community economic development. Political networks, not for partisan electoral purposes but for local and national purposes of community economic development, are an essential element of social infrastructure activity. Such networks may be hastily carpentered for a single issue, as in the OFC case, but, as in all community development, the CDC needs to plan for long-term institution building and must have the tools for articulating, translating, and promoting the community-based approach to economic development. Of course, the CDC in both Canada and the United States develops ongoing relationships with political officials as a means of ensuring a chance for government funds. But the overall purpose of strengthening the community's influence is not just to get government grants. Established political connections are the lever by which many varieties of decisions made outside the community but affecting it can be shaped, deflected, or even initiated as necessary.

The importance of political development is so obvious and the tactics are so dependent on the local situation, that I will not dwell on this aspect of social infrastructure any further. It is perhaps worthwhile to emphasize only that the CDC itself may not be the most appropriate instrument for organizing this dimension of the community. Some insulation from the necessary rough-and-tumble of influence building may be necessary for the rest of the CDC's program; therefore, here, as elsewhere, the CDC may wish to play a catalytic rather than a direct role. This role is particularly easy when overlapping membership in the leadership of a community political group and of the CDC itself allows the same persons to speak from different platforms, so to speak. The political independence of the CDC must be safeguarded. The formulation once enunciated by a director of the Hough Area Development Corporation, a black leader who had spearheaded a successful voter registration program in the neighborhood, has often recurred to me. "No permanent friends and no permanent enemies," he intoned. He meant that a CDC has to avoid becoming identified with any political faction or party or leader. Yet this was said at a time when Cleveland had recently elected the first black mayor of any major American city, a man who was known personally by some of the HADC people as a fellow pool player in their younger days.

Another CDC, TELACU of Los Angeles, might deny the force of that formulation, for TELACU has been pretty much identified with the Democratic party in California and nationally, and it has certainly created an impressive multimillion-dollar program. Whether its success is based in part upon its political connections or whether it might have managed as well or even better without those close relationships is hard to answer. It seems easier to recognize that, as mentioned before, TELACU's intimate relationship with the United Auto Workers union *has* been critical. And surely political networking through unions and other organizations that are more directly involved in partisan influence is a useful, and presumably less risky, tactic than direct political activity.

Both in Canada, which has seen a number of national political upheavals during the inception and buildup of local community economic development groups, and in the United States, where the presidency has swung back and forth between the two parties in the same period, it has been essential that, whatever the local alliances, the development movement has maintained communications with the outs as well as the ins. For example, in the United States, while the federal program and authorizing law explicitly for support of low-income community economic development groups had Democratic sponsorship in a Democratic administration, it was under a later Republican administration that it was significantly strengthened. Here again, community groups have something to offer elected and political officials besides the coin of political endorsements. Every politician wants to be identified with a potentially successful approach to the recalcitrant problems of the depleted communities in his or her district; and if CDCs can make a promising case on the basis of actual performance, they do not need to attach themselves to a limited partisan connection. Today that promise and that performance have been established here and there in Canada and the United States, but they remain to be systematically formulated and exploited.

TEN

Matching
Financial Capital to
Community Needs

F INANCIALLY strip-mined, a depleted community staggers under a hidden debt burden of an undetermined size and distribution which nevertheless has to somehow be paid off. It is as if everything has been mortgaged to the hilt, the cash and profits exported, and only the debts left behind—some debts visible in abandoned properties, other invisible in the deterioration of institutional resources. Continually sucked dry of the sweet juices, the depleted community is unloaded onto those with the least resources to pay for its upkeep and financial rejuvenation, the residents. The community leadership faces the complex task of reversing this outflow of capital by mobilizing and maintaining the financial resources that still exist locally and by finding or inventing varied means of attracting outside capital of all kinds to return to the community.

Mobilization at the community level can create a vision of comprehensive renewal and an inventive program for development, but somewhere, somehow, the program must find the capital to carry out that vision. How much capital will ultimately be needed over the years for any one community is impossible to say. Since community economic development is a very long process of recovery that must stretch over many, many years, the local conditions and opportunities will change too much in that extended period to predict the costs in detail at the beginning, much less to specify the probable sources and types of capital. Indeed, if all the dollars for a complete development plan for any depleted community had to be totted up at once, the large-scale financing needs might bewilder the most imaginative resident and discommode the most optimistic. Perhaps it is as well that the full scope of the task is not readily interpreted in dollar terms. Yet some planning and foresight are required of a CDC, which would usually use one-, two-, and five-year projections. In these projections, each specific infrastructure or business development project must be matched with a set of potential financiers, specific organizations or individuals who might be interested in that particular project.

Some potential capital sources—major foundations, such as Ford, or national religious organizations, such as the headquarters programs of the Presbyterian Church, U.S.A.—are interested in a wide range of possible community development activities and can be approached for general-purpose financing as well as for specific projects. Occasionally a small local foundation, a local church group, or a corporation with local headquarters can become broadly interested in community projects if they are carried out in the local area.

Most financing sources, however, limit themselves to a single, rather specific type of project. Thus, even though federal, state, provincial, and local governments may have a wide range of interests, each particular agency at any level of government is categorically organized and must be approached separately on a project that might attract them. Even different divisions within a single agency will have separate budgets for restricted purposes. One finds, for example, that money is available from one agency subdivision for counseling unmarried pregnant girls under the age of eighteen, but that sometimes the same dollars cannot reach out to the fathers-to-be or even to other mothers-to-be over the age of eighteen. For an integrated and comprehensive program, then, community leaders need to be experts in piecing together, over time, monies from a variety of sources.

It is an added complication that the potential sources of funds change in their degree of availability and in the kinds of interests the fund sources have. Accordingly, a descriptive matrix of capital sources and their permissible applications of funds should optimally be constructed and updated annually by each local CDC. However, to be candid, it is unlikely that any one local group will be able to develop a thorough list of potential capital sources or to keep such a list really current. Some years ago, the Institute for New Enterprise Development produced such a matrix for U.S. CDCs, but even that was basically limited to a single slice of possible projects—business expansions and start-ups—and even it became rapidly outdated as some of the government programs it discussed were changed or discontinued. Nevertheless, a CDC must take the time and thought to review systematically what is or might be available for capital, in what forms, and for what purposes.

This chapter offers an overview of the extensive spectrum of capital sources and forms that CDCs have used in the past. The examples should be a stimulus for local groups to range broadly in their thinking, for it is one of the incredibilities of this world that financiers and their clients have created and can continually create new unexpected ways to fit dollars to investment needs. Many observers insist that in North America there is rarely any shortage of capital for a reasonably good project; instead, the task is to structure the project so that it can attract the capital it needs from the sources that have capital available for such projects. That may be a slight exaggeration, but it is indeed my own experience that, despite the disadvantaged position of the depleted community, troubles in financing come all too often from inadequate conception and presentation of the local project. Under all circumstances, the responsibility and burden of effort fall upon the CDC to design its projects to justify the investment to be made in them by the appropriate sources and types of capital.

Sources of capital can be considered according to whether they are *internal* or *external* to the community. In either instance, the capital should be differentiated by the purpose to which it might be applied and the specific forms and particular sources of the financing.

It is common for community groups to begin their financing plans with some idea of getting a grant from a government agency or a charitable organization—that is, with the idea of getting external capital. But I would like to begin here with a discussion of raising *internal capital,* because even the most depleted community has its own capital to invest. And even low-income families within the community can be a source of some of that capital. It is incumbent upon the community economic development organization to recognize that the community is not without its own resources, because that recognition generates an invigorating sense of the community's own capacities and will help to mobilize all the other kinds of capital needed.

Internal capital is obviously not going to be available in large chunks. It will have to be aggregated from the small amounts that each local source will be able to allocate. Such allocations may differ according to the form of capital required and the purpose to which it is to be put, but usually local capital is more *flexible*.

Perhaps the most outstandingly successful single effort to mobilize *general-purpose* or flexible local capital is illustrated by the Zion Investment Associates, Inc., a community economic development fund based originally in the members of the Zion Baptist Church, a large black congregation in the north Philadelphia district led by the Reverend Leon Sullivan. Their capital-raising technique, invented in June, 1962, became known as the "10-36 plan" because it entailed individual contributions of $10 per month for 36 months. Initially, Sullivan persuaded about two hundred of his parishioners to join the plan in order to establish resources for a community development corporation. Their monthly contributions would go toward paying for a single stock share priced at $360. After the first round of shares was sold in the ensuing three years, another round was begun, to be purchased by four hundred more church members. Only after this second round was completely subscribed (for a total of over $200,000) did Zion open stock purchases in 1968 to people outside the church and outside the community. (However, some church members and stockholders were affluent residents of other parts of the city.) Today stockholders number in the thousands, and Zion has used the fund as seed capital to lever additional capital.

The initial project of Zion Investment Associates was a low-income garden apartment development. It was built in 1964 with 90 percent government financing but was then refinanced by another government mortgage fund, which enabled Zion to recover its entire local capital. At the conclusion of the project, Zion's new mortgage returned all the local dollars that it had initially put into constructing the garden apartment complex. After that experience, Zion went on over time to lever additional millions of dollars to create a shopping center, various manufacturing and other businesses, and more housing.

There are three lessons to be reviewed here. First, even in a low-income community, there is general-purpose capital available if the overall community development mission can be made meaningful. In the case of Zion Investment Associates, undoubtedly the leadership of a charismatic minister was crucial. (Sullivan had already multiplied the membership of his church many times over in the dozen years before his 10-36 plan was set up.) Moreover, Zion Baptist Church did have some affluent members, and perhaps another community might not be able to raise as much. But even one-quarter as much can be a very powerful seed capital fund.

The key term *seed capital* implies the second lesson—namely, that the internal capital must be regarded as merely the means of germinating other, outside capital. Just as the Zion group used its investment fund initially to lever outside money for its first housing project, so *leverage* must be the aim of any internal capital, drawn as it is from the very limited resources of the community. While all capital can be regarded as a means to additional capital, the capital generated from residents of a depleted community must always be so regarded and must not be spent for operating expenses or even invested in a project from which the community will not derive the fruits of further capital for local investment.

A detailed example should be helpful here. Suppose that a CDC had raised some money locally and decided that the money should be used to help local businesses expand or improve their cash position for working capital—in short, used for lending purposes to strengthen existing local enterprise or even to help start new ventures. Lending the money would generate a return (of interest charged) and eventual replacement of the principal, so such use of the capital would create permanent or renewable assets—in terms of both the businesses themselves and the loan fund.

But what about using that money even more powerfully for the same purpose? For instance, in the United States, a CDC can establish—and several have established—a so-called Small Business Investment Corporation, or SBIC, by which the CDC investment can be multiplied many times over with matching federal funds when lent to local small businesses. Thus many more thousands of dollars are pumped into the local economy by priming the pump with some local dollars. Similar programs occur at the state level. And Canada has its own versions.

Perhaps the CDC's own capital is not a large enough sum to qualify for starting that kind of investment subsidiary. Even so, there are other different structures that the CDC might build to fully use the power of its dollars. Instead of lending the money directly to the local businesses, it might, as did the East Boston CDC, establish a revolving *loan guarantee* fund. In this structure, the CDC joins a local private business in going to a bank for a loan and tells the bank that if it lends the money to the business, the CDC will back the loan—will guarantee repayment if the borrower defaults. Of course, the CDC prefers not to guarantee the entire amount, for then it would not raise any more money for local business than the original CDC fund. Indeed, guarantees of as little as, say, 35 percent of the bank's loan may get the right amount of credit for a local venture that could not have otherwise qualified for what it needed. So the CDC fund raises much more capital for community businesses than its original or base amount.

Yet the multiplication of capital need not stop there. In the guarantee process, the CDC will deposit the requisite dollars at the lending bank, that is, the amount that will cover 35 percent of the bank's loan. While on deposit (and not used because the borrower is faithfully repaying his loan), the money will earn interest for the CDC, though probably at a lower rate than a standard deposit for the same length of time. Details of the guarantee agreement can, however, produce a less reduced return to the CDC. For example, in parallel with the dollar amount of the principal being paid back by the borrower, the bank agreement for the CDC's deposit can provide that an increasing proportion of the deposit will begin to earn a higher interest; in short when the *first* 35 percent of the total principal is repaid, it might fully free up the CDC's linked deposit to earn the full interest for such a deposit—until the CDC finds a new loan to be guaranteed. These or more complicated arrangements can be designed to achieve the most powerful possible use of the CDC's original capital. Exploring such possibilities is critical to getting the most impact from the dollars that the CDC has raised.

Seeing the possibilities of leverage leads finally to the third lesson to be garnered from the Zion case. The concept of leverage helps to reveal that a dollar is not just a dollar, that there are different kinds of dollars. Money comes in different forms and has different powers and potentialities. Some money is quite weak, some is quite powerful; and the community group that examines the form of capital to which it has access and that uses it for the highest and mightiest potential will have learned to make one dollar do the work of many. Thus, single-purpose money (dollars raised to be allocated only to one limited task) is usually the weakest of all, while general-purpose money, which can be plugged in anywhere, is clearly the most powerful. It behooves the community group not to use powerful money for tasks for which targeted weaker money can be raised.

For example, locally generated general-purpose capital— whether raised in substantial amounts by a 10-36 technique or in small amounts by a series of bake sales—has a special power and attraction. It demonstrates local strength to outside sources of capital. Being able to join local capital is highly prized by outside grantors like foundations, but even the most conventional bank will look for what the local community group is providing. Thus raising internal capital is not an alternative to raising external capital; it is often simply a first step. Several millions of dollars of government and bank money imported into Cape Breton by New Dawn had a beginning in the few hundred flexible dollars contributed by each of the original members of the Cape Breton Association for Cooperative Housing four years before the CDC was incorporated.

Since this type of capital has such special power and is relatively scarce, it must be carefully allocated. There is nothing more discouraging to a community group and its supporters than the evaporation of those scarce local dollars. Therefore, while the particular application of the funds may not have been formulated while raising the money, certainly everyone involved will need to know that the money is properly handled as seed capital, and monitoring procedures must be in place.

Eventually, the community development group can look forward to the regular generation of its own flexible all-purpose dollars, when the individual projects or enterprises themselves begin to generate a profit stream. Again, even small profits can lever dollars for projects totally unrelated to the original source of the profits. For example, the Roxbury Action Program realized $25,000 in unencumbered proceeds when in 1971 it closed papers on its first project, $490,000 worth of scattered-site family housing rehabilitation, which incidentally began with the donation of two dilapidated, abandoned buildings owned by neighborhood residents. The $25,000 proceeds helped RAP defray the expenses of moving on to a second project, which included commercial property rehabilitation and which cost about twice as much as the first project. Eight years later RAP closed papers on another development project, from which it generated several hundred thousand dollars. Unfortunately, at that point the organization had previously undergone some major program failures, and the proceeds of that project had to go primarily to the repayment of debts. Nevertheless, because these funds were flexible—as opposed to some specific grants RAP also had—they were free to be allocated to pay off the debts and to keep RAP from certain dissolution.

Flexible, general-purpose dollars, however, are not the only local capital that can be raised. *Limited-purpose* money is what is generated by, for example, organizing a credit union, where the pooling of local savings provides capital specifically for financing member loans, including home mortgages and business loans. Here too, gathering the local capital can lever additional resources for specialized lending purposes. When the Hough Area Development Corporation established the local credit union, it solicited large "public interest" deposits. Such deposits in insured accounts are often available from the regular investment funds of outside church groups which are willing to take a lesser rate of return when a deposit will offer social benefits to a needy community. Brooklyn Ecumenical Cooperatives, a CDC that evolved out of an energy supplies and services cooperative sponsored by a network of churches, used its church connections to garner outside deposits not only for a credit union, but also for two revolving loan funds to finance the purchase, rehabilitation, and resale of residential properties for small low-income housing cooperatives. Community Development Credit Unions, organized exclusively to serve specific low-income neighborhoods, have spread throughout the United States and have become powerful tools for local finance. The more ubiquitous general credit unions of Canada still are not viewed as an instrument for business development and remain a sleeping resource for community-based economic development purposes.

Internal capital, whether limited-purpose or general-purpose, comes in three forms: *equity* (as in share purchases in Zion Investment Associates), *debt* (as in citizen deposits in the Hough credit union), and *gifts* or grants (as in the property donations to RAP). The same three forms occur in *external capital,* and different considerations arise, depending upon the form, when a CDC seeks external capital. The broad category of external capital is most conveniently discussed by treating each form separately, although some considerations apply to all forms.

Let us begin with *debt* financing—that is, financing for which the local group usually pays at least some interest and is liable for full repayment at some point. "Friendly money," represented by outsiders who make less than the conventional demands in interest rates and repayment conditions, is of course what any development group will prize. Inquilinos Boricuas en Accion (IBA), a very successful Puerto Rican CDC in Boston, has created hundreds of low-income housing units and many other community amenities, using the low-interest capital offered by the Local Initiatives Service Corporation (LISC). LISC, founded by the Ford Foundation and financed especially by a consortium of U.S. corporations and insurance companies, requires well-planned projects that can reasonably predict repayment; but the LISC interest rates may be only half the conventional rates. Sometimes, with friendly money, interest can be even less. The Roxbury Action Program obtained a no-interest loan of $20,000 from Boston's Episcopal City Mission to finance the land purchases for its second project until permanent mortgage money could be obtained and the loan repaid; the permanent mortgage money itself came from a Massachusetts state finance agency at below-market rates.

A welcome development in the United States has been the recent rise of the so-called Community Loan Fund (CLF). These funds have spread along the East Coast from New Hampshire and Maine to Pennsylvania and are beginning to appear in other sections of the country. CLFs are local, independent, nonprofit organizations that lend money to feasible local community projects which cannot qualify for conventional loans or which cannot pay current interest rates. They are capitalized by private individuals, church organizations, foundations, and others who lend that capital to the CLF at very low rates, sometimes at zero interest. These borrowed funds are re-lent, typically at only a slightly higher rate to cover administrative costs, to projects within the community area of the group of CLF backers.

CLFs generally concentrate on housing projects and relatively short-term loans—the first because housing projects offer more security, and the second because the CLF's own funds are usually on relatively short-term deposit from their backers. The typical CLF loan is probably some sort of bridge loan, money to tide a low-income housing project over until more long-term money will be available—for example, a construction loan until a bank mortgage can be obtained on the completed structure. CLFs fill a capital need for other small nonprofit organizations that are regularly turned down by banks or that cannot afford bank rates and still produce or maintain housing for low- and moderate-income people. Yet CLFs operate in a businesslike fashion, use skilled specialists for loan screening, and provide technical assistance to community groups so that they can make projects financially feasible. CLFs maintain policies that keep their funds safe and experience a very low default rate, on the whole perhaps better than conventional banks; and still they make affordable money accessible for community purposes.

It is psychologically customary and natural for community development groups to seek and expect bargains in external debt capital. Since there is public interest to be served in the lending of money at below-market rates to facilitate the community-building process in a deteriorated area, both borrower and lender can justify concessionary charges for debt capital. Moreover, when borrowing money, any CDC should, of course, look for the best deal. Still, a community economic development program should not be totally dependent upon bargain money. If every project is financially planned so close to the margin that it requires the cheapest possible interest and easiest possible repayment conditions, it will be vulnerable to the vicissitudes of chance and unable to survive the unexpected crises that any business or infrastructure project will inevitably face. The planning and conception of community development projects ought to entail expectations of virtually conventional costs; then, if friendly money can actually be found, the project will have an additional reserve to surmount the crises ahead—or perhaps it will be able to offer greater benefits in some other way. Further, if a community development group chooses and plans its projects on the assumption that they will require friendly money, it effectively cuts itself off from the much wider pool of potential external debt capital that can be available to it. After all, there is only a very limited amount of debt capital for community economic development at bargain rates, and of course there is competition for that amount.

The major potential source of external debt capital is where everyone else goes—the banks—and community development groups, like any other potential bank customer, must play that borrowing game by the bankers' rules. It is helpful to consider the banking community as if it were some kind of exotic South Sea culture—that is, its rules of behavior are sometimes very hard to understand, rather odd, sometimes funny to those outside the culture, but worth knowing about if you want to get along with the natives. First of all, banks, as I have mentioned before, are wary of the usual nonprofit community organizations because typically they are less likely to be administered in a businesslike manner.

But CDCs, after all, are organized to be businesslike, and this message has to get across. Second, it is well to remember that a bank is made up of people, and the CDC simply has to get to know them as such. The first contact that can be used in this campaign occurs when the CDC establishes its own checking account. But if that opportunity happens not to be used to become acquainted and to explore the bank's personnel and perhaps its policies for lending, then a prominent CDC board member (perhaps accompanied by a staff member) should make another special opportunity, simply to get the bank officers acquainted with the community group and to begin to get over the mutual strangeness that creatures from different cultures have for each other.

Establishing a relationship with the particular banks or bank that will hold the most promise for possible capital at some later date may take some time for a nonprofit community group. How that campaign is carried out will vary from locale to locale, and what is effective in one setting to overcome the stigmata of nonprofit low-income organizations may not be useful in another.

The Mexican-American Unity Council of San Antonio was once engaged in lengthy negotiations with a local bank to get them to consider the idea of lending several hundreds of thousands of dollars for the CDC's projects. The bank officers were very pleasant, but nothing seemed to impress them. The MAUC officers went to pains to be businesslike—for example, by arriving promptly for any meetings with the bank people in their downtown offices—but all they got was a bland, noncommital response. Then MAUC requested a meeting at their own headquarters, and the bank officers came out to the barrio, which in itself, of course, was no great inducement to risk their bank's money. But the meeting was held in MAUC's board of directors' room, which had all the characteristics of a bank boardroom—paneled walls, leather chairs, a long, gleaming, well-polished table, quiet carpeting, and even some dignified portraits of former MAUC board chairpersons on the walls. Suddenly, the atmosphere of the relationship changed. The bankers could recognize what they had not really seen before—namely, that the CDC could be a reasonably appropriate customer. At that point, MAUC's careful financial planning and presentation of the project for which it had sought bank credit could also become visible. MAUC had reassured the visiting natives that it would abide by the rules of the game.

When even the most assiduous cultivation of the banking sector has produced little for the representatives of the depleted community, CDCs can turn to intermediaries. The most impressive intermediary is a potential new bank customer who will agree to make a substantial "linked deposit" in the bank. The link that gets the deposit is the bank's agreement to work with the CDC. The offer of a linked deposit is a powerful attention getter, because a bank is allowed, of course, to lend many times the amount of any dollars deposited with it. If the deposit is substantial, the bank's resources for making money are nicely enriched. So if the CDC has contacts in the corporate world who are willing to deposit some corporate funds in a potentially helpful bank, the image of the CDC changes in the eyes of the bank, and business plans not appreciated before become potentially interesting. Note that I am only talking about the CDC's getting a real hearing from the capital source; the quality of the CDC's project and presentation must thereafter bear the burden of attracting the necessary capital.

There are a variety of possible linked-deposit arrangements. The new corporate customer may simply deposit an agreed-upon total, or the total might vary from time to time as a so-called compensatory balance, in which the amounts loaned and paid back for CDC projects call for increases or reductions in the deposit. The corporate intermediary can be depended upon to negotiate its own suitable terms with the bank, so long as it and the CDC are clear on the link—on what benefits the CDC seeks.

The intermediary does not always have to be an impressive depositor. Sometimes it can even be a subsidiary of the nonprofit group itself. This is the case in Halifax for the Human Resources Development Association, which has learned never to approach banks directly, only through its for-profit subsidiary, HRDA Enterprises, Ltd., a holding company that owns and runs small businesses. In another similar case, the Community Development Corporation of Kansas City (CDC-KC), a black neighborhood CDC, had had a hard time establishing itself with local banks, even though it had obtained considerable sums in government grants for economic development purposes. Using some of their grant money, CDC-KC at one point bought a business that had already had a good credit relationship with one of the local banks. It discovered that this purchase made a difference. The credibility of the business firm apparently was transferable, because the formerly reluctant bank thereafter accepted the nonprofit CDC-KC as a good customer. To many banks, a nonprofit CDC is a very strange being and not at all a likely customer. A CDC thus may need a for-profit intermediary to do the job of introductions and interpretation of the foreign languages that the two sides seem to speak.

When regular business relationships with banks still elude the community group and the residents generally, then it is incumbent upon the CDC leadership to organize their campaign on a political level. This campaign can include public demonstrations at bank offices and petitions to the biggest bank customers to change their bank. Banks are vulnerable to a well founded and well publicized allegation of poor service. A bank, after all, is chartered to provide service, and governments at different levels offer supports and subsidies to make banking more profitable. For example, two federal agencies (in Canada, the Canada Deposit Insurance and, in the U.S., the Federal Deposit Insurance Corporation) use taxpayers' money in the process of insuring banks and encouraging depositors to place their funds in the insured banks. There is a right of access to bank services implied in such government activity, and community development groups should claim that right. In the United States, the rights have been specifically shored up by the federal Home Mortgage Disclosure Act and the Community Reinvestment Act, as previously noted, and these laws offer leverage against nonperforming banking institutions.

This special federal legislation has been effectively invoked in Massachusetts by a consortium of community groups known as the Massachusetts Urban Reinvestment Advisory Group, or MURAG. MURAG has established itself both as an adversary to be reckoned with and as, ultimately, an aid to bank prosperity. Two examples will demonstrate MURAG's influence and suggest analogous actions by other community development groups. In one case, MURAG's actions were basically adversarial. It objected to the expansion of a bank to another branch, citing the bank's lack of community responsibility as evidenced in its redlining practices. On these grounds, the bank did not receive approval from the necessary federal agency to open its new branch—which represented a considerable financial loss. To protect itself in the future, the bank thereupon changed its practices to develop a record of making loans where it had not before. In the other case, MURAG was actually helpful to the bank. A bank had decided to close a neighborhood branch because of unprofitable operations there and was gradually reducing its staff, hours, and services at that location, with announced plans to close entirely. MURAG, in cooperation with a neighborhood organization and neighborhood business establishments, dealt directly with the bank, insisting that the branch be kept open and pointing out that the management of that branch had long before stopped providing adequate services to the area—for example, by rejecting reasonable loan applications from the local businesses. The bank reconsidered, shifted management and policies at the branch, and within a short period discovered that the branch was turning out to be above average in profitability. In short, MURAG had alerted the bank to its own internal business mistakes that were threatening the neighborhood.

Private sources of external debt capital, like banks, can be supplemented significantly by tapping public and government programs of credit assistance. Since government programs change regularly in policy and form, one of the CDC's tasks is to keep informed. Moreover, early warnings, so to speak, of such changes can be a great advantage for preparing a strategy to deal with the changes and to take advantage of them. Consulting the publications that specialize in keeping track of all the particular government programs and policies in which the CDC is interested is one measure; there are some very useful newsletters to be subscribed to or consulted in a major library. Probably the most useful source of information, however, is the staff members of the legislative representatives for the CDC's own district. Developing a relationship with the legislators and their staff will be crucial in facilitating an information flow that can mean thousands of dollars to the community development group. Of course, a CDC can develop a relationship directly with civil servants in one or more key government program offices, but those sources naturally know much less about what is happening in other offices that might also be relevant to the CDC. That is why the CDC needs the more general access that legislators can provide.

Information tends to be an eagerly proffered legislative constituent service because it requires spending very few political chips and returns a great deal in constituent appreciation and publicity. For that reason, community development groups can get valuable assistance if they keep the legislator (and her or his staff) specifically informed of local projects and local needs. And if the legislator's tips on possible government funds turn out to be productive, there is nothing that will warm the heart of the legislator more than being able to announce a government grant or release of credit or other assistance to some organization in the legislator's district. Thus the community development group and the legislator can exchange much of benefit to each other—and can do so without involving commitments on either side that might be too costly. Of course, some community development groups are also adept at gaining the intervention of legislators to make sure that the government assistance programs specifically place the available dollars in the local development project. But, as I have earlier implied, this activity requires a greater expenditure of the legislator's political influence and thus may involve a risky identification of the group with the legislator.

A third source of information on government loans and other funding programs are fellow community groups. Often they offer a more sophisticated analysis just because they share the same perspective. However, they too have to rely upon intermediaries, of course, so they may not be as immediately informative as the direct source at the government agency offices which the legislators can more readily tap. Nevertheless, when community groups can systematize their own information services for each other—especially by establishing a specialized newsletter and an information-gathering office—they improve their access to government (and other) capital by a quantum jump over the process of relying upon their own individual contacts.

Of course, everything that has been said here so far applies to all programs of government financial assistance. Governments at all levels can be a source not only of loan funds but also of outright grants and, occasionally in Canada but only rarely in the United States, of equity investments, share purchases in local business ventures. However, before turning explicitly to these other two forms of external capital that a CDC might seek—whether from government or from other sources—I want to emphasize that community development groups ought to consider an activist approach with government to recover the capital that has been exported over the years from their depleted communities. Instead of just focusing on existing government funding programs that might be available for local economic development, there is no reason why, in concert with other community development groups, a CDC might not work to create new programs that can benefit local communities. And in fact groups in both Canada and the U.S. have done so. In Canada the LEAD (previously LEDA) program was surely instituted particularly because New Dawn and other Canadian groups stimulated the interest of civil servants (and members of Parliament) in the concept of community-based economic development. Now LEAD provides grants for venture capital and for the administrative expenses of community groups in many small rural communities. Keeping up contacts within the government services in different agencies and promoting a network of people interested in community economic development was an essential part of gaining a critical mass of energy to launch that program. I do not mean that government officials did not have their own sources of interest, but only that whatever was there was assiduously stimulated and maintained by the community development groups—even through three different cabinet governments.

On the federal level in the United States, the most outstanding consequence of concerted action by CDCs was probably the reactivation of the federal Rural Development Loan Fund (originally $100 million) and its redirection to community development groups. In this instance, the CDCs actually instituted suit against the U.S. government to start operating the fund again, and they eventually won a settlement. The settlement led to the financing of the private (controlled by the community development network) National Rural Development and Finance Corporation, which makes loans and offers technical assistance to rural low-income community organizations. Some of the fund money also went to finance the lending operations of the Southern Cooperative Development Fund, owned and controlled by low-income agricultural cooperatives in southern U.S. communities. And some went directly to a few rural CDCs for the operation of their own local revolving loan funds.

At the provincial level, Native American groups in Canada have also generated funding to establish their own new development finance institutions in Saskatchewan and Nova Scotia, and in several American states CDC groups have successfully sponsored various kinds of legislation for community economic development assistance, including the Community Development Finance Corporation of Massachusetts, the first state development bank for CDC ventures. In short, community development groups can increase the forms and amount of external capital available to them at all levels of government if they work together to design and promote such new programs.

Even though the government intervention traditions of Canada and the United States are different, community development groups in both nations can get ideas from what has happened across the border. HRDA managed to get welfare regulations readjusted to provide legal authority for its use of social assistance money for small business investment. Its technques can be studied profitably by U.S. groups for gaining access to welfare funds in their own states. Similarly, the tax credit and deduction techniques instituted by state and federal laws that support various types of projects by U.S. community groups can be examined for adoption in a Canadian province or even in Canada as a whole. For example, Pennsylvania offers a tax credit to corporations for corporate dollars that go to an approved project sponsored by a community group. Called the Neighborhood Assistance Program, it provides 50 to 70 percent tax write-off of the corporate contribution to the project. When a community group registers its project with the Pennsylvania state authorities, it can go to any corporation paying taxes in Pennsylvania with something valuable to offer in exchange for corporate support. Several other states have the same kind of program.

Such corporate contributions illustrate another form of external capital, namely, *grants*. Although grants, unlike loans, do not have to be repaid, they are not without cost. In fact, as I have suggested earlier, whether the grants come from government or from a private institution such as a foundation or large corporation, they ordinarily entail both dollar and nondollar costs to a community organization. Just preparing forms and proposals can be expensive, particularly since the effort sometimes fails in its purpose. Even a successful grant proposal implies new program and administrative obligations—for example, detailed monthly financial reports by project, reports that the group may not be accustomed to produce and which will require additional bookkeeping services. Thus grants are not free money, and the community development group must clarify for itself what any particular grant implies for the group's goals and resources.

In any case, not all grants can really be considered external capital for local investment, quite apart from the question of whether they cost more than they produce. After all, most grants are made for service purposes (to operate a senior citizens center, for example) and also for annual operating expenses; that is, they are designed to be exhausted in the year for which they were granted. Such grants may be said to be externally derived *working capital* or operating capital only if they will permit the service to be set up in a format that will generate replacement funds on an annual basis to continue operating. If, on the contrary, the grant program is designed so that the dollars will be exhausted and the only replacement will be a new grant, if any, then this type of grant cannot be considered capital in any form. It is very weak money. However, the community development group might be able to figure out how to expend these weak dollars in such a way that—though the grantor did not so design it—the dollars or some part of them can be transformed into capital. For example, if the grant contains dollars for rent, perhaps the monthly rent can be paid in such a way that it will actually defray all or part of a monthly mortgage payment, thus building up the CDC's capital base of property owned. Or perhaps certain CDC-supplied services (such as bookkeeping) can be charged against the grant in such a way as to replenish the central working capital of the CDC.

Good accounting requires that the CDC charge each of its grant program budgets for all the costs that might be overlooked but that are actual costs in carrying out the grant purposes. Moreover, the charges against each grant budget can, in many instances, be made on commercial rates—that is, including a profit margin to the appropriate administrative services division of the CDC. Creative accounting, so to speak, can be a small but significant capital accumulation technique for community groups, even when the service grants received would not otherwise represent a long-term investment for the community.

Paradoxically, the community development group can run into difficulties by trying to be businesslike in its accounting procedures. The following example, while not involving a grant program but rather a government loan program, illustrates the dilemma often faced by the nonprofit organization trying to conserve and build its capital. New Dawn Enterprises used to construct, with its own staff, a good deal of low- and moderate-income housing, using the subsidized mortgage programs of the federal Canada Mortgage and Housing Corporation (CMHC). CMHC requires the itemization of all expenses, of course, in the construction and development of the project to which it will offer financing, and New Dawn provided the same types of expenditure itemization as the commercial firms with which CMHC was accustomed to doing business. However, CMHC would not recognize as real the same costs for New Dawn that it would for a conventional construction firm. It insisted that since New Dawn was a nonprofit organization, it should contribute the internal administrative services for which the commercial businesses charged CMHC. Essentially, CMHC refused to recognize so-called overhead costs, assuming that they did not really exist for a nonprofit community group in which members often contribute services. Such bureaucratic problems finally led New Dawn to retire from the actual construction of housing and to maintain only a sponsor relationship to CMHC-financed housing. Now New Dawn contracts with local firms to do the work for which CMHC will pay when it is performed by a for-profit business. In this instance, the community group would otherwise have had to deplete its capital in order to take advantage of a government program. (Alternatively, of course, New Dawn might have been able to launch a for-profit construction firm if CMHC had been willing to accept this structure.)

Devising ways to use a grant so that it will do double duty within the community is tougher for all those types and sources of money that were not designed directly as a contribution to the revitalization of the depleted community. But even when grants and gifts are in the form of capital and are intended to reinvigorate the community, they challenge the community development group's ingenuity in investing the sums at the most productive leverage. The availability of a grant from city funds to redevelop an abandoned industrial building, for example, should spur the neighborhood leadership to design the project to establish a permanent community asset, to generate additional capital both from income and from the asset appreciation of the property, and to provide for the best use of the real estate for neighborhood purposes. All of these payoffs do not necessarily fit together, and may have to be traded off against one another. Getting a grant is only one step in the institution-building process on any particular project.

The final type of external capital to be discussed is *equity*. Equity capital is simply financing that actually buys stock or stock equivalents as a way of creating or expanding a business venture. It is almost always garnered from private individuals or corporations. Canadian government agencies, both federal and provincial, have from time to time made equity investments in private businesses, but none of these arrangements has yet involved the business of a community economic development group, so far as I am aware. In the United States, it is only at the state level, as with the Massachusetts Community Development Finance Corporation, that equity investments have occasionally been made in CDC ventures. So community groups must ordinarily look to nongovernment sources for this type of capital.

Equity, like debt capital, has different degrees of friendliness, but, generally speaking, equity investors who are at all willing to risk buying stock in a CDC business venture are, by definition, more friendly than otherwise. Nevertheless, the degree of risk involved in any equity investment (in which, after all, the investor is potentially liable to total loss) means that somehow the investor expects to receive a very valuable benefit. That benefit may be the satisfaction of doing a socially responsible action, but ordinarily it also includes some financial return—and sometimes a very high return. Otherwise, the investor would simply make a gift to express his or her social commitment. Assuming, then, that the outside investor expects a financial return, the CDC plans a venture that reasonably predicts such a return; and since outside equity investors rarely accept a risk all alone, the CDC will also be investing and will also be at risk, and therefore at the same time will be planning a financial return for itself on its own investment. In short, the CDC and the outside investor essentially become partners in the venture, sharing an interest in all the valuable outcomes of the venture. Indeed, some community development enterprises are structured legally as partnerships rather than as corporations, and the investments are in "partnership interests" or percentages of ownership of various specified returns and risks rather than in shares of corporate stock.

In the United States, the partnership structure has been used quite frequently over the last decade or so in the development of low-income housing and other projects because U.S. tax laws have offered an inducement to wealthy outside investors to join a nonprofit community group in such projects. For example, the so-called 167k provision (referring to a section of the tax law) has allowed a partnership to deduct as a business expense in the short space of five years the entire cost of rehabilitating buildings for low-income housing. That can be a substantial benefit to an investor in the 50 percent tax bracket, and since the CDC, as a nonprofit organization, ordinarily does not pay income taxes, the benefit can legally go virtually in its entirety to the outside investor.

Affirmative Investments, Inc. (AI), a new social investment advisory firm located in the Boston area, specializes in helping socially responsible wealth join with community groups—with this sort of tax advantage or other financial returns in mind. AI charges its investor clients for this service because it is able to screen and recommend community development projects that have a reasonable chance of a good market rate of return simply on financial grounds. The investor then has the double satisfaction of doing well by doing good.

The point, in general, is that the CDC itself can bring something of value to partnerships or corporate joint ventures, and therefore it can be an attractive colleague for outside equity investors. The attraction varies according to the potential partner's interests. It can be, as with the Kentucky Highlands Investment Corporation and the entrepreneurs of Outdoor Venture Corporation, the matching capital from the CDC's own funds. Or, for others, it might be control of a valuable piece of property deeded by the city to the CDC for development purposes; or a responsible management team ready to carry out the project; or the ideas and a well-worked-out plan for the venture; or influence with those (for example, government officials or departments, other possible investors, etc.) who can help make the project profitable; or many other possible advantages, such as the nonprofit, tax-exempt status.

The advantages that the CDC can offer derive one way or another from its special position as a neighborhood development group, and thus it may successfully use these advantages instead of cash to match in some measure the equity capital it seeks from outsiders. Moreover, just because the outsider brings the financial capital does not mean that the outsider calls the tune on how the project is to be designed and managed. As I have pointed out in the earlier discussion of business development projects, the community development group can attract capital, offer even majority ownership, gain financially as well as institutionally, and still obtain the nonmonetary community benefits that the group envisions the project will provide.

The powerful capital represented by outside equity—powerful for the community because it is willing to take risks that other investors providing debt capital will not—should be a target for any community economic development program. Obtaining that financial resource depends upon recognizing what must be offered in return, while at the same time protecting and promoting the community aims for which the capital is sought.

ELEVEN

Operational Challenges

T HE inherent conflict between what external capital seeks and what the local projects require is only one of the major operational tensions at the local level. These common operational problems are inextricably imbedded in the very nature of the community economic development strategy. In a sense, these problems could be considered existential. That is, they are a natural ingredient of the community economic development perspective and program; they are inescapable; there are no definitive solutions; and the fundamental key to their management is simply to recognize that they are there. Like the tensions between capital mobilization and capital allocation, all existential tensions of the community economic development strategy will be more successfully managed at one period and less so at other times.

Perhaps the most general of these local operational problems is the task of strengthening and maintaining a relationship between the community itself and the development program and organization. The magnitude of this task can be highlighted by asking, Can a depleted community truly determine its development by exercising control over the CDC, the instrument for carrying out the development program? Or is the CDC doomed from the beginning to become merely another elite or special interest group?

The fundamental conundrums of democratic control are no different in a community economic development organization than in any other organization or instrument of self-governance. Perhaps, in fact, it is more difficult to maintain community governance of a community development group because the depleted community has traditionally been blocked from achieving and growing in self-governance. It has fewer resources in time, energy, and money to devote to maintaining control over its own organizational tool. Too many of the residents of the community are themselves without a full complement of experience that will help them grasp this task and grapple with it effectively. Moreover, a city neighborhood or rural district is never completely united in its goals and policies, and the development organization will naturally reflect ongoing disagreements if it is representing its community in full. Control over the tool will therefore be shared by a coalition of different interests, whose influence over the CDC itself will ebb and flow. In this sense the CDC will always remain an essentially political institution with all the problems of translating democratic control over it as the core institution in a community economic development strategy.

The ebb and flow of effective democracy at each CDC offers lessons in the use of specific techniques for sustaining community participation in the policies and projects of the development program. Those techniques rest upon *shared information* and *readily accessible channels* by which ideas and criticisms as well as information can flow *to and from* the organization and its constituency. Some of these techniques can only be learned the hard way in the course of action, but perhaps others can be systematically constructed by using the experience of other groups. In any case, success is not based on a one-time set of decisions on how to facilitate information flow between the core organization and its constituency.

In a previous chapter I noted some of the structural features of this core institution and therefore the potential channels for information flow. For example, five broad categories of responsibility and activity (corporation members, board members, chief board officer, chief staff officer, and other staff and consultants) offer opportunities for access by the community. How available each of the posts and the occupants of these posts are to those in the community provides a measure of potential broadly based local control. A complementary measure asks how active these persons within the organization are in both passing on information to others outside the organization and seeking views from them.

The particular pattern of techniques for access must vary from one occasion to another, and they are indeed so varied that it is not practical to review them here. But, for example, access in one community may mean that the chief staff director has to have been a long-time community resident, but at a later stage of development the organization and its constituency, having gained in experience and self-confidence, can tolerate or even seek an outsider. For example, a new CDC in a black community may insist on having a black staff director, but in the natural course of turnover a few years later it may settle upon a replacement who is white. Or quite the contrary, in the beginning the board may be so anxious to get the most technically qualified person possible that it will choose someone outside the community or ethnic group instead of waiting until an insider or coethnic can be found. Later on, the group may feel that a replacement must fit local as well as technical criteria.

I do not believe that any one structural pattern for the core organization is best for ensuring community control, simply because cultural and historical precedents differ in each setting. For example, the traditional European forms of democratic political control, such as universal suffrage elections, when used for tribal board members in a Native American reservation, probably mismatch the electoral procedure and the local tradition. Non-Indians often seek the reassurance of promoting their own familiar structures in the Native American community, but that is a costly tranquilizer and may blur the outsider's view of what is really happening. Even in an ordinary urban U.S. setting, the familiar electoral forms are no guarantee of protection from special interests. That is as true for a CDC as it is for a city government. In a CDC with which I once worked closely, a local board election was planned and carried out in order to force dismissal of a staff director who had sturdily resisted diverting CDC resources to the individual benefit of a corrupt board faction.

There are certain choices to be made in view of a community's cultural and other features. For example, scheduling a yearly community panel hearing on the work of the CDC and inviting contributions from different sectors of the community as well as from residents at large can be useful in an urban setting. However, even if that method of exchanging views is also familiar to residents of a rural area, a single annual meeting which requires people to come to the meeting from far-flung corners of a large dispersed community may be a dubious practice. In the rural case, one might want to schedule a series of such hearings in different locations around the district if one sought broadly based local participation. Conversely, hearings on a nonurban Micmac or other Indian reserve might be geographically convenient and accessible to all residents, but since speaking out controversially in public is not culturally familiar, such a hearing would mainly offer access to those who have adjusted their ways to European styles. Another means of ascertaining views and needs would be required for the more traditional residents of the reserve, who might indeed attend the meeting but say nothing. Their input would have to be ascertained *after* such a meeting, perhaps rather indirectly through a number of informal opinion leaders, each of whom is recognized as being in touch with a subgroup or even a single family.

Furthermore, the rather technical nature of much economic development activity poses a special challenge for broadly based participation within a low-income organization, as well as for adequate controls over the technicians on which the organization will rely. This dimension of the problem of local control often causes eyes to roll heavenward among the technocrats who doubt the value of community control. Their skepticism is sometimes well taken, but again there are means by which a community board can effectively guide its own program. First of all, outsiders in any case tend to overestimate the technical qualifications necessary to guide the process and underestimate the human resources available for the task in the depleted community. Such doubts sometimes make the community residents underrate their own capacities and help confirm the technocratic viewpoint. But when CDC leaders join their skills and recruit within the locality those who do have specialized experience and training, all the bases can usually be covered. It is not necessary that everyone on the CDC board of directors, for instance, be able to critically review a financial report. It will only be necessary for a responsible and technically proficient board committee to spend the necessary review time and to report to its colleagues on the results and implications of its examination. Exactly the same structure can be used for any other specialized task. For example, when undertaking housing programs, a board will have recruited perhaps a building contractor, or an architect, or a master carpenter, or the like to its membership and will charge that person or persons to develop an expert monitoring committee (including people who are not board members) which will report regularly to the rest of the board.

Moreover, there is a learning process that all generalists go through to gain the proficiency and sophistication to guide the specialists reporting to them. Thus CDC boards, like the nonmedical boards and administrators of hospitals, do learn how to ask the right questions and break through the jargon of the specialists who are involved with them in the greater enterprise. Concurrently, to a large extent, technical experts can be expected to develop a certain identification with that greater enterprise which makes them want to do their jobs in the best way possible for the good of the community and to work hard at communicating the issues. Boards can become adept at judging consultants on the basis of their ability to relate both to the nonspecialists representing the community and to the broad community goals.

Another factor makes community control, even of technical specialists, not only possible but sometimes required for technical success. Residents very often have crucial knowledge about local conditions without which a specialist from outside the area would founder. This is particularly true when the success of a project depends upon alliances among local figures, but it may even be a matter that is directly within the scope of the expert. For example, experienced loan officers may know how to judge an applicant so long as the applicant belongs to the usual universe of bank customers but may not know as much as neighbors do about the reliability and resources of someone who is strange to that universe. Thus, a CDC loan fund needs more than an M.B.A. to administer it.

Because local residents bring in resources of knowledge, skills, and information about the community that are basic to a successful program, community control is necessary. And because community control is possible, it remains a reasonable basis for economic development—despite the inescapable problems associated with it.

The processes of local control offer the best means of dealing with the second major existential problem of community economic development—namely, trade-offs among the multiple and often at least partially conflicting goals and objectives inherent in that enterprise. Even single-purpose organizations will have the task of choosing among priorities. The board of a business firm making only one undifferentiated product, for example, still must choose between satisfying stockholders with a dividend or reinvesting surpluses for expansion. But a CDC confronts the trade-off problem at every turn because it seeks so many different community benefits. Local, democratic control offers the justifiable technique for *making* the choices, even though it does not offer standards for *weighing* them.

To promote local manufacturing jobs, the Bedford-Stuyvesant CDC, Restoration, once got the city of New York to give up plans to use a large parcel of land for public housing and a new school in Bedford-Stuyvesant. Instead Restoration persuaded the city to sell the land to IBM, which built a new facility there. IBM had outgrown its other Bedford-Stuyvesant facility and would have moved away in order to expand. Without the community support that Restoration symbolized and could mobilize, the city certainly would have been in no position to justify to local people its selling to IBM instead of building new low-income housing and a new school. Restoration had to make that trade-off into a community trade-off.

Another good example of a trade-off also comes from the Restoration experience. The CDC coventured a supermarket with a major chain, which agreed to supply and manage it, as well as to guarantee that prices at that store would be at the same level as at its other stores in the New York City area. Within a few months, this pricing policy brought down food prices for residents at the other competing stores in the area. Thus residents began to see cheaper prices whether or not they shopped at the CDC store. However, the installation of a supermarket in an area which has none—which was Restoration's motivation—also has the effect of depressing incomes for local food store entrepreneurs. This can be especially costly in a neighborhood in which small food stores are a way of life, as in Puerto Rican districts, but it also would be costly for black storeowners that live in a black neighborhood like Bedford-Stuyvesant. Only a community-based group can confront such issues directly.

The most acute form of trade-off occurs when the CDC must choose between generating new resources or distributing short-term benefits. The same conflict is faced by an individual business—namely, to build for the future or to satisfy the needs of the present, to reinvest or to declare a dividend. Quite analogously, the CDC is continually faced with choices (between or within projects) on a scale of returns that ranges from institution-building reinvestment to direct services for the community. Even a CDC's choices between some business goals and social goals often turn out to be the same choice between future and more immediate benefits; and neither the business nor the social category is at the same pole of this dichotomy in each case of conflict. Although it is common to hear people say that CDCs are always torn between business goals and social goals, the reality is that the choices are ordinarily between long-term benefits and short-term benefits in different patterns of varying benefits.

Let us suppose that a CDC has a modest amount of venture capital to invest. Shall it be in a manufacturing business that is projected to produce a small number of jobs and substantial profits (either by appreciation or by income), or shall the investment be made in a supermarket business that will offer convenient low-price shopping and produce more jobs, but only very small profits? Or shall it be in a housing project that will offer much-needed affordable shelter, some appreciation of assets, rather small suplus income, and very few jobs, apart from temporary construction work? Or shall it be in the construction of an office building that can house (at reduced rents) clinical and social services that will not otherwise be available locally—while rentals on other space in the building return an adequate cash flow to compensate for the rent reductions? Or shall it be in capitalizing a daycare center, which will give a steady though small dollar return?

Clearly the issues here are not business versus social goals. The trade-offs are much more complex, and, depending upon the dimensions considered, have some short-term and some long-term benefits. Moreover, the choices just described occur between very different sectors of the community economy—food, shelter, medical services, and so on. How the CDC board makes the choice—bearing in mind which arrangement of priorities, based upon which assessment of community needs, derived from which basis for determining those needs, etc., etc.—expresses the ineluctable tension of a multipurpose program. Who is to say in any one instance how that tension is to be resolved? No one except the representatives of the community through its community development organization.

Another operating problem is whether to spend time monitoring prior operations or developing new directions and new ideas. Perhaps it might be conceptualized as the difference between a managerial and an entrepreneurial task. Both are carried out within the CDC, the first for an orderly and sure exploitation of the efforts and money invested in the projects already established, the second for continuing to move forward energetically in the local development program.

A disastrous form of this conflict occurs when a board slights its responsibility for monitoring financial statements and focuses instead on new programs, on organizing new political resources, or on any of the other kinds of community entrepreneurial tasks that boards must do. The fact is that no board can operate safely unless it maintains a monthly review of the financial status of the organization as a whole and of each individual project within its program. The monitoring process may not take long; it may be delegated in detail to a committee or to a specific specialist, but it must be considered each month, and for that purpose monthly financial reports must be available.

Yet even energetic and productive CDCs have run themselves to the brink of bankruptcy just because no one has been watching the books. Unfortunately, community-based organizations often downgrade financial controls. They hire an inexperienced book-keeper (perhaps in a well-meaning intent to offer a job opportunity to someone who needs help), but then they do not give the person access to expert supervision to ensure that the necessary figures are reported. Time after time I have seen a community board accept the fact that they have met together for still another month without the financial reports to tell them where the organization is or where it will probably be the next month. Sometimes, only after a long-overdue audit, they find out that they have inadvertently overspent, misspent, just plain lost money, or perhaps let money stay idle that should have been productive.

Once I was making this point in a panel discussion with other panel members from community development groups and was immediately confirmed by a fellow panelist's candid remarks. She told the audience that only weeks before she had discovered that her organization had overspent by $500,000 because of inadequate reporting procedures. This person was a nationally respected and successful staff director who was managing a well-known and well-financed program of varied local projects in her urban neighborhood in California. Luckily, her organization had the means to retrieve itself, but of course that retrieval meant reprogramming a half-million dollars that could have been much more productively used. The same fate befell the Roxbury Action Program, as I mentioned before, and they had to use several hundred-thousand dollars of proceeds from their most important housing development project to pay off a debt that would not have built up had they been regularly receiving financial reports. Virtually the same prospects faced the board of New Dawn in 1983 when they finally obtained an audit that showed imminent bankruptcy, after they had tolerated months of incomplete or nonexistent reports.

In one organization I have worked with, this sort of inattention and dire results happened *twice* in a period of six years. That organization now, I am happy to report, has so tightened its procedures that it is probably one of the best monitored of any community group and will not fall into the same trap again. In this and in most other instances, the boards have members from the ordinary business world, successful businessmen, bankers, accountants, and others, but at the CDC they seem to leave behind the tools they would never forget in their other work.

I have suggested that such events occur when a board ignores managerial for entrepreneurial duties, but there can be other reasons. Sometimes board members may be overworked because they have not adequately divided and delegated tasks, and they operate in such a sense of crisis that they slight the mundane task of financial reports and do not care whether they receive them. Or sometimes a board's genuine concern for people and for pressing community needs takes precedence, and no one wants to change the subject and thereby appear to others as being unconcerned with those needs. In still other instances, board members simply do not take their responsibilities seriously enough to risk being charged with cantankerousness if they criticize someone for not providing the financial reports.

Still another operational problem in resolving conflicts among CDC goals has been alluded to in an earlier chapter: the problem of handling an unexpected opportunity that does not fit into the CDC's adopted plan. When a CDC has gone through the exhausting task of planning and allocating its resources for the coming year, all too often it is confronted by an attractive project opportunity that will deflect it from carrying out that plan. Perhaps the potential project was not contemplated originally because at the time no one thought it was practical, but suddenly a new set of circumstances makes the project attractive. The trade-offs between pursuing a well-thought-out plan already well under way and taking after the new opportunity are difficult to weigh, with hidden costs that can be substantial. Each case is different, and there is no pat resolution to this dilemma. Of course, other organizations outside the community development field confront the same tension, but again, the CDC is more vulnerable to this conflict because of its multiple interests.

This subject brings up another set of common operational problems: the whole issue of making time for planning in the first place. It must be done, and yet every CDC finds it terribly difficult. There really is no solution to the tension between the insistent pressures of ongoing activities and the need for planning, and so the CDC must simply establish a routine for doing planning and stick to it, despite those pressures. One technique is to build into the bylaws of the organization an all-day internal quarterly review session to be attended by both board and staff, as well as an annual weekend retreat session. The quarterly reviews offer an opportunity to update timetables and to revise subsidiary objectives, as well as to monitor progress. The annual weekend retreat (at a location away from the community, if at all feasible) is the setting at which the board, with or without participation of the entire staff, can make the final decisions for one-, two-, and five-year projections. These plans can be economically made when the meeting is based upon staff papers which have previously been read by board members even if not yet discussed by them.

To prevent the board from being diverted by other problems—pressing though they may be—a group facilitator, someone from outside the organization and even from outside the community, may be necessary. The facilitator can help the board make a plan for solving a demanding problem that suddenly comes up rather than waste time trying to solve the problem at the planning session. Other special roles may be needed within the staff or may be played by consultants in producing preliminary reviews of an issue or project so that the board can concentrate on making program plan decisions with the necessary information well in hand. One specialized function that can be extraordinarily helpful is the development by an outsider of a history of the organization's affairs over some selected period of one year or more; this review can pinpoint issues around which planning needs to be focused. In general, having to produce a plan focuses the efforts of the organization on carrying it out (or revising it as necessary), and thus makes more efficient use of the organization's resources. TELACU, in East Los Angeles, came to the conclusion that its plans ought always to concentrate only on one major project per year, and they feel that much of their success has derived from that tactic.

Closely related to the planning problem is the problem of internal renewal and regeneration for the organization and its board and staff. The annual planning retreats are an opportunity for all participants to get a new sense of where the organization is going and how they can best contribute to future progress. The traditional twin problems of personnel burnout and organizational ossification in a community organization are usefully attacked in the planning process. For one thing, plans force everyone to be fairly rational about where the resources in time and people are going to come from, and this focus prevents overcommitment on the part of those vulnerable to burnout. The annual review also infuses new enthusiasm because people recognize how much they have actually accomplished now that they look back on it.

There are, however, a good many other helpful measures that will contribute to keeping the organization and its participants fresh and energetic while contributing to the ongoing work of the group. Annual panel hearings in the community on where the organization is going and what new objectives ought to be selected can be effectively organized so that new people and new ideas are brought forward; in this way hearings can do something other than offer a forum for complaints. Such hearings provide an opportunity to discover articulate residents who can be recruited onto new committees and advisory groups and perhaps later to board or staff positions.

Equally important are annual occasions for ceremonial awards for outstanding contributions from board and staff members—so long as awards are made for real performance. Such occasions can be organized in connection with some holiday celebration to which a broad spectrum of community residents can be attracted. The occasion thus offers the community organization good publicity as well as an occasion for rewarding good work. Of course, if the occasion can include affordable food and drink—either free from the organization or individually paid for by ticket sales—so much the better.

Structural features of the organization also have their impact on self-renewal. For example, if built into the bylaws, a limited elected term of, say, three years for board members with a required one-year interval before being eligible for reelection will help to bring in new blood. And for long-term staff, required vacations or even paid sabbaticals can often be designed into the budget and operational cycle.

If turnover in board (and staff) is a means of garnering new resources in energy, ideas, and contacts, it also produces problems of continuity, and so there is the inescapable tension of novelty versus stability within the process of regeneration. In practical terms, a CDC will need to make provision for bringing new board members and new staff up to speed as fellow contributors to the work of the organization. I have previously discussed this task within the context of the board committee structure, noting that the issues of self-development and new members ought to be delegated to a special committee. I will now go into a little more detail about the means by which new directors and new staff members may be integrated.

The task is not just to orient board and staff members to their new responsibilities, but also to acculturate them, so to speak, to the values and goals of community economic development as pursued by the organization. One of the most practical means of accomplishing this task is the intensive experience of the annual planning retreat. There the new participants see in vivid colors the play of issues that community economic development embodies. However, the organization probably ought not to rely solely upon such natural events to acclimate its new people. A set of focused orientation sessions, deliberately scheduled and designed, can also be used to provide a better grasp of the history of the organization, its current planning documents, its current projects, and so on, as well as the conceptual tools and vocabulary of the revitalization process for the depleted community.

In short, taking a paid or unpaid job at the CDC ought not to be handled like taking any other job. The commitment required is a commitment to a mission, not merely to the performance of a limited set of tasks. That commitment cannot be assumed; it must be fostered. The role of the CDC is too complex and too demanding for the organization to be administered like any other office or business. Perhaps it is more analogous to a political group or a religious institution in its concern for the entire round of life of the local community. As such, then, the integration of new people is a critical procedure for ensuring the necessary energy and dedication and the organizational renewal of that energy and dedication.

Finally, I cannot emphasize too much the benefits for both staff and board members of getting out of the community to meet others in other communities who are engaged in the same enterprise. There is probably no more effective influence for organizational renewal and refreshment than regional or national meetings with others in the community economic development field. Not only are new ideas to be discovered, but one can have the satisfaction of contributing one's own experience and ideas to interested others who are seeking the same stimulation. Of course, such meetings involve some expense to the organization, but the costs need to be weighed against the returns in the renewed enthusiasm and enhanced skills of those who have participated. When these meetings are prohibitively expensive, less expensive substitutes can be considered. Exchanging site visits with a nearby organization can be a useful technique, even if the potential benefits are less extensive.

Undoubtedly, others might emphasize different issues as being among the major universal challenges or tensions of community economic development. Nevertheless, no CDC is likely to escape the constant pressure to justify the programs of the organization in terms of the community as beneficiary; to make tough choices among the multifarious community goals and among the benefits to be realized; to maintain adequate managerial controls while surging into new projects; and to find the time and techniques for long-term plans and for internal renewal that long-term plans demand.

PART
THREE

TWELVE

Evaluating Community Economic Development

T HE future of community economic development as part of a national strategy for a healthy economy depends upon the careful documentation of the results of the community economic development approach wherever it has been systematically tried. Without such documentation, policy makers at local, state, and national levels will be disinclined to commit public funds for ongoing programs, as contrasted to occasional projects. That documentation has to include more than illustrative cases; it must include research that has produced firm dollar figures or other statistics demonstrating the efficient use of public funds. Moreover, the research must permit the replication of results in standard scholarly or scientific procedures. At this time, there is already some systematic evidence that demonstrates the usefulness of the community economic development approach, but additional evidence will be needed over the long haul.

Perhaps the most attractive relevant systematic research was carried out in 1980 by a single CDC under the leadership of its director, who was a certified public accountant. Tom Miller and his associates at the Kentucky Highlands Investment Corporation (KHIC), a CDC in the Appalachian backwoods of southeastern Kentucky, designed a simple statistic to demonstrate how a community economic development program contributes directly to national economic strength. The procedure they used computes a "return on taxpayers' investment," or ROTI. They took the records of KHIC's start-up ventures to compute, at first, three different contributions that the ventures made to the federal treasury. The first was the corporate taxes paid annually by each company. The second was the personal taxes paid on the wages of those companies' workers *who were previously unemployed.* The third was the savings on the federal welfare contribution that would otherwise have been made for those workers who had been on public assistance transfer payments before they joined the companies. For the year 1980, for example, these three figures totaled $1.447 million. By the end of that same year, the total federal funds ever received from all federal sources for all purposes (not just for venture creation) by KHIC since it began in 1969 amounted to $7.7 million. In short, the national government received $1.447 million in 1980 on a total investment in KHIC of $7.7 million, or a "Return on Taxpayers' Investment" of 18.7 percent that year. In previous years, the statistic was as high as 25 percent, and there is no reason to suppose that the ROTI statistic does not stay at high enough levels to continue to document an excellent return on federal dollars at that CDC.

The ROTI statistic is so conservative in methodology and so easy to compute that, when applied to all CDCs receiving federal funds, it can stand alone as a quick measure of what they can produce. However, to my knowledge it has not been computed for other CDCs, and so the overall impact of such federal investment is not known. Certainly KHIC is one of the most successful of CDCs, and one would not expect the same high returns at all other localities, although there are other CDCs as successful as KHIC. Because ROTI has the advantage of simplicity and easy audit, it can be very useful in making cost/benefit decisions. It has one disadvantage—namely, it deals with only one activity of a CDC, launching new businesses, and makes that activity bear the burden of all the payback for all federal funds granted to the CDC, even though CDC grants are concurrently being used for other CDC activities. Since those other activities are also designed to serve the public purpose, there should probably be some analogous payback statistics designed for them. In the meantime, the ROTI statistic is an enormous encouragement to all those seeking a new commitment to the future of the forgotten community.

ROTI is not the only research approach that has been taken, and indeed its results are reinforced by several other more extensive studies, some of which meet the need for at least some quantitative findings. All of the extensive studies are on the U.S. experience. There do not appear to be any similar Canadian studies, although there have been qualitative case evaluations made by Canada Health and Welfare of two of its first grants—to New Dawn Enterprises in Sydney, Nova Scotia, and to the Human Resources Development Association in Halifax, Nova Scotia.

Qualitative assessments are typical and useful in all situations when one is exploring new research territory, and the first major study in the United States was a qualitative evaluation, comparing a CDC with three other types of economic development projects. This study was conducted by the Westinghouse Learning Corporation under contract with the antipoverty agency, the Office of Economic Opportunity (OEO), in 1968. The aim of the study was to assess projects carried out by four different government agencies operating under a single congressional mandate, the authorization for "special impact programs" (SIP) for deteriorated inner-city areas and impoverished rural areas subject to high out-migration. Among the individual projects reviewed were the Hough Area Development Corporation, OEO's first grantee under its community control program. HADC was compared with two rural projects carried out by the Agriculture Department (one in Kentucky, near where KHIC was later to be founded, and one in North Carolina); a demonstration loan fund, privately incorporated with Commerce Department funds, to lend money to minority and other businesses that would hire workers in the deteriorated Watts area of Los Angeles; and a number of plant location subsidy projects administered by the Labor Department for high unemployment areas in New York City and Los Angeles.

All of these projects were financed as a kind of experiment to test different approaches to economic development and the creation of jobs in depressed communities. Each of the various government agencies, in bureaucratic competition, sought to demonstrate that it was the one that ought to receive SIP appropriations to carry out its type of program. However, with the exception of the two indigenously controlled projects, in North Carolina and Hough, all of the economic development efforts were eventually judged to be failures. For example, the Labor Department grants seemed to create new jobs very quickly, but the program actually turned out to be merely a form of easy and lucrative subsidy for quickly setting up low-wage plants with high employee turnover in dead-end jobs. Most of the plants had little likelihood of longevity because the owners of the businesses were not particularly committed to them once the subsidies were spent. In one case, instead of serving a designated pocket of low employment, the subsidized firm actually moved its facilities further away from the target group of unemployed.

The Commerce Department loan fund dissipated its money swiftly in loans to businesses that did not survive, and the Agriculture project in Kentucky that was supposed to attract businesses there never managed to do anything at all. No doubt some of the failures could be laid at the door of the project administrators rather than the project designs, but mostly it was clear that the locality-targeted programs that did not involve the residents of the locality in the design and execution simply could not serve the purposes for which they were established. The commitment and the knowledge just were not there.

The North Carolina project, as contrasted to the failed Agriculture Department project in Kentucky, was run by a local group of small businessmen, professionals, and representatives of the low-income black and Indian communities, all from the four-county target area. Thus, it represented fairly well a range of interests in that rural district, and the investment projects in which it engaged touched base with those interests. The North Carolina group spent its government funds on very small infrastructure projects scattered throughout its target area. These projects included assistance to a black village development organization to complete the renovation of a theater that they wanted to recycle as an industrial building; water and sewer connections for a number of small-town mini-industrial sites; the renovation of a baseball park that allowed a baseball-conscious town to attract a franchise for a farm club team for the Minnesota Twins, thereby encouraging a group of small businessmen to join together to build a motel to accommodate the expected sports fans from other communities; and similar modest projects.

This group resisted the initial Agriculture Department pressure to concentrate its funds on one or a few large projects, and its smaller projects could be considered reasonably successful in promoting community development, local business sector involvement and leverage, and increased job opportunities. The community-based structure and the encouraging results of the North Carolina project matched the pattern of the Hough project. This result convinced the U.S. Bureau of the Budget (now known as the Office of Management and Budget) that the program model based on the CDC had a good chance of working in both urban and rural areas, and the Office of Economic Opportunity was eventually given full responsibility for developing the program further.

In the period 1970–1973, a very different and more extensive evaluation study was undertaken by Abt Associates, a firm under contract with OEO, to see how all the CDC projects funded by that agency were performing. The various reports of the studies make tedious reading and are occasionally confusing, partly because the study was first designed to last eighteen months and to include sixteen CDCs but then was expanded to last three years and to include thirty CDCs. The cumulative reports therefore do not build logically on each other, and it is difficult to integrate their conclusions. Very likely another obstacle to coherence was that the evaluators seemed to have trouble finding their way among three possible and very different assessment tasks: evaluating the agency's execution of the program, evaluating the program model as such, and evaluating each CDC's performance in the use of program funds.

The CDCs which had received program funds insisted that they should help design the study, especially to include the way that the government agency operated, since that operation and its shifting demands shaped their own results. The agency, however, was naturally ambivalent about that idea, and the sharpness of the evaluation focus suffers from Abt's apparent responsiveness to the multiple definitions of the research task by different actors.

Abt's report also suffered from its methodological choices—probably urged by the agency—for measuring certain variables, such as venture profitability, that are more meaningful in a long-term perspective even though only a short term could be studied (the life of the ventures averaged 1.8 years). Choosing variables for long-term significance was particularly a problem since most of the CDCs in the Abt sample were themselves only two or three years old.

Even so, Abt felt it could project performance on the basis of the data it gathered. And one key finding was a projection that was indeed borne out some years later by another study on the same group of CDCs. The projection was that the CDC ventures would have no more than a 50 percent failure rate; that is, 50 percent of CDC ventures would at least be breaking even after four years. This is about twice the standard survival rate for small businesses. It was a very impressive statistic for businesses established or expanded in the hostile economic environment of a deteriorated community in the then-current period of national slowdown. The standard failure rate cited in small business circles is 80 percent after five years, with most failures occurring in the first two or three years. The evaluators nevertheless expressed the opinion that the CDC rate was too poor, a position to which the CDCs understandably objected in commentaries appended to two of the Abt reports. The CDCs pointed out that a community economic development strategy requires multiple goals in the activity of business development and that even traditional economists and business theorists debate whether profit is (or could be) the prime objective of a business firm; they cited the standard literature on this point and complained of the evaluators' myopia.

In a final report, Abt's position evolved somewhat, and its recommendations urged that each CDC "be allowed and encouraged to pursue" its own strategy—apparently recognizing that the maximization of profits was not necessarily appropriate in every case. Moreover, with additional data, Abt concluded that the tactic of using business development for broader community development aims had been "comparatively successful." For example, CDC businesses that employed "higher percentages of previously unemployed workers were as profitable as those with lower percentages." And the report even decided that "the comprehensive nature of the [community economic development] approach to the development problem appear [ed] to be associated with some—however small—gains in terms of business efficiency."

Another Abt argument for the community economic development approach was "strong evidence for the positive effects of community participation and control on CDC performance." Community control (measured by the percentage of representative and resident community board members versus outsiders) alone explained about 40 percent of the variation in an aggregate achievement measure for each CDC that combined such things as job creation, wage improvement for newly hired employees, capital leverage, and so on. Among other positive findings was that CDC venture investments were in businesses that hired 65 percent of their employees from the local target area community, and 29 percent of the employees had been previously unemployed. So there appeared to be evidence that the business development activities had a real local impact, although Abt recommended that CDCs achieve a higher percentage of previously unemployed— between 30 and 50 percent—while at the same time achieving profitability. Among other criticisms leveled at the CDCs generally were "excessive debt/equity ratios" and "inexperienced managers," although Abt recognized that CDCs also had "human development" goals in upgrading local managerial skills.

Abt found it difficult to discover directly comparative data on other government economic development programs, but even here it was able to document that the cost per job created through CDCs was less than that of the federal public works program of the Economic Development Administration. Its summary conclusion, then, was that "overall, the experience of the [community economic development] program validates the key concepts of the approach."

In 1974 the Ford Foundation sponsored a study by the Urban Institute to get an outsider's report on whether or not Ford's grant program, then under way only for three CDCs, was working. The Urban Institute reported and the foundation was convinced that the CDCs were in fact effective managers of the foundation grants and that the CDCs did achieve the purposes for which the grants were made—namely, the conclusion of specific projects and the self-development of the CDC itself. Yet the evaluation report was by no means a glowing account. It was flatly critical of the performance of each of the three Ford-funded CDCs it reviewed, using such terms as "disastrous" and "serious and as yet unresolved problems." The three CDCs were the Bedford-Stuyvesant Restoration Corporation of Brooklyn (also receiving federal SIP support), The Woodlawn Organization of Chicago, and Zion Investment Associates of Philadelphia. When I will cite some of the figures for each of them from the Urban Institute report, I will do so in the order in which they have been named here.

The institute finessed the dilemma that Abt had faced—that is, how to take in the differing perspectives of grantor and grantee—by simply measuring each CDC's performance against its own goals, its own projected outputs. This tactic effectively assumed that those goals took into account at least some of the vagaries of the grantor to which the grantees would be trying to respond, and so both grantor's and grantee's performance would be entwined in the grantee's ultimate progress. The choice of self-defined goals also ensured that tangible and measurable performance indicators were studied and that those indicators could be considered appropriate for different conditions at each of the three sites. The institute specifically chose outputs that the various individual CDC managers themselves had projected. A total of 95 program milestones were selected—including such items as the number of housing units to be rehabilitated by a certain date, the permissible tenant turnover per month, the number of mortgage loans to be placed, and so on. Of course, these items varied in type and level at each site.

For each CDC, the various project managers had projected that about 80 percent of the total number of their different CDC outputs would be increased over the level of the same outputs of the previous year, which was an extremely optimistic prediction for any organization. They did not achieve 80 percent. The results at the three sites, respectively, showed that 54, 52, and 42 percent of the output measures actually increased over the previous year's performance. While the CDCs' own projections were clearly over-optimistic, one might well consider that the actual increases in performance were outstanding, especially since the evaluators "found little effort on the part of the CDC managers to set unduly low targets for themselves." This conclusion was borne out by findings that although, as noted, the year's results were very frequently better than the previous year's, the higher individual output targets themselves were met or exceeded for only 22, 37, and 9 percent, respectively, of the chosen indicators. In sum, performance improved substantially from one year to the next, but in only a minority of instances was the full degree of projected improved performance reached.

The evaluators pointed out that neither overoptimism nor management faults (though they noted the impact of both these factors) were fully adequate explanations for the shortfalls in performance records. The performance at all three CDCs also suffered from the fact that their funding sources, foundations and federal agencies, shifted priorities and policies. The evaluators pointed out that the complex programs of the CDCs are vulnerable to such vacillations in their capital sources, since the CDC is always juggling the demands of its capital sources against the priorities of local needs and plans.

In the end, the Urban Institute concluded that each of the CDCs "provided positive indications of its staying power in the face of a deteriorating national economy [in 1974] and the elimination and cutback of many public and private sources of support." The institute interpreted these findings as "strong evidence of institutional strength and 'self-sufficiency.'" Perhaps the most significant implication of the Urban Institute study is that clear targets of performance can be set and reached by community groups, and that therefore any government policy maker or other funder or investor can and should exact and expect specific self-set program objectives by local groups that are grantees or investment partners.

Increasingly, some ten years after this evaluation report, the Ford Foundation concentrates a mjaor portion of its domestic grants and its program-related investments in the field of community economic development. It does so now under the direction of a foundation president who was once head of Bedford-Stuyvesant's CDC.

The same year that the Urban Institute report was published, in 1976, Rita Mae Kelly published her path-breaking book, *Community Participation in Directing Economic Development*, based upon data collected about the same time as the Urban Institute's but on a larger number of CDCs. Kelly's study was perhaps less evaluation than fact finding about the leadership of CDCs, in both board and staff, but she found a positive statistical correlation between high performance and strength of the community boards— that is, the better the community control, the better the performance. This discovery confirmed the Abt finding that statistically linked an aggregate measure of CDC performance with degree of community control. In short, then, there is considerable evidence that CDCs should rely upon local community control for better results in economic development programming, and that too should be a policy principle. That finding was of course the conclusion also of the first assessment of the programs of the four government departments in 1969 by Westinghouse, even though it was based only on impressionistic evidence from very few cases.

Chronologically, the next study of CDCs was performed by the National Center for Economic Alternatives (NCEA). Again, the research was sponsored by the agency that offered grants for broad community economic development programs, and, again, its methods were different from those that preceded it but nevertheless generally confirmed earlier findings. On the one hand, the significance of this methodological variation from study to study lies in the value of what might be called the "triangulation of findings." Coming at the same issues with different methodologies helps to free findings from questions as to whether they were simply an artefact of the research technology used; when different technologies come to the same conclusion, it is easier to feel confident of the findings. On the other hand, of course, because of the lack of replication of techniques, one is left without confirmation that one use of a technique has not been subject to accidental influences.

In any case, this next study, published in early 1981, was in some ways the most careful and systematic, probably because, in contrast to the other government-financed studies, it had the sole full-time commitment of the research director, an accomplished program evaluation specialist in economics. It deliberately chose a sample of fifteen CDCs out of thirty-seven in the federal program for community economic development support at that time (1980). The fifteen CDCs were certainly a cross section. They included some CDCs that had obtained funding through the program for most of the program period from 1968 to 1980 and some that had been financed by other sources but had only recently been receiving federal community economic development grants; some had been generally successful, and some were in "probationary" status with the agency for poor performance; some were rural, some urban; and they came from every section of the country and from every ethnic category of community that had ever received aid under the program.

The cross section of fifteen CDCs was characterized as a "quota sample," chosen to be representative rather than random; but as it turned out, it represented more than the average number of years of program support and more than the average dollar support per year compared to those not chosen and especially compared to those no longer within the program. In short, it probably overrepresented the more successful CDCs, even though there were three in the sample of fifteen, that is, one-fifth, whose grants had just been or probably were about to be discontinued for poor performance. At the same time, the measures used by the evaluation team were cast in very conservative terms; the report used "Draconian conventions to limit the opportunities for overstatements," particularly with respect to employment and business development. For example, the study considered no "multiplier effects," made virtually no estimates or projections, and relied on an audit firm to document actual current jobholders through personal income-tax-withholding reports.

NCEA confirmed the Abt results on business development, finding that the (non-real-estate) ventures had a business survival rate of about 50 percent, but it pointed out that CDCs tolerated a level of loss in ventures that would not conventionally be accepted. Nevertheless, the data on all bankruptcies and other losses, as well as on gains, offered the conclusion that "overall the [288] CDC ventures have generated a small net profit."

Unable to get the specific data from one of the larger urban

CDCs in the sample, NCEA documented employment figures from only fourteen CDCs. At that time, those CDCs, in their own offices or in business, property, or social ventures, were employing about 3,700 people, the vast majority of whom were local residents. In all, about 23,000 person-years of direct employment had been created, a figure that included the shorter-term employment in CDC ventures that had eventually failed or been sold. The evaluators did not want to use a jobs-created figure because it seemed to them too difficult to justify over the time period concerned; in addition, they avoided claims for indirect employment, although they added to the 23,000 person-years a supplementary figure of 6,400 person-years due to the CDCs' business loan programs, the construction and provision of new commercial and industrial space, and the recruitment of businesses to the local area. In addition, the statistic for those hired who were previously unemployed was 45 percent; for residents overall in nonmanagerial jobs, 71 percent; and for residents overall in managerial jobs, 53 percent.

Investment capital granted from the federal program was about $109 million, which had levered an additional $237 million, most of that in bank credit. An additional $118 million was levered by CDCs through their own financial subsidiaries—for example, by their loan guarantee funds. The agency had granted $100 million for general administrative expenses, for a total agency grant cost for the fifteen CDCs of $209 million. There was a great deal to show for that amount. The current asset base accumulated by these fifteen CDCs was about $183 million, and gross annual revenues were about $153 million. These two figures were the only significant estimates used in the study, but they appear to be conservatively based; for example, real estate was valued at cost, without any appreciation.

Within the 288 investments (in businesses, physical property, and financial institutions), the median investment was in the range of $75 to $200 thousand, excluding real estate ventures. However, approximately 60 percent of investment capital had gone into physical development, that is, real estate undertakings. Some of the results from these projects were three thousand units of new or rehabilitated housing and 2.3 million square feet of commercial and industrial space. This account did not include more limited projects, such as weatherization or assistance to other housing development organizations. The largest of the property development projects was a joint venture in a $35 million Hyatt-Regency hotel in San Antonio, where the CDC (the Mexican American Unity Council) expected to ensure a large-scale, permanent, Hispanic-oriented work force. Up until 1981, 187 of the ventures were still maintained by the CDCs; the others were sold off or closed out, mostly as failures, with nevertheless a small net overall profit, as noted earlier.

Two other major CDC activities—key parts of any community economic development strategy—were dealt with in the report: social programs (of which there were forty-eight) and the general political and other institutional development work by the CDCs. For the forty-eight social ventures, an additional $63 million (not included in the agency support figures previously cited) had been raised from public and private sources. About 65 percent of the social programs were in training or other employment-related services, about 20 percent in the health field, and the rest in miscellaneous activities such as day care, transportation for the handicapped, and the like. At the time of the evaluation, about two-thirds of the social program activity was still going on.

In institutional development, the evaluators provided descriptive materials to illustrate that the CDCs had "worked to build more effective systems for development" in their communities. This effort included collaborative work both with other local groups and with public agencies, as well as community campaigns and political pressure for local improvement. With maturity, it was "not unusual for a CDC to be a major, if not the only, repository of technical community development capacity" in its district, and to be relied upon by state and local government for basic services as the institutional bridge to the community. A striking example was the Kentucky Highlands Investment Corporation, the grantee in Kentucky, which was in virtually the same district where the earlier Agriculture Department project had failed in 1968, the year before KHIC was founded. The Kentucky state industrial development finance authority told evaluators that it found its investment opportunities in the grantee's nine-county area almost exclusively through KHIC's recommendations.

The CDCs had also built access to politically controlled resources at all governmental levels; this access meant that CDCs were getting more and more financial support from different sources and therefore were less and less dependent upon the federal agency for such support. Since the federal agency was in fact abolished just two weeks before the evaluation report was published, that was a key finding.

In its final pages, the report posed the basic question, which by that time seemed moot, whether, "in an era of [federal budgetary] belt-tightening," a federal community economic development support program ought to be continued. The report answered the question with "an unqualified 'yes.' " The evaluators further suggested that, even with a reduced program budget, considerable impact on impoverished communities was still possible as long as grants were continued for investment funds as seed money for newer, less established community groups. The assumption was that the more mature CDCs could manage to find other resources.

Whether or not the report was specifically influential, a program of support for community economic development groups has been continued by Congress despite the express disapproval each year since then by the Administration; it was lodged by Congress in another agency, the Department of Health and Human Services, to substitute for the agency that the Administration abolished. In addition, it is reassuring to report that, for the most part, grants under the (much reduced) program have generally gone to newer groups, as the evaluation report had recommended.

A similar program in another agency, Housing and Urban Development (HUD), however, did not survive, perhaps because the rationale was not so clear. In 1981–1982, an evaluation study of the HUD program of support to self-help development groups looked at a sample of thirty of the ninety-nine HUD grantees and found mixed results. This study was also conducted by the Urban Institute, and it included organizations that restricted themselves to housing or to some other single focus in community development. The institute reported that those groups that focused on commercial or other economic development projects have a much tougher job and are less successful than those that focus only on housing. While this finding is probably not news to most community leaders, it does document the ambitious character of the community economic development strategy and sets up warning signals that the strategy is not to be adopted lightly just because it is the thing to do. A further finding underlined this warning. More than two-thirds of the groups, at the time of the retrospective evaluation of progress on the grants, had no "significant internal expertise" in the financial economics of the development projects they were undertaking, and some groups had no staff at all with relevant experience. Yet all of these groups had been screened for and had received federal funding, two-thirds also had some local government funds, and one-half had some private support. This finding must indeed raise questions about the uncritical award of funds for local groups, even though the Urban Institute researchers did find that the projects developed local capacity where there had been little before. The policy implication must be that if the aim is local capacity building, then organizations should be encouraged to undertake initial projects that are less ambitious and to develop their sophistication about the skills needed for successful operation. Only after a group has demonstrated that basic capacity should they be encouraged to take up more challenging projects, and only much later enter the field of comprehensive local development.

However, it is apparently unnecessary to require prior experience in *all* development areas when judging the capacity of a group to engage in a development project. The Local Initiatives Support Corporation (LISC), a financial intermediary sponsored by the Ford Foundation and financed also by insurance companies and other major private industries, has a reputation for being a "hard-nosed philanthropist" in its loans and grants to community developers. On the basis of a study of twenty groups assisted by LISC, researchers at Harvard University in an evaluation of the LISC projects reported the following: "Overall, LISC has invested in projects that perform successfully and has structured its investments in ways that produce predictable financial returns; 'at risk' funds [i.e., loans] are typically recouped as anticipated." Nevertheless, LISC-assisted groups took on activities that departed "significantly from their previous base of operations" and raised the skill levels of the staff, especially increasing their "financial sophistication." In short, with a businesslike screening process, it *is* possible to fund successful projects and concurrently to increase the local capacity level, which after all is the aim also of community leaders in the CDCs.

All of the systematic research on community-based economic development can probably be summarized in one significant conclusion: this approach to local renewal is effective, but efficiency in the use of this strategy is threatened by inadequate attention to managment skills. Given the general concurrence of the evidence, it seems incredible that there has not been a wider recognition and evolution of the strategy and its necessary external resources. Community economic development is not simply an interesting idea generated in some university nor an abstract strategy devised by technical specialists. It is one name for a painful discovery by concerned residents of a troubled community that they must and can do something about local renewal themselves. Government and other outside actors cannot do what is necessary and in fact are or have been part of what has gone wrong. Yet outside actors must be an important source of assistance, especially of seed capital. Inside the community there are resources to be discovered; outside the community there are resources to be mobilized.

THIRTEEN

Beyond the Community

W ITHIN each depleted community, the capacity to build local coalitions and to pool skills for local development must, in time, be turned to new and broader levels of coalitions. These new coalitions must erect buttresses of supportive groups and practices that concurrently aid community economic development in many different communities. Building those wider coalitions ultimately targets highly complex public policy matters entailing a sophisticated knowledge of how federal, state, provincial, and local government regulations and funds can be mobilized for the forgotten communities. In the process, local leaders who have been concentrating on their own, usually isolated ethnic or racial, communities first have to evolve toward a wider perspective so as to encompass people and problems different from their own.

Sometimes this essential preliminary evolution may take a fairly simple form that conceals a real crisis for the leader and his or her local constituency. In the early 1970s, the East Boston CDC was scheduled to host a meeting of the national association of CDCs, which had only recently been organized. At that time, East Boston was one of the crisis areas in the stormy process of school desegregation that was taking place in the city. Many of the Italian American people of East Boston were strongly against the entry of blacks bussed in from other parts of the city as part of the court order for desegregation. Yet the membership of the CDC association, of course, included a high proportion of black groups, whose board members and executive officers would be descending upon the East Boston neighborhood for the meeting. One of the chief of-

ficers of the East Boston CDC, himself an Italian American who
had no racial animus, confided to me his anxiety that the black
visitors would not be treated hospitably and might in fact be a
target of hostility and demonstrations. Some of his board members had tried to prepare their constituency for the occasion, but
he worried what would happen. And of course there was no question that blacks all over the United States already knew of the at-
tacks upon blacks in the Boston crisis, so the CDC visitors would
have been all too aware that their presence could be a problem.

As it turned out, the conference was a huge success. Early on,
there was a basement banquet in the style of church suppers, with
which everyone was quite familiar, except that this one featured
lasagna and more unusual Italian specialties that piqued the
curiosity of the visitors. In no time at all, people were exchanging
ethnic recipes with representatives from other races and cultures
attending the meeting. Ziti in a tomato-hamburger sauce was compared with black-eyed peas and ham hocks, and the ice was broken
for the discussion of serious issues then facing all of the CDCs,
particularly how to deal with the antipathy of the Washington administration for federal aid to depleted communities. In the
course of encountering differences in their own approaches, essential understandings were reached on common goals in the
national struggle to protect and revive depleted communities
everywhere. It had not been without risk to choose the East Boston
site for a meeting that had to bridge the chasms of ethnic and racial fears and parochialisms, but it had worked.

It is true that our own communities make our lives with each
other humanly satisfying, but often much of what we find satisfying actually derives from relations to institutions external to the
community, whether that is a touring theater company or a federal
policy. Moreover, no matter how economically and socially integrated and self-reliant a community may hope to become, the
community arena of socio-economic development is after all an
abstraction from the entire universe of socio-economic processes
stretching out through the community's surrounding regional,
national, and international setting. Thus, although the community
base is convenient and efficient as a focus for development, its sur-
roundings must be reconnoitered for their potential as an aid or
hindrance to local development.

Keeping in mind the same institution-building perspective
that makes sense on the local level, local leaders must work to
create or stengthen institutions external to the locality, insofar as

these will fill needs in the local community. In doing so, the leaders go beyond what they can reasonably expect to do or to obtain just for their own community needs; they enter into a larger battle for many communities and for transcommunity institutions. Essentially, they must join together and enlist others in an effort to influence public policy on the national and state or provincial level. I am assuming here that public policy at the local level is already very much a focus of attention for community economic development people, but to become engaged in the wider arena requires somehow a stronger definition of the community's capacity to get things done. Local leaders and their constituents naturally tend to be more comfortable with their grasp of the local situation, and to become engaged in matters quite far out of the community means taking off in a new direction. Yet that is exactly what must eventually be done in the revitalization process.

The first and essential transcommunity institution is a tool for promoting joint consultation among community economic development groups, for exchanging experiences and for evolving common perspectives and goals, as was the aim in the East Boston conference. A working association of groups must grow up on a state or provincial level, a national level, or, closer to home, on a metropolitan level, in order to gain better access to the resources at those levels. A certain competitiveness, perhaps, or some other insecurity may make it difficult to come together, as if one might endanger one's own access to those resures by encouraging others to go after them. Therefore some leaders from different CDCs will have to get out front to inspire their peers in still other CDCs and to raise everyone's horizons just the way they were raised locally in the original task of building a home-base CDC. It takes common sense and enthusiasm to lay out the vision of a larger pie when all join to bake it. In watching the formation of national organizations in Canada and the United States, however, I have had the impression that community leaders are moved first by altruistic motives and then by the bread-and-butter issues—that is, a sense of common commitment to equity and fairness for those who have been left behind begins the search for a joint strategy, and then the specific aims in resource access are detailed. Again, if there is not a sense of hope that something can be accomplished, then very little does in fact get done besides the mundane chores of electing a secretary and chairperson.

There is today in the United States an active national association, the National Congress for Community Economic Development (NCCED). But this association was a long time in coming. A precursor organization had been formed by some community groups in 1969, but it did little, and its leadership proved unsatisfactory. Those who might have provided the inspiration over the long term were still too bound up in making their home organizations work, and it was not until a few years later that a completely new association was established to make a clean start, with the commitment of CDC leaders who were highly respected by their peers. Since then, NCCED has had a considerable history of sometimes more, sometimes less collaboration among the community economic development groups nationwide. There remains a tendency for each local group to look solely after its own welfare, and collaboration at a broader level is renewed only as someone who is recognizably concerned with the welfare of all the groups takes leadership to bring them together.

A Canadian association, the Federation of Community Development Corporations of Canada (FCDCC), has been in existence for about five years; it has sponsored regional meetings, carried out a survey of community groups throughout the country, provided, on contract, policy analysis and recommendations to a federal agency, the Canada Employment and Immigration Commission, and promoted informal joint consultations and some lobbying activity. It no doubt exerted a positive influence in getting the federal LEAD program (Local Employment Assistance and Development) established to provide venture capital to community groups in small communities under 50,000 in population. However, once that program was under way, a parallel association of Canada's LEAD corporation grantees was promoted by the federal administrators of the program to operate quite independently of other community economic development groups, and it has not been particularly active except to hold two or three conferences for its members. Instead of gaining strength together, the LEAD association and FCDCC remain in isolation, less active and less influential than they might be.

In the United States, NCCED activities have stressed the sponsorship of workshops led by technical experts who are drawn mostly from the staffs of member organizations. These workshops have generally focused on practical issues in project development, such as the financing of real estate development projects. In this way, CDCs are explicitly sharing their information with each other, with the more advanced CDCs providing excellent technical assistance through the workshop procedure. Ordinarily, these technical workshops are held in conjunction with national or regional meetings, which also allow for informal contacts as well as a variety of formal panel discussions by members and outside resource persons, including foundation executives, government officials, bank officers who have sponsored innovative development support programs, and so on.

Other practical services offered by NCCED include newsletters, technical monographs, a computer network, and a roster of technical assistance providers. NCCED also carries out research and information projects on contract with state and federal agencies. One of its most significant activities has been working with other like-minded umbrella organizations in monitoring federal legislative and executive actions that can be expected to aid or hinder local programs. As a tax-exempt group, NCCED is restricted from substantial lobbying activity, but through the years its members have established a succession of parallel organizations without that restriction—following a common practice for national associations with governmental interests.

The joint political campaigns of the community economic development groups have been relatively successful—in concert with other associations of community-based groups—in protecting and promoting U.S. federal support for local projects. The clearest success was the congressional rescue of the antipoverty agency in 1973 when it was to have been abolished by the Nixon administration. The agency survived under a new name, with strengthened provisions for support of community economic development, including special legislative authority for venture capital for CDCs. With the advent of the Reagan administration in 1981, a new rescue operation had to be launched. This time, however, partly because of destructive management of the agency program over the previous three or so years, the CDCs succeeded only in maintaining the community economic development appropriations on a reduced level and in still another government agency. In the meantime, however, CDCs had gained proficiency in getting access to other better-funded federal programs, especially the Community Development Block Grants that funnel federal dollars through city and state governments. In short, CDCs, by joining forces, have mastered the national political process well enough to ensure at least some potential return of resources to their depleted communities, and this is indeed a crucial exercise of common influence.

Yet there are a good many other necessary joint projects that do not focus on gaining federal money. In Canada, in 1981, a technical study prepared for the federal Task Force on Labour Market Development suggested that a network of supportive institutions was necessary outside the communities in need to facilitate a "community-based development system for the 1980s." These institutions would carry out information, training, advocacy, finance, legal assistance, and technical consultation functions.

In the United States, national institutions have from time to time been created to perform just these functions. Some have been jointly established and run by CDCs, others have been taken over by representatives of the community economic development movement, and still others have been independent but quite directly related to the field of community economic development. In 1977, for example, NCCED sponsored the formation of the National Training Institute for Community Economic Development with the express purpose of helping CDC board members improve their skills for governing the CDCs. Although this organization was dissolved five years later, it had in the interim produced training films and slide and sound shows, training manuals and workbooks, and other materials still useful today; it had also conducted numberless workshops and other training sessions for individual CDCs at their own local settings and for groups of CDCs at regional centers. Both staff and board members took advantage of the institute programs. Today NCCED itself conducts the systematic training activities. It should be emphasized that under both organizations the training has been carefully consumer controlled, has been responsive to the needs defined by the CDCs themselves rather than expressive of only an academic or theoretical perspective on what CDC people ought to be taught.

A research and advocacy center also flourished in the 1970s, the Center for Community Economic Development, which was directed by a board of trustees comprised mostly of a national cross section of CDC board and staff members. This organization provided much of the basic research and literature on which practitioners rely today. But again, its functions were eventually taken over directly by NCCED, whose members had previously been running the center. Under funding from a variety of sources, a legal assistance group still functions independently—the National Economic Development and Law Center in Berkeley, California. And the Institute for New Enterprise Development carries out specialized research, issues publications, and offers consultation to community groups in Canada and the United States.

In several states, there are state associations of different degrees of activity. Formal associations in Florida and Massachusetts arose after, rather than before, the state governments there initiated a program of support for CDCs, but there was informal coordinated action by some groups in the process of promoting legislation for such programs. In other states, like Ohio, formal associations were established in order to press for state support. No formal associations have, as yet, been organized for metropolitan areas, although the CDCs of the Boston area established a coordinating council to bid (strongly though ultimately unsuccessfully) for the cable television franchise from the city. In southwestern United States, Chicano CDCs joined together to create a financial intermediary, a so-called MESBIC, or Minority Enterprise Small Business Investment Corporation, to lever up to fourteen federal dollars for every local dollar to be loaned to a small minority business.

It should be abundantly evident from this account so far that a central concern of joint action in the associations, however geographically based, has been and must be the promotion of institutional arrangements to ensure access to capital for community economic development. Thus, although the first essential transcommunity institution is a consultative forum for CDCs, an ultimate aim of such a forum will come to be the creation of other institutional practices that will funnel outside capital to meet the needs of the reactivated but still depleted community. CDCs have met with some success in certain limited situations—for example, as described earlier, in the founding of the Opportunity Funding Corporation, the rescue of the Rural Development Fund, and the creation of the (Massachusetts) Community Development Finance Corporation. Moreover, a number of individual states now have different types of programs that provide financial support to CDCs. And in Canada, the Provinces of Saskatchewan and Nova Scotia, for instance, have some kind of accessible and specific support for selected community-based economic development groups. Yet neither Canada nor the United States has evolved an integrated and rationalized system for providing capital for community economic development. It remains the task of development groups in each nation to help create a system of public structures and procedures for the capital needs of the forgotten community, not simply to meet those needs as such, but also to supply an essential ingredient in the recipe for a strong national economy.

Today national economic policy in both nations grapples uncertainly with the *macroeconomic* techniques of monetary, trade, and fiscal controls in a kind of rearguard action against recession. At the same time, a national policy consensus emphasizes the *microeconomic* arena of private sector business as the basis for positive growth. On the assumption that the private sector's response to markets is the essential motor for a strong economy, deregulation and tax incentives have become the major public tools for the microeconomic arena to achieve a steady growth in productivity, employment, and output to match population growth and the aspirations of the citizenry. Unfortunately, in the rhetoric and theory of national economic policy, there is an unrecognized gap between the macroeconomic controls and the microeconomic incentives. This gap ignores the base of all economic activity, the community systems of local institutions, as if somehow that base will automatically flourish with proper national controls and a free enterprise environment. Any such assumption puts the cart before the horse, as is so dismally apparent in the vicious cycle within which the depleted community is caught.

Indeed, the problems of the depleted community give the clue to what builds strength on the national level. When a community is healthy, it attracts productive business activity. When a community is unhealthy, it not only does not attract private enterprise, but it becomes a drag on the entire economy, both public and private. To the extent that any community operates at less than the level of full health, it is a reservoir of untapped resources and a negative influence upon its economic environment—regional, national, international. It behooves policy makers, then, to guide capital and other resources in such a way as to reinforce the community base of the national economy. Public policy at the national level, as well as at the state or provincial level, must concern itself with the means by which a rational steering of capital into the depleted community can be engineered.

A modest number of such techniques are already in place. Although they are currently at risk because of concern over national budget deficits, they should be maintained and made more efficient. If I point to the need for something like the current federal funding sources, I recognize at the same time that they are not as effective as they should be and that they are often inefficiently targeted. So I am only locating the places where some impact is presently being achieved and where more could be effected. I do insist, though, that the gap between the public policy initiatives of macroeconomic controls and microeconomic business incentives ought not to be widened by sacrificing the now quite minimal national tools that are currently in place to bridge that gap in the United States and in Canada.

There are two general classes of tools presently in use. One is the direct federal program of appropriated funds, and the other is the indirect federal program of tax law structure. Preeminent among the direct programs in the United States is the Community Development Block Grant, (CDBG), the revenue-sharing procedure by which an eddy from the broad stream of federal dollars is channeled to needy areas for community-building projects, pretty much on the basis of decisions by city and state governments. That decision making is often inefficient, and therefore the CDBG program itself is vulnerable to budget-cutting initiatives. But this channel of funds should not be blown up because it is expensive to maintain; instead the costly faults ought to be repaired. Similarly, in Canada very reasonable criticism can be leveled at the many categorical programs of the Department of Regional Industrial Expansion or the Canada Employment and Immigration Commission, for example. The resolution of these criticisms, however, cannot be simply budget retrenchment; it must be a rationalization and integration of programs to achieve precisely targeted aims. In neither country will the dollars be efficiently used unless policy makers recognize and support the struggle of each community to make itself a viable setting for business development. They cannot approach that recognition unless community leaders help them do so, pointing out the necessary division of labor between different levels of government and between public sector government, private sector industry, and the third sector, that is, community economic development groups. To a great extent, that means helping policy makers realize that maintaining or improving community infrastructure is required not so much to meet some abstractly conceived needs of potential business, but to keep the community a livable place for self-respecting human beings, most of whom, even in depleted communities, do, after all, seek the satisfaction and challenge of good jobs, well done.

To *prevent* decline where it threatens probably requires the simple measure of established maintenance procedures for physical infrastructure rather than the usual policy of wear it out and then think about replacing it. To *correct* the decline of the forgotten community, attention to infrastructure has to include special aid for social resources, particularly support for the organizational energy of an existing community economic development group and accessible capital for its programs. In this manner, the cost of regenerating business within a given community would be reduced at all levels of government as well as in the private sector. In short, there must be some sort of funding that provides CDCs with the working capital to administer their programs as well as with investment capital for infrastructure and business projects. In the United States, the Community Development Block Grants, skillfully used, have offered the flexibility for such a wide range of uses.

There are those who would question whether any assistance—federal, city, state, or provincial—really means an increase in business activity or whether the local increase is merely a displacement from other localities where it would have otherwise taken place. The argument is at the same time valid and vacuous. The validity arises from the fact that there must indeed be a new market demand somewhere for the increased production coming from the new or expanded venture; otherwise a mere shuffling of resources has occurred. The vacuity of the argument lies in its failure to recognize that any demand springs from the fuller use of existing resources, including people. To the extent that each forgotten community mourns fallow fields and jobless citizens, to that extent national opportunities for increased growth or business activity are being bypassed. When those opportunities are bypassed in any locality for too long a time and over too wide a swath of community life, that local community will sink into the forgotten realm and pull down with it additional national resources. But any locale can do more than merely participate in the redistribution of jobs; it can create new ones. It can do so because available financial capital is not, in the end, a finite quantity with strictly limited effects. That capital is capable of being levered by other forms of capital—unused human skills, unused physical facilities, and so on. If opportunities for this kind of leverage are foregone in preference for concentrating on an area already well developed, the whole society pays. It is easy to be blind to those opportunity costs, but that does not mean they have disappeared.

The particular form of displacement or redistribution that is called the "footloose factory" is an extreme case. Almost always the movement of a facility from one locality to some other is at least marginally useful for the economy of the particular firm but nationally costly in the abandonment of physical and human capital, since the initial locality suffers from the substitution of transfer payments for wages, the eventual deterioration of closed facilities, and the reduction of personal health and community stability. This is no more true for overseas relocation than for internal relocation.

The public policy issue is not how to block any locality from stealing another locality's industry or even how to block firms from opening branches in Taiwan and the like. The policy issue is how to prevent the community depletion and decline that encourages abandonment, for if one facility leaves, it is more costly to retrieve that loss at the bereft locality and to prevent further abandonments than to prevent the initial abandonment by enhancing the community as a base for continued business development. Similarly, encouraging all residents of a community to abandon it for employment elsewhere is to jettison still more irrecoverable capital, especially the capital implicit in known relationships of trust. When local resources are appropriately used in the depleted community, internal capital begins to emerge and can combine with whatever imported capital is necessary. Properly matched in amount and kind, local resources can contribute to national economic health by supplying the essential element missing from the microeconomic incentives and the macroeconomic controls upon which Canadian and U.S. policy makers seem fixated. It is up to community economic development leaders to make that argument strongly and repeatedly.

I will now turn briefly to the indirect supports for business activity that can serve as another potential model for bridging the gap in national policies that promote a healthy economy. They are essentially provisions in law for tax exemptions or reductions. These provisions offer quiet assistance to private sector firms through liberal depreciation allowances, investment credits, employment credits, and the like. Theoretically, the same provisions are now accessible to CDCs for their taxable businesses, but the law is skewed for particular industries and does not fit the varied ventures of the usual development strategy pursued by a community development organization. Where the tax laws have been targeted to the need for low-income housing, they have worked exceedingly well for the community development organization, as previously described.

The same targeting for other kinds of development projects can make a real impact for the community that is prepared to use them.

One relatively new idea that has been advanced by both conservative and liberal proponents is a variation on the location incentive—the so-called enterprise zone. Special tax incentives are proposed for firms that will open facilities in distressed areas and for investors who channel their capital to such firms. For more impact, the tax benefits are supposed to be accompanied by a relaxation in local or other regulatory measures that businesses would otherwise have to honor. Variations on this idea were originally developed in Great Britain, and other forms have been instituted by about fifteen states in the United States. Provision in federal law has also been promoted but not yet enacted.

Evidence for the positive effects of this particular combination of location incentives is hard to evaluate, especially since a great many other supporting measures were included in the apparently more effective projects. Some fundamental limitations raise questions in the case of the depleted community. For example, regulatory restrictions (zoning ordinances, pollution controls, and the like) are not peculiar to the depleted community but in fact are usually less enforced in such communities, ordinarily making lack of regulation one of the drawbacks of living there. So local deregulation would not appear to be a powerful tool and could even have negatively reinforcing effects. Taxes, as I have already argued, presenting the overwhelming evidence, simply are not the significant element in location decisions. For the large corporation, company policy pretty well reduces the tax bite to mosquitolike proportions, making it a marginal consideration; for the new firm, where taxable profits are rarely projected in the critical initial years, freedom from taxes is even less significant. To the contrary, infrastructure development is critical, and enterprise zones as used, for example, in Baltimore have relied upon infrastructure projects financed by federal programs. For example, Control Data agreed to work with the city of Baltimore to establish an incubator mall only if the city went after a variety of substantial federal subsidies. Moreover, it appears that the collaboration of local CDCs may also be required.

Perhaps the public sector use of the enterprise zone concept can be justified in a very special situation, in which many other incentives (including infrastructure upgrading) will make a difference. For example, one might combine free trade zone incentives and a local development plan for interrelated industries. Suppose, for instance, that firms in a selected locality were relieved of a range of taxes in a locality where other local industries, similarly relieved, are suppliers and customers of each other, and all would make use of substantial physical infrastructure improvements in an atmosphere of added concern for supportive human services. It might then follow that the reduced costs of production and sales (in taxes, transportation, and concentrated expertise, as well as in public supportive services) for the location could be a decisive element in a broadly based locality incentive program. The large scale of such an industrial development plan at one locale, however, militates against the use of this variation for the revitalization of any considerable number of depleted communities. And I am inclined to believe that that sort of public sector project would in any case too often suffer the fate of other big-bang projects. Somehow we human beings can rarely pull off extremely large-scale complex projects at any cost that seems reasonable.

A similar but much more modest approach has been proposed and used by William A. Duncan, president of the Mountain Association for Community Economic Development (MACED). He stresses the beginning assumption that institutional change, not projects, is the overall goal for CDCs, and he urges strategic "sectoral intervention" in a selected economic sector—that is, building technical expertise and many projects within the single sector until it is molded to serve the CDC's constituency. "Depending upon the nature of the specific situation . . . it might be practical to mount a sectoral intervention on a city, county, state, or national level," he states. As an example of national intervention, he cites the way community groups, under the leadership of Gail Cincotta, "immersed themselves" in the operating details of the commercial banking world until they and their allies were able to formulate and pass the Community Reinvestment Act. In his own Appalachian area, Duncan points to the sawmill industry, where a MACED venture has made an impact by offering improved market access for the small sawmills; the venture "buys, agglomerates, processes, and resells the lumber of small mills in eastern Kentucky" and has begun working similarly with loggers. He notes: "The goal here is to use a number of mechanisms to make the industry more viable, not because it offers high pay rates or growth potential, but because sawmills and loggers are critically important employers of poor people in the most rural parts of the area.

Any increase in hardwood sales from the area translates directly into additional days worked by underemployed men who are supporting their families on incomes from a variety of patched together sources." The sectoral intervention approach is illustrated in the emphasis placed on the fishing industry by Coastal Enterprises, Inc., a CDC in Maine. Coastal Enterprises began with helping to develop and strengthen a cooperative of fishermen. It has also constructed a processing plant, sponsored a fishery employment training program, and established an export company, among other activities in the fishery sector. And Coastal Enterprises is recognized as one of the most successful CDCs in the United States.

The local community economic development approach thus has a different and more encouraging, if modest, prospect than the enterprise zone idea. The years it has been quietly tested have shown its limits and its potential for success. It has the merit, in any case, of being small scale in any one test, so that the financial costs of failure are easily borne. Even a million-dollar failure in a CDC project is practically unheard of. That record compares very favorably with what unfortunately happens elsewhere in the use of government development assistance at home and abroad. One reason for the low cost of failure is the low cost of success. Community economic development programs cannot and should not try million-dollar efforts in the early stages of their evolution, and by the later stages, the curve of local learning and the increase in local institutional support make it less and less risky to venture more and more dollars in public support. Contrary to the psychology of public sector projects and the demands of the private sector or corporate world of substantial investment resources, a CDC project can start small and be rewarded by success in small-scale efforts, thereby enabling the CDC to strike out more ambitiously in succeeding years. I would stress again that the evolution of community capacity implies testing and developing strengths on modest projects for the purpose also of avoiding the immense costs of reinforcing discouragement in the depleted community. As a community development leader once told me, "We've had too many busted dreams to go that route again."

It may be that the modesty that marks the community economic development strategy has kept CDC leaders from venturing more effectively into the wider arenas outside the community. Yet the ultimate promotion of community economic development will depend upon an efficient integration of public policies at each level of government, as well as upon the creation of innovative ways to latch onto the microeconomics of conventional business activity. CDC leaders need to recognize and use the opportunities that will become available at every level of government. For example, at the local level, major municipal governments can catch directly the benefits of the free market development that is attracting capital to growing areas and shunt some of that capital to those areas of the city which are not currently attractive from the market standpoint. Boston and San Francisco have pioneered in this effort, promoting the concept of "linkage." In this policy, city government facilitates financially attractive private projects, such as a major new downtown office plaza, in return for the private sector developer allocating some of his financial return for investing in poorer neighborhoods, especially for housing.

Exactly how the linkage concept should be managed in different cities should usually be a local decision, fitting local needs and traditions. Neither the Boston nor the San Francisco model has been entirely successful and should not be slavishly followed. The allocation might pass through the city by way of a special tax fund drawn from the downtown project, or it might flow directly by way of collaborative projects between the private developers and the low-income community organizations. Slightly different techniques are being used on the county level by Dade County, Florida, and Montgomery County, Maryland—both metropolitan areas (Miami and Washington areas)—where there are new fees on real estate development which are set aside for low-income housing.

State and federal laws can be tailored to fit a local linkage policy and to provide neighborhoods and private developers with additional tools for collaboration. For example, something like Pennsylvania's tax credit for private sector corporations engaged in neighborhood assistance projects could be designed to apply directly as a supplement to a linkage project. Moreover, where states or provinces have established a capital pool for redevelopment of distressed areas, offering capital for new and expanded businesses or for the refinancing or repair of physical infrastructure, a federal role might be found in rediscounting the relevant state or provincial bonds; or other federal development banking functions might be considered, not as an independent action on behalf of the depleted community, but as a supplement to the work of the low-income community organization when that work is backed by state or provincial action.

To be both consistent and practical, I would not want to promote any specific new program measure at this juncture. Instead I would urge that a variety of potential measures be thought out and considered in a process in which community development leaders participate. Perhaps what we need first is a national process of local and regional workshops for the exchange of ideas among the three sectors—public officials, private industry, and community development leaders—on the ways in which integrated government action can be designed. In its initial phases, this workshop process can be conceived of as a brainstorming session. Naturally there would not be complete agreement within each sector or between sectors. Later on, therefore, the sectors would have to set some proposed priorities and begin a national debate on these issues and on the general issue of local development and its place in the society.

The basic evidence for the urgency and meaning of a community economic development approach is available, and each nation must consider carefully the place that this strategy can have within its national program for a healthy and growing economy. In the industrialized countries like Canada and the United States or in Third World nations, community economic development can fill a political and policy gap between international and national macroeconomic policies and the international and national microeconomics of conventional business activity. Locally controlled development by nonprofit organizations, as the third sector of any economy, must take its place between public sector monetary, fiscal, and trade measures on the one hand, and private sector response to market opportunities on the other.

The controversies about supply-side and demand-side and about how free a market can be tolerated in a gyrating world economy leave untouched the reality of a local economy that must somehow survive in the course of the battle of the giant forces around it. The experience of community economic development groups in low-income communities provides both ideas and practical and technical procedures that need to be evolved further. Whether one wishes to consider the debt crisis of the Third World or the rising percentage of Canadian and American federal budgets spent on transfer payments, surely the most reasonable perspective for national action begins with recovering the lost resources embodied in the lives and energy wasted in the impoverished and forgotten community. There are uncounted people in these communities all over the world who can contribute mightily to national and international stability and growth. Without tools to do their work, their potential contribution is lost.

Low-income communities can and will create tools for themselves, as they have in the past, but they will need support from public and private forces outside the community for recovering and levering the expatriated human and financial capital necessary to revitalize their own resources. History will also expect community economic development leaders in the United States and Canada to see that impoverished communities in the rest of the world learn that local people, with prudent outside assistance provided them on their terms, can start their communities on the way to dignity and equity.

Notes and Sources

Prologue

Most previous examinations of community economic development have been published as collections of rather brief comments, some of them indifferently edited and without reliable bibliographic references. There are two exceptions to this picture, one on the United States and the other dealing with Canada. The U.S. volume unfortunately dates from about fifteen years ago: John C. Weistart, ed., *Community Economic Development* (Dobbs Ferry, NY: Oceana Publications, 1972); this was a republication of two 1971 issues of *Law and Contemporary Problems*. The introductory book on Canadian experience is Susan Wismer and David Pell, *Community Profit: Community-Based Economic Development in Canada* (Toronto: Is Five Foundation, 1981).

There are two traditions in social studies that underlie my approach in this book. One is the community development tradition represented by Paulo Freire. Freire insists that change in the community and the history of a community begin with reflecting upon one's own history and responding to that reflection. I think that anyone seriously concerned with communities should make use of his *Pedagogy of the Oppressed* (tr. by Myra Bergman Ramos; New York: Herder and Herder, 1970). The other tradition is that of participant observation in social research, which was originally recognized by William James as early as 1904 and called by him the Chicago School of Thought. It evolved into the Chicago School of Sociology and included the social philosophy of George Herbert Mead and others, but there was no more sophisticated articulation of this position than that by the psychiatrist Harry Stack Sullivan. A few pages from his works provide a basic insight. See his *Con-*

ceptions of Modern Psychiatry (New York: Norton, 1953; pp. 11–12); and *The Psychiatric Interview* (New York: Norton, 1954; pp. 19–25, and see index entries for participant observation); see also the index entries in *The Fusion of Psychiatry and Social Science* (New York: Norton, 1964) as well as in *The Interpersonal Theory of Psychiatry* (New York: Norton, 1953).

The classic reflection upon the self as observer in a particular social research project is William Foote Whyte's methodological appendix "On the evolution of *Street Corner Society*" in his *Street Corner Society: The Social Structure of an Italian Slum* (2nd ed.; Chicago, IL: University of Chicago Press, 1955; pp. 279–358). A recent collection of papers that extends the concept of participant observation with many illuminating examples is David N. Berg and Kenwyn K. Smith, eds., *Exploring Clinical Methods for Social Research* (Beverly Hills, CA: Sage Publications, 1985).

Chapter One

For the unusual case of the San Francisco garbagemen, see Stewart E. Perry, *San Francisco Scavengers: Dirty Work and the Pride of Ownership* (Berkeley, CA: University of California Press, 1978).

For the essential significance to us all of the economic and other experimentation inherent in the Haight-Ashbury episode, see the perceptive account by Helen Swick Perry, *The Human Be-In* (New York: Basic Books, 1970). The colonial American tradition of economic compacts like CDCs is discovered in Patricia M. Lines and John McClaughry, *Early American Community Development Corporations: The Trading Companies* (Cambridge, MA: Center for Community Economic Development, 1970). More general is the book by Rosabeth Moss Kanter, *Commitment and Community: Communes and Utopias in Sociological Perspective* (Cambridge, MA: Harvard University Press, 1972). It brings together the threads in the history of various American economic communities such as Oneida. "A city upon a hill" was the moral, social, political, and economic community of Boston, projected in a sermon on Christian charity delivered on shipboard by Governor John Winthrop as the Massachusetts Bay colonists neared their new home in the year 1630; he took the phrase from the Sermon on the Mount.

A readable and indispensable record of the 1960s period of acute crises in the black communities of the United States is, surprisingly, a government document: *Report of the National Advisory Commission on Civil Disorders, March 1, 1968* (Washington, D.C.: U.S. Government Printing Office, 1970). There has been a long history of periodic rises in the intensity of black consciousness, especially with regard to economic solidarity; this history is reported in E. Franklin Frazier, *Black Bourgeoisie* (New York: Free Press, 1965, originally 1957). For a contrary view of the meaning of black history in the 1960s, see Edward C. Banfield, *The Unheavenly City* (Boston: Little, Brown, 1970). Banfield sees the rioting as "mainly for fun and profit." He states: "That racial injustice may have had less to do with the riots than is generally supposed is strongly suggested by the fact that a major riot . . . occurred in Montreal in 1969 during a sixteen-hour wildcat strike of policemen" (p. 198). This quoted passage is dropped in the next edition of his book, which was issued in 1974 under a new title, *The Heavenly City Revisited,* but the book still reveals an inability to follow out the full implications of discrimination against an economically disadvantaged group—francophone, black, or just general welfare recipient.

The fears in whites about "Black Power," a rallying cry raised by the civil rights leader Stokely Carmichael and then others in the 1960s, are hard to imagine today, in this time of routine black political mobilization. Yet even at the Office of Economic Opportunity, which was so directly concerned with the rights and progress of black people, the concept of black self-determination in local economic development (and other organizational or neighborhood matters) seemed to raise anxiety that the agency was encouraging "black separatism." President Lyndon Johnson himself worried about "kooks and sociologists" in the agency, located then within his own Executive Office of the President. On the day that this quoted remark of his appeared in the press, I pointedly noted to my colleagues at OEO who were *not* sociologists that while I most certainly belonged in that category, they were obviously lumped together in the other. Several months later I wrote a paper designed to answer some white anxieties; it was published eventually as "Black Institutions, Black Separatism, and Ghetto Economic Development," *Human Organization* (1972) 31:271–279.

Daniel P. Moynihan provides a lively contemporaneous, if somewhat sour, report of the War on Poverty and the then-current zeitgeist of local self-determination: *Maximum Feasible Misunderstanding* (New York: Free Press, 1970, paperback edition with a new introduction). A more sympathetic and careful account can be found in Robert A. Levine, *The Poor Ye Need Not Have with You* (Cambridge, MA: MIT Press, 1970). Although he has a negative view of economic development, he applauds the Hough Area Development Corporation for institution building in the economic sector. Compare also Frances Fox Piven and Richard A. Cloward, *Poor People's Movements: Why They Succeed, Why They Fail* (New York: Pantheon, 1977). For other contemporaneous reports, see Sar Levitan, *The Great Society's Poor Law: A New Approach to Poverty* (Baltimore, MD: Johns Hopkins Press, 1969); and Kenneth B. Clark and Jeannette Hopkins, *A Relevant War on Poverty* (New York: Harper & Row, 1969). The critical comments of the latter work are echoed in Steven Rose, *The Betrayal of the Poor* (Cambridge, MA: Shenkman, 1972).

A brief history of the beginnings of the CDC program at OEO can be found in Stewart E. Perry, "Federal Support for the CDCs: Some of the History and Issues of Community Control," *Review of Black Political Economy* (1973) 3: 17–42. Zeroing in at a later date on OEO's community economic development program is Lawrence F. Parachini, Jr., *A Political History of the Special Impact Program* (Cambridge, MA: Center for Community Economic Development, 1980). This is the basic analytical and historical record, written in a readable style. For the beginnings of the Bedford-Stuyvesant project, see Jack Newfield, *Robert Kennedy: A Memoir* (New York: Bantam, 1970) or Newfield, "Robert Kennedy's Bedford-Stuyvesant Legacy," *New York* (1968) 1, No. 37: 25–34. In the same general period as the CDCs were being organized, the United States government, through its Department of Housing and Urban Development, was launching a Model Cities program. This was intended to recognize the interdependence of problems in a deteriorating neighborhood and take a comprehensive approach to revitalization. However, it was to be carried out by city governments and originally had no commitment to new grass-roots structures for the neighborhood constituencies concerned, although there was supposed to be "widespread citizen participation." See Peter Marris and Martin Rein, *Dilemmas of Social Reform* (New York: Atherton, 1967).

My friend and colleague during my time at OEO and since then, Jeff Faux, as rapporteur for a foundation task force, prepared the first general treatment of CDCs: [Geoffrey P. Faux], *CDCs: New Hope for the Inner-City* (New York: The Twentieth Century Fund, 1971). He gives an insider's view of some of the problems of launching and administering the OEO program in "Politics and

Bureaucracy in Community-Controlled Economic Development," *Law and Contemporary Problems* (1971) 36: 277–296. The issue in which this article appeared is devoted to community economic development and was reprinted as John C. Weistart, ed., *Community Economic Development* (Dobbs Ferry, NY: Oceana Publications, 1972). A detailed presentation of several case studies and an examination of some legal considerations may be found in an excellent report by Nels J. Ackerson, Lawrence H. Sharf, and Robert M. Hager, "Community Development Corporations: Operations and Financing," *Harvard Law Review* (1970) 83: 1558–1671.

The term community development corporation has been adopted for development organizations quite different from those that are central to this book, particularly with respect to control by the community to be developed. Differing on this dimension are, for example, the CDCs initiated by federally chartered banks in the United States. See Beth Siegel, Peter Kwass, and Andrew Reamer of Mt. Auburn Associates, *Financial Deregulation: New Opportunities for Rural Economic Development* (Washington, DC: National Center for Policy Alternatives, 1986), pp. 55–58.

The papers, statements, and discussions of the Dalhousie conference were issued as *A Report on the CDC Workshop* (Halifax, Nova Scotia: Dalhousie Legal Services, 1975). Gregory J. MacLeod, the founder of New Dawn Enterprises, has recently published a book that draws an analogy between the status of Cape Breton and Third World underdevelopment: Greg MacLeod, *New Age Business: Community Corporations That Work* (Ottawa, Ontario: Canadian Council on Social Development, 1986). He reports on community-based programs in Quebec and in Spain (the Mondragon co-op complex), as well as on New Dawn. He properly places the co-ops of Mondragon in the context of community economic development, rather than looking at them merely as successful worker-owned firms, as previous observers have.

Chapter Two

Social invention was the theme of the annual meetings of the American Sociological Association in 1981 in Toronto; it was selected by the incoming president, William Foote Whyte. Whyte's presidential address of that year provides a context for the idea of social innovations like CDCs: "Social Inventions for Solving Human Problems," *American Sociological Review* (1982) 47: 1–13. Not so incidentally, CDCs were analyzed in one of the thematic sessions of that annual meeting. Whyte himself has been deeply involved in community-based development, although this involvement has been primarily in the context of a Peruvian project. I find his conceptual approach very meaningful. See Whyte and Lawrence K. Williams, *Toward an Integrated Theory of Development* (ILR Paperback No. 5; Ithaca, NY: New York State School of Industrial and Labor Relations, Cornell University, 1968).

There is so far no conventionally published account of HADC, but a consultant firm's report to a few government agencies and others is a perceptive piece of work. See Sam Harris Associates, Ltd., *Community Development Corporations as the Vehicle for Inner-City Economic Development: A Case History of Cleveland's Hough Area Development Corporation* (Washington, D.C.: Sam Harris Associates, Ltd., June 1973; 140 pp.), photocopy available through the Institute for New Enterprise Development (INED), Box 360, Cambridge, MA 02238. Only brief accounts may be found in more available sources. See, for example, Faux, book cited, pp. 67–71.

Since HADC is not presented here as typical of all CDCs, other more available case studies might be pursued. A series of case studies was issued by the Center for Community Economic Development, Cambridge, Massachusetts, and while the center itself is no longer in existence, its publications are sometimes available in academic libraries. Other case studies have been issued by INED, some of which are available in condensed form in Stewart E. Perry, ed., *Cases and Issues in Community Economic Development*, forthcoming. Perhaps the most accessible case studies will be found in a previously cited *Harvard Law Review* article by Ackerson et al. Very brief but more current notes on eighteen CDCs can be found in Robin J. Erdmann, Harlan Gradin, and Robert O. Zdenek, *Community Development Corporation Profile Book* (Washington, D.C.: National Congress for Community Economic Development, 1985). This publication has the advantage of presenting certain information about each CDC in tabular form, a presentation which permits comparative examination; it also offers an excellent survey of the variety of projects in which CDCs have been involved.

A detailed study of a failing CDC is reported by Harry Edward Berndt, *New Rulers in the Ghetto* (Westport, CT: Greenwood Press, 1977). This book presents a thoroughly critical view of the community economic development approach, characterizing it as a failure in general and as a fraud upon the poor. The author's point of view should be considered carefully since he was a staff member at the CDC in question, the Union Sarah Economic Development Corporation. However, Union Sarah EDC has since gone on, under new leadership, to become a very successful operation. For a somewhat later view, see Lynette Benton, *Union Sarah: A Community on the Move* (Cambridge, MA: Center for Community Economic Development, 1978). My own site visits to the CDC indicate that it changed its strategy from primarily business development to primarily property development—both commercial and housing—with excellent results.

I have not brought the story of HADC up to date, partly because, of course, it is a changing and continuing account. But it may be worth noting that DeForest Brown eventually left Hough and after a variety of community development posts returned to his ministerial profession; Burt Griffin is now a judge in the Cleveland area; Frank Anderson succeeded Brown at HADC but is now in business in North Carolina, having obtained a degree from the Harvard Business School; Ahmed Evans is still serving a prison term; Carl Stokes became a radio news commentator, his brother Louis carrying on the family political tradition as an influential member of the Congressional Black Caucus; and HADC, after many vicissitudes with other projects, including some wholly owned businesses that were promising for some years but rarely profitable, has reduced its concerns, presumably temporarily, to the administration of its real estate properties, including the King Plaza.

A pioneering report on New Dawn was sponsored by the Canadian federal agency (Health and Welfare) that gave New Dawn its original grant support. See John Hanratty, *The New Dawn Story: An Experiment in Economically-Based Community Development* (Sydney, Nova Scotia: Highland Resources, Ltd., 1981), available through New Dawn Enterprises, Box 1055, Sydney, Nova Scotia B1P 6J7. A shorter but later account can be found in Greg MacLeod, already cited. Today New Dawn sponsors as its main business development activity an investment program for new or expanding private enterprises, and it has continued to build low- and moderate-income housing until the recent cutback in federal mortgage financing. MacLeod continues to teach at the University College of Cape Breton and remains involved in many development activities, but a couple of years ago he left New Dawn's board of directors when its automatic board rotation policy called for replacement of original members who had already served the maximum number of terms.

Chapter Three

The argument of this chapter follows that of Michael Harrington in *The Other America* (rev. ed.; Baltimore: Penguin, 1971), except that he also ends up defining the poor as individuals (or as families) who are poor, even though he emphasizes the systematic nature of their status. His diagnosis and solutions do not truly include the community dimension. He recognizes that an antipoverty program must be comprehensive and "along the lines of establishing new communities, of substituting a new environment for the inhuman one that now exists" (pp. 177–178). But he saw housing and national and city planning and a federal department of urban development (not then in existence) as the keys—not the community as the active agent. It seems true that poor housing itself has a major influence on the maintenance of poverty. See Alvin L. Schorr, "Housing Policy and Poverty," pp. 113–123 in Peter Townsend, ed., *The Concept of Poverty* (London: Heinemann, 1970). But it should not take center stage as the fundamental solution.

Harrington rightly says of "the other America" that the poor are entangled "in a vicious circle," in a "culture of poverty," which includes more than bad housing. Thus he states: "The individual cannot usually break out of this vicious circle. Neither can the group, for it lacks the social energy and political strength to turn its misery into a cause. Only the larger society, with its help and resources, can really make it possible for these people to help themselves" (see pp. 16–17). This position clearly left the initiative to those outside the depleted community, and it was, after all, Michael Harrington's human and eloquent work, originally published in 1962 (and still *immediately* relevant today), which stimulated President Kennedy to order an inquiry into possible federal action. Of course, after Kennedy's assassination, Johnson pressed on with the creation of a federal program.

The so-called War on Poverty, launched by the Johnson Administration in 1964, stimulated considerable examination of exactly what was meant by "poverty." Certainly, long before that, there had been serious and detailed examinations, of which Henry Mayhew's *London Labour and London Poor* (4 vols.; New York:

Dover, 1968; a reprint of what was originally published in 1851–52 and 1861–62) is classical and fine reading. But when new attention by many economists and other social scientists was engendered in the 1960s, the definitions of poverty took off, almost exclusively, from the base of asking which individuals should be counted as poor.

This census type of definition could itself take many forms. Williamson and Hyer reviewed sixteen different measures of individual poverty, used over a ten-year period, and noted their divergences and statistical intercorrelations. All these measures centered on the individual, although they came from sociological studies. See John B. Williamson and Kathryn M. Hyer, "The Measurement and Meaning of Poverty," *Social Problems* (1975) 22:652–663. On occasion, absolute measures have been rejected by social scientists in favor of relative ones—so that being poor can be defined and measured differently in different locations. Peter Townsend, "Measures and Explanations of Poverty in High Income and Low Income Countries: The Problems of Operationalizing the Concepts of Development, Class, and Poverty," in Townsend, ed., *The Concept of Poverty* (London: Heinemann, 1970). Some such measures are, of course, administratively essential for income transfer programs, and I don't mean to derogate them. I simply wish to point out that reliance upon them can obscure the significance of the depleted community.

It is the presupposition of this book that the understandable concern with the individual poor person has distracted observers from the role played by the community in which that person participates, and despite the focus of the War on Poverty upon community action, the idea of the community as the base of poverty, rather than individual characteristics, has not received detailed scholarly attention. Before leaving the issue of definition, I should note, finally, the idea that poverty should be defined by some measure that indexes its cost to the society as a whole. See E. Smolensky, "Investment in the Education of the Poor: A Pessimistic Report," *American Economic Review* (1966) 56: 370–378. Smolensky asserts that a poverty line that "considers only the needs of the poor may not be the most pertinent guide to federal policy" (p. 371), and he urges a definition that considers the "disutility" of poverty to the rest of society—which would guide public expenditures on education for those who have no entry into the job market anyway. This focus does transcend the individual focus in an interesting way, but again it also leaps over the community context as an impoverishing environment.

A somewhat different dimension was introduced when some social scientists looked at the culture of poverty and argued that people were poor because they participated in a special and debilitating culture of poverty, were caught up in an impoverishing set of attitudes, values, and norms of behavior deriving from their life situation. See, for example, Charles A. Valentine, *Culture and Poverty: Critique and Counter Proposals* (Chicago: University of Chicago Press, 1968). Yet this conceptual view still remained abstracted from the depleted community. The idea of a culture of poverty is useful in considering the general nature of poverty as an interlocking network of mutually reinforcing influences; the concept could be used especially to consider the effects of chronic discouragement, as Harrington emphasized, and it could also point to the lack of institutional tools.

The evidence of this interlocking network can be discouraging in itself, and it can be distorted into a Social Darwinism by those who would counsel no efforts at change. Years before the U.S. society rediscovered poverty and thought to do something about it, the political scientist Edward C. Banfield pointed out the role of cultural barriers to change, but his pessimism barely avoids a prediction of inevitable poverty. He reported on the values and attitudes of an impoverished Italian village which was caught in a chronic helplessness. See *The Moral Basis of a Backward Society* (Glencoe, IL: Free Press, 1958). In his book, *The Unheavenly City*, previously cited, he returns to the idea of a culture that keeps people poor in the lower classes of American cities, particularly lower-class blacks. His pessimism is more evident in that context, in which he sees no feasible policies that have a chance of being instituted to combat poverty.

Looking at the problem with a more optimistic perspective, one might come up with other data on the psychology and resources of the poverty stricken. Still concentrating on the individual American poor person, Leonard Goodwin rebuts those who would insist that the poor you will have with you always because they prefer to be poor rather than work. See Leonard Goodwin, *Causes and Cures of Welfare: New Evidence on the Social Psychology of the Poor* (Lexington, MA: Lexington Books, 1983). In this and a previous book, *Do the Poor Want to Work?* (Washington, DC: Brookings Institution, 1972), Goodwin documents the capacity for change in the poor in U.S. communities, showing especially the strong motivation to get off welfare, for example. In short, it should be quite possible to demonstrate both conservative elements and change elements accessible in any specific population. That discovery should not be so surprising, but it does make things more complicated.

Fried and Gleicher have documented the commitment of low-income people to their impoverished neighborhood even in an urban setting where migration to a better neighborhood is presumably only a matter of moving a few blocks. See Marc Fried and Peggy Gleicher, "Some Sources of Residential Satisfaction in an Urban 'Slum'," *Journal of the American Institute of Planners* (1961) 27: 305–315. See also Fried and collaborators, *The World of the Urban Working Class* (Cambridge, MA: Harvard University Press, 1973). Incidentally, the resistance to moving can be seen as a conservative factor, but it can also be viewed as a resource for community renewal, if the commitment to the neighborhood can be used as a citizen mobilization device.

There are standard guides to making a community inventory. See, for example, Charles M. Tiebout, *The Community Economic Base Study* (New York: Committee for Economic Development, 1962). As I have suggested, however, these guides omit absolutely essential elements of the community's base for economic revitalization. The disastrous record of economic development efforts in most Native American communities offers a dramatic example of the error in ignoring available social, psychological, and cultural tools. In this connection, a most insightful and instructive examination of why economic development efforts have so often failed in the Native American case is contained in Bill Hanson, "Stratification and Economic Development in Native American Communities," in Perry, ed., *Cases and Issues in Community Economic Development*, forthcoming; the paper is also available from INED as a separate publication. Hanson focuses on the fractionation of Native American bands which, in a forced reservation setting, distorts and handicaps their capacity to make decisions, especially regarding economic resources. His analysis of how this division occurs and how it has evolved from the Indians' historical and cultural heritage is superb.

I have not found any general treatment of the cultural variations in capital accumulation, although commentators on any particular economic development setting might rail against the peculiar habits of the people in valuing, for example, provision for burial insurance over other savings and investment opportunities, as is the case in many black communities. Yet even this practice might have significant benefits for community development. See

Thomas C. Atkinson and W. M. Davis, *The Savings and Investment Function of Life Insurance Companies in the Sixth Federal Reserve District* (Atlanta, GA: Research Dept., Federal Reserve Bank of Georgia, 1956). For attention to the special problems of capital in black urban low-income communities, see Theodore L. Cross, *Black Capitalism* (New York: Atheneum, 1970), from which the banker's comment on lending to blacks is taken (p. 45). However, Cross's commitment to a particular program for development in the black inner city leads him to say, "Under present conditions there is absolutely no basis on which loans can be exported to black areas on a basis fair to the lender and his ghetto borrower" (p. 55). Events have proved him wrong for those forgotten communities that have come alive again.

The capital restraints of mortgage redlining are documented in a study by A. Thomas King, *Discrimination in Mortgage Lending: A Study of Three Cities* (New York: New York University, Graduate School of Business Administration, Salomon Brothers Center for the Study of Financial Institutions, 1981). An extended list of studies was prepared by the Library Division of the U.S. Department of Housing and Urban Development: *Red-Lining: A Bibliography* (3rd rev. ed.; Washington, D.C.: United States Department of Housing and Urban Development, Library Division, 1978). Cross, already cited, notes that insurance redlining compounds the problem of change in the low-income area (p. 133).

The initial report on the disaster of the West End project may be found in Herbert J. Gans, *The Urban Villagers* (updated and expanded ed.; New York: Free Press, 1982). This book, originally published in 1962, is credited with focusing so much attention on the human costs of the urban removal practice that subsequent urban projects were more vulnerable to this critique from their onset. The actual relocation had not begun when Gans left the area, and for data on the resulting psychiatric disabilities, he relies on colleagues who continued to study the process. See, for instance, Marc Fried, "Grieving for a Lost Home," pp. 151–171 in Leonard J. Duhl, ed., *The Urban Condition* (New York: Basic Books, 1963). The works by Fried and collaborators (previously cited regarding attachment to the home community) grow out of the same major study of the West End.

Chapter Four

I used to think that my application of the concept of triage to the economic development context was an original, if sardonic, comment. I discovered, however, that it was seriously used and recommended by an urban specialist, Anthony Downs, as cited in Robert Goodman, *The Last Entrepreneurs: America's Regional Wars for Jobs and Dollars* (Boston: South End Press, 1979; pp. 70–71). Goodman's book is a fine critique of the location strategy in regional economic development. Recently, Nancy Kleniewski reviewed the use of the concept by other urban planners as well as critically examined its application in Philadelphia. Nancy Kleniewski, "Triage and Urban Planning: A Case Study of Philadelphia," *International Journal of Urban and Regional Research* (1986) 10: 563–579.

Since in this chapter I rather summarily reject some specific formulations of economic development practice, readers may want to review for themselves what the general field offers. For a view of conventional practice and theory in economic development, which focuses on overseas settings, consult a standard text such as that by the University of Toronto economist, Benjamin Higgins, *Economic Development: Principles, Problems, and Policies* (new ed.; New York: W.W. Norton, 1968). Comparing the 1959 and the 1968 editions of his book will reveal some previous evolution in the traditional idea of economic development. Another authoritative text is by MIT's Everett E. Hagen, *The Economics of Development* (5th ed.; Homewood, IL: Richard D. Irwin, 1986), and similarly, a quick look at previous editions can be instructive.

It is worth recalling that the field of economic development is a post–World War II phenomenon generated in part by the U.S. government activity in the lesser developed nations—such as President Harry S Truman's Point Four program—and in the establishment of international finance mechanisms. True, there had been some classic works on economic change that can be considered within the rubric of economic development, like those of Weber, Schumpeter, and Marx. Such grand theories have been a significant part of modern thought, but the tremendous upheavals consequent on World War II and the institution of the United Nations organization brought an entirely new dimension into the picture, raising questions about the future of the newer nations freed from overt colonialism. These questions really defined what economic development was to consider. As a modern field of inquiry and practice, it has thus had that overseas focus from the beginning.

In the United States, however, domestic economic development had already been around for some decades in crude and rudimentary form as a practice but not a very self-examining one—that is, there was virtually no conceptual development of the field. See Donald R. Gilmore, *Developing the 'Little' Economies* (New York, NY: Committee on Economic Development, 1960). At the time of Gilmore's book, he could report that local programs of economic development, some of them dating back to the turn of the century, had little or no connection to the main problems that the directors of those programs themselves were then formulating in response to Gilmore's interviews and questionnaires (p. 22). Interestingly enough, a more systematic attention to such problems can probably be dated from federal action, the Area Redevelopment Act of 1961, much as work on the definition of poverty got its impetus from the Economic Opportunity Act of 1964. The programs deriving from the Area Redevelopment Act and from subsequent federal activity are reviewed in Sar A. Levitan and Joyce K. Zickler, *Too Little But Not Too Late* (Lexington, MA: Lexington Books, 1976). A brief but more recent review is by a senior staff member of the Center for Community Change, an outstanding source of technical assistance for community development groups: Norman C. DeWeaver, "Federal Infrastructure Programs for Area Economic Development: A 25-year Retrospective," prepared for the National Neighborhood Coalition Conference, November 1985. The field of so-called regional economics stems from the onset of government interest. There are a number of texts, of which Avrom Bendavid-Val, *Regional Economic Analysis for Practitioners* (rev. ed.; New York: Praeger, 1974) may be of most interest to readers of this book.

Evidence that there has been little progress in the conventional field of economic development applied to local communities may be gleaned from briefly reviewing Curtis H. Martin and Robert A. Leone, *Local Economic Development* (Lexington, MA: Lexington Books, 1977) and George Sternlieb and David Listokin, eds., *New Tools for Economic Development* (New Brunswick, NJ: Center for Urban Policy Research, Rutgers, 1981). In the latter work, perhaps the newest idea is a minor wrinkle on tax incentives for locating industries in depressed areas. Under the jazzy name of *enterprise zones,* it suggests federal and state location tax advantages, blithely dismissing evidence of the failure of previous similar tax incentives, and adds a few details like freedom from zoning restrictions and other bureaucratic requirements—as if these too are critical issues for business location. However, I should not weigh in too loudly against those who place their faith in tax incentives; I have to admit that before I knew differently, I once proposed an experiment to demonstrate their efficaciousness if they were targeted for a low-income area. See Elliott Sclar and Stewart E. Perry, *Preliminary Notes for a Field Experiment to Simulate Anti-Poverty Tax Incentives* (Cambridge, MA: Center for Community Economic Development, 1970), a proposal that at the time was taken seriously by potential government funders, but other events intervened.

Some of the difficulties in economic development thought derive directly from the primary presuppositions of the particular brand of basic economic theory being used, whether that is the so-called neoclassical school or the Marxist school. Compare Thee Kian Wie, "Historical Research and Economic Development," pp. 53–60 in L. Blusse et al., eds., *History and Underdevelopment* (Leiden: Leiden University, 1980). See also P. T. Bauer, *Dissent on Development* (London: Weidenfeld and Nicolson, 1971), especially chapter 7, "Economics as a Form of Technical Assistance." Bauer, incidentally, probably represents what could be called the "right wing" in economic development, since he sees much to be gained from colonialism. For a leading spokesman from the opposite wing, see Gunnar Myrdal, *The Challenge of World Poverty: A World Anti-Poverty Program in Outline* (New York: Pantheon, 1970). Presuppositions, reflecting power relations between the lesser developed and those helping or commenting on them, are embodied in terms and labels used in the field, according to a book edited by Geoff Wood, *Labelling in Development Policy: Essays in Honor of Bernard Schaffer* (London: Sage, 1985); see especially the chapter by Edward Horesh, "Labelling, and the Language of International Development," pp. 161–172. The book is a reprint of an entire issue of *Development and Change* (1985) 16, No. 3.

Some Euro-American views of economic development have included cultural dimensions but from a quasi-colonial viewpoint —that is, have focused on the cultural factors operating in the resistance to development within overseas settings. The economic development of the bypassed communities of the industrialized nations do not receive that same attention. Compare Ralph Grillo and Alan Rew, eds., *Social Anthropology and Development Policy* (London: Tavistock Publications, 1985). It is not the task of this book to provide a thorough review of economic development thought, but I hope that the brief remarks and the citations offered here will serve as a springboard for those whose interest is whetted to do their own reconnaissance.

Limiting assistance to growth centers is not a practice restricted to Canada and the United States. For a critique of the practice in Norway, see Vilhelm Aubert, "Rural Poverty and Community Isolation," pp. 236-250 in Peter Townsend, ed., *The Concept of Poverty*, already cited.

The National Film Board of Canada and the Extension Service of Memorial University of Newfoundland produced a film in the "Challenges for Change" series on one of the Newfoundland resettlement stories, *Fogo Island*. Other materials on the Fogo Island story may be found in Robert L. Dewitt, *Public Policy and Community Protest: The Fogo Case* (Newfoundland Social and Economic Studies, No. 8; St. John's, Nfld.: Institute of Social and Economic Research, Memorial University of Newfoundland, 1969); the series has other materials on resettlement. For a description of the J.A.L. group in Quebec, see Greg MacLeod, book cited, pp. 27-36. The practice of governments urging citizens to burn their houses and move seems hard to believe, but, after all, there is also the time-honored practice of urging farmers to plow under their crops or kill their pigs and cows—another economic policy of desperation that sometimes makes sense to a few economists and government officials but not to others.

The costs to relocated residents of the West End are described in Gans, especially pp. 378-381.

The quotation on orderly decline is from a report for the Economic Development Administration that I have somehow misplaced. The quotation from Levitan and Zickler about trickle-down is from p. 141 of their work previously cited.

The quoted conclusions from a review of studies of location incentives are drawn from Bennett Harrison and Sandra Kanter, "The Political Economy of States' Job-Creation Business Incentives," *Journal of the American Institute of Planners* (1978) 44: 424-435.

Grumman's location considerations were reported in a trade newsletter, *Economic and Industrial Development News*, August, 1985. A later report, from which the quotation was derived, appeared in *Expansion Magazine*, June, 1986.

The Santa Barbara study may be found, in abridged form, in Richard Appelbaum et al., *The Effects of Urban Growth: A Population Impact Analysis* (New York: Praeger, 1976). See also Harvey Molotch, "The City as a Growth Machine: Toward a Political Economy of Place," *American Journal of Sociology* (1976) 82: 309-332.

My information on the Sebastopol case comes from unpublished research by Susan Wismer and David Pell. I should note that the vulnerability of Sebastopol was also due to its small size, a vulnerability shared also by rural farming villages in a time of severe agricultural depression—as currently in the U.S. Midwest.

Avrom Bendavid-Val's experience with the New England small town is quoted from his *Local Economic Development Planning: From Goals to Projects* (Planning Advisory Service Report No. 353; Chicago, IL: American Planning Association, 1980). This excellent monograph is refreshingly sensible and insightful; it should be read by any practitioner.

There are no publications yet on the Point St. Charles group, but the Roxbury Action Program is described in Stewart E. Perry, *Building a Model Black Community* (Cambridge, MA: Center for Community Economic Development, 1978). For a full account of the construction project, see Hunt C. Davis and Stewart E. Perry, "Marcus Garvey Gardens: A Case in Community-Based Property Development," in Perry, ed., *Cases and Issues in Community Economic Development*, forthcoming.

Chapter Five

The conundrum of "growth" in economic development apparently can confuse even the specialists trying to distinguish between economic growth and economic development. Growth, says Hagen in the first edition of his (previously cited) text published in 1968, is simply a rise in per capita income, while economic development is that rise plus changes in economic and social structure; but then he says that growth is always accompanied by changes (p. 29). In the fourth edition (1980), he says that "technically" economic development is the result of growth, but it is really growth plus improved distribution of income. Gary Fields in *Poverty, Inequality, and Development* (Cambridge University Press, 1980; p. 245) says that growth can occur without change, especially without change in income distribution.

The confusion probably stems from reliance upon overly simple measures when dealing with conceptual issues in the field—measures like an increase in per capita income to show progress in economic development. Yet Hagen quite well recognizes the systemic nature of the impoverished way of life. See his seminal *On the Theory of Social Change: How Economic Growth Begins*

(Homewood, IL: Dorsey, 1962). But he and others are apparently beguiled by the ease of using the standard measures of income, so they tend to stick with change in the distribution of income as the indicator of change in general. That approach will not satisfy the practitioner of local economic development because so much improvement in other community indicators must and can take place before there is much change in income distribution; thus progress along the way has to be measured by other sorts of indicators, such as new institutional resources.

In 1971 a sociologist and an anthropologist working in a rural sociology department conducted a path-breaking attempt to assess various indicators of development. They chose a whole range of indices, from the number of flush toilets and median family income to a scale of institutional differentiation and a scale of medical specialities available locally, and applied them to two time periods for a selection of very small towns in the state of New York. They concluded that, whatever the potential of other measures, the structural indices (such as institutional differentiation as such or in a particular field as in medicine) had critical relevance, and they offered an opening for empirical-theoretical links in economic development at home and abroad that has still not been exploited. This is a key if somewhat demanding report: Paul R. Eberts and Frank W. Young, "Sociological Variables of Development: Their Range and Characteristics," chapter 5 in George M. Beal et al., eds., *Sociological Perspectives of Domestic Development* (Ames, IA: Iowa State University Press, 1971).

It is not just the economists who have trouble agreeing on a key concept that undergirds local revitalization. The concept of community is certainly elusive and is not unanimously defined by sociologists and other students of the community. In fact, there have been dozens and dozens of definitions. To begin a review, see Jessie Bernard, *The Sociology of Community* (Glenview, IL: Scott, Foresman, 1973). Roland Warren's works will be especially relevant, and a recent text by him might be consulted.

Operation Life is described in one of five brief case reports in a publication by members of the Tufts University Department of Urban and Environmental Policy. See Rachel G. Bratt, Janet M. Byrd, and Robert M. Hollister, *The Private Sector and Neighborhood Preservation* (prepared under HUD contract No. 7180–82; Cambridge, MA: Neighborhood Policy Research, 1983).

Chapter Six

On municipal activity in local economic development, the following works should be consulted. On small town efforts, see Nancy T. Stark, *Harvesting Hometown Jobs* (Washington, D.C.: National Association of Towns and Townships, 1985), which has a bibliography; and the 1986 conference proceedings of the Center for the Small City, University of Wisconsin-Stevens Point, Stevens Point, WI. The *Economic Growth and Revitalization Report*, published in Silver Spring, Maryland, is a useful, though expensive newsletter. The National Council for Urban Economic Development (1730 K Street, N.W., Washington, D.C. 20006) is a kind of bridge organization between municipal development agencies and others; it has a publications program as well as regular conferences. Perhaps the latest general book is Emil E. Malizia, *Local Economic Development: A Guide to Practice* (New York, NY: Praeger, 1986). It stresses public-private partnerships but does not mention CDCs; it is, nevertheless, a useful book.

A sensitive and trenchant treatment of the abuse and ineptitude of the Canadian unemployment compensation allowance system may be found in *Building on Our Strengths*, Report of the Royal Commission on Employment and Unemployment (St. John's, Newfoundland, 1986); see especially Chapter 12, "A New Income Security System."

The case of ECCO in Georgia and its impact on local government has an unhappy ending. The organization fell under attack for poor administration of its private and public grant funds, with accusations of fraud. In that context, the chief executive officer, a forceful and charismatic leader, was killed in an airplane accident, and the CDC never recovered its momentum, its projects falling into disarray. The depleted community is especially vulnerable to the loss of its critical leadership.

The quotation from the Canadian federal document comes from a 1974 staff paper prepared for Canada Health and Welfare, Welfare Grants Division; the paper also premised the CDC as "accountable to the local government," as if that were its constituency rather than the residents of the depleted community.

The Featherfield Farm/New Communities, Inc., project was described in a publication of the University of South Carolina Graduate School of Social Work, by Shimon Gottschalk and

Robert Swann, "Planning a Rural New Town in Southwest Georgia," *Arete* (1970) 1: 3ff.

A perspective on the stages of evolution for a community group that moves into development projects can be found in a special issue of the newsletter *Conserve Neighborhoods* (October, 1985), called "Building on Experience." A brief case study in the issue, describing the Broad Park Development Corporation of Hartford, Connecticut, is instructive. There is also a bibliography that would be useful for emerging groups. The newsletter is published by the National Trust for Historic Preservation, based in Washington, D.C. The trust is of course mostly concerned with the protection and rehabilitation of historical properties, especially in inner-city areas, but it has been a helpful source of grants and loans for low-income neighborhood projects. It issues an annotated "Bibliography for Neighborhood Leaders" and a "Directory of Useful Organizations."

For a detailed account of the East Boston CDC, see Peter Bateman, *Who Represents East Boston? A Case History of the East Boston Community Development Corporation* (Cambridge, MA: Institute for New Enterprise Development, 1982); this work is reprinted in an abridged form in Stewart E. Perry, ed., *Cases and Issues in Community Economic Development*, forthcoming. Related materials can be found in John N. MacPhee, *Local Government and Community Autonomy in East Boston* (Cambridge, MA: Center for Community Economic Development, 1973).

Chapter Seven

On the legal forms for a CDC in the United States, see *A Lawyer's Manual on Community Economic Development*, a massive compendium prepared by the National Economic Development and Law Center, Berkeley, California. Lawyers working with those seeking to organize a CDC in the United States can get some limited assistance from the center and update the advice of the manual, which was published in 1974. There is no comparable publication for Canadian law, but the U.S. manual would be useful.

A general manual for organizing a CDC is issued by the state of Massachusetts: *How to Organize a Community Development Corporation: A Manual for Community Organizations* (Boston, MA: Office of Community Economic Development, Massachusetts Executive Office of Communities and Development, n.d.). Although this publication, a revision of one issued in 1980, is designed to guide the organization of groups so they will meet the requirements of Massachusetts state laws to qualify for state grants and loans to CDCs, almost all of the information and advice would be helpful for a group in any state.

An early report on United Durham, Inc., is Barry Stein, *United Durham Inc.: A Case Study in Community Control* (Cambridge, MA: Center for Community Economic Development, 1972). Stein published a somewhat disguised version of his study as "The Centerville Fund, Inc.," *Journal of Applied Behavioral Science* (1973) 9:243–260. See Geoffrey Faux, "Politics and Bureaucracy in Community-Controlled Economic Development" (previously cited) for the political trials UDI had with the White House in getting started. HRDA of Halifax is described by Suzanne Strickland, *HRDA Enterprises, Ltd.: A Case Study in Productive Alternatives for Public Transfer Payments* (Cambridge, MA: INED, 1982). For TELACU, see Lawrence Parachini, *TELACU: Community Development for the Future* (Cambridge, MA: Center for Community Economic Development, 1977).

In the case of the Harlem Commonwealth Council, the board is made up of eight members who represent block associations, ten members representing other community organizations like churches or the Urban League, and twelve prominent individuals, such as a president of the New York City Board of Education, who were the originators of the CDC. See Barry Stein, *Harlem Commonwealth Council: Business as a Strategy for Community Development* (Cambridge, MA: Center for Community Economic Development, 1974). Barry Stein also prepared a report on the Bedford-Stuyvesant group, *Rebuilding Bedford-Stuyvesant* (Cambridge, MA: Center for Community Economic Development, 1975).

The widespread use of a *combination* of both for-profit and nonprofit forms in the organizational tools for a given community is documented in a report by the National Center for Economic Alternatives, *Federal Assistance to Community Development Corporations: An Evaluation of Title VII of the Community Services Act of 1974* (Washington, D.C.: NCEA, 1981).

Chapter Eight

Four publications can offer an introduction to business development in the context of community economic development, listed here in ascending order of detail. *Business Ventures for Nonprofits*, a special issue of *Conserve Neighborhoods* (June 1986), offers primarily a wide range of illustrative projects—which can be useful to a group that is just beginning to think about business development. Canadian examples are featured in Susan Wismer and David Pell, *Community Profit: Community Based Economic Development in Canada* (Toronto: Is Five Press, 1981), but this book also has a good deal of specifics on community business planning. In 1984 the Women's Institute for Housing and Economic Development (92 South Street, Boston, MA 02111) issued *A Development Primer: Starting Housing or Business Ventures By And/Or For Women*, which is as effective for other organizations as it is for women's development groups; it has a useful annotated bibliography. Finally, Linda M. Gardner's *Community Economic Development Strategies: Creating Successful Businesses* (Berkeley, CA: National Economic Development and Law Center, 1983) is comprised of three volumes, *Building the Base, Choosing the Business Opportunity*, and *Developing the Business*.

The Small Business Administration in the United States and the Federal Business Development Bank in Canada offer many helpful pamphlets. The Institute for New Enterprise Development has a series of "Venture Development Aids" that have been written to be used in CDC operations, either by independent entrepreneurs considering a joint venture with a CDC or by CDC business development staff themselves. For example, *The First Stage Analysis* provides a form with specific questions to guide an initial feasibility study for a service or manufacturing venture; *How to Prepare a Business Plan* has received wide use both inside and outside CDCs; and *An Introduction to Investment Agreements* is especially targeted to the typical items that might be involved in a CDC joint venture with an entrepreneur.

The idea of incubator malls (as contrasted to the conventional industrial mall) is a relatively new one. An early version was promoted by Control Data with the expectation that the new businesses in the mall would have computer access, training, and facilities through them. Control Data marketed its concept under the name City Venture Corporation to cities in Canada and the United States, and the results of its approach, from the standpoint of low-income communities, have been negatively evaluated in Calvin Bradford and Mihailo Temali with the assistance of Karen Branan, *The Politics of Private Sector Initiatives: The Case of City Venture Corporation* (Minneapolis, MN: Hubert H. Humphrey Institute for Public Affairs, University of Minnesota, 1982). A survey of variously sponsored malls throughout the United States was reported in Mihailo Temali and Candace Campbell, *Business Incubator Projects: A National Survey* (Minneapolis, MN: Hubert H. Humphrey Institute for Public Affairs, University of Minnesota, 1984). Although the use of the incubator mall has been attractive to CDCs, very few have undertaken such a project; for this reason, a workshop conference, cosponsored by the National Congress for Community Economic Development, the Humphrey Institute, and the Pratt Institute for Community and Environmental Development, was held in 1985. An evaluation of the effectiveness of business incubators for job creation and economic development in Canada, the United States, and western Europe is currently being conducted for the Mott Foundation by Candace Campbell at the Humphrey Institute.

Chapter Nine

Housing development, the most significant of all infrastructure activities for a CDC, is of course an entire field in itself. A basic source of information is the Low-Income Housing Coalition (1012 14th St., N.W., Washington, D.C. 20005), as well as the National Trust for Historic Preservation. The National Housing Law Project (1950 Addison St., Berkeley, CA 94704) has a newsletter and offers assistance through Legal Services groups. The Enterprise Foundation (600 American City Bldg., Columbia, MD 21044) has a publication program through its Rehab Work Group, and it also offers grants and loans for housing development. A brief but authoritative, if somewhat dated, overview in the context of community economic development may be found in Paul G. Garrity, "Community Economic Development and Low-Income Housing Development," *Law and Contemporary Problems* (1971) 36: 191–204; this work is reprinted in Weistart, previously cited.

The story of the crisis in launching the Opportunity Funding Corporation is told in a slightly different version, which perhaps relies more on the viewpoint of the official sponsors, in Samuel I. Doctors and Sharon Lockwood, "Opportunity Funding Corporation: An Analysis," *Law and Contemporary Problems* (1971) 36: 227–237; reprinted in Weistart. See also David K. Banner, Samuel I. Doctors, and Andrew C. Gordon, *The Politics of Social Program Evaluation* (Cambridge, MA: Ballinger, 1975), which is a case study of an evaluation research study of OFC.

For a systematic look at the use and development of the human capital embodied in the CDCs, minority or otherwise, see Arabella Martinez and David B. Carlson, *Developing Leadership in Minority Communities,* an unpublished study for the Carnegie Corporation, 1983. The authors are currently preparing a more extensive study to be published by the Ford Foundation. Consult also my "Notes and Sources" for Chapter Twelve for some unpublished data on human capital development in CDCs, derived from the study of the National Center for Economic Alternatives.

The relative aggressiveness of community development leaders in the United States versus Canada may be a cultural feature. It is certainly a trait often found in U.S. CDC directors. One CDC leader is said to have interviewed an antagonist, a high-ranking corporate executive, while lying on the floor, as a means of putting his antagonist at a disadvantage. The same CDC leader who suggested the use of the Lord's Prayer to his antagonist in the government is the subject of another tale that I want to repeat. When his CDC was first awarded a federal grant, the actual funds were delayed for several months, and the CDC leader came to Washington to track down the clerk who was not releasing the funds— because, as it turned out, certain forms had not yet been reviewed in her bureau. "He told her that the people in [his community] had concluded that he had taken the money himself and that if she didn't release the funds, they would kill him when he got back to Georgia. . . . The clerk released the funds." (Faux, "Politics and Bureaucracy in Community-Controlled Economic Development," work cited, p. 290).

Chapter Ten

My emphasis on looking to internal sources of capital first is underlined by an examination of special programs of low-interest external capital in the most depressed countries of the world. See Dale W. Adams, Douglas H. Graham, and J.D. Von Pischke, eds., *Undermining Rural Development with Cheap Credit* (Boulder, CO: Westview Press, Frederick A. Praeger, 1984). This book's authors, many different specialists working with many different countries, make the startling point that local savings would be available and would be effective if they were not discouraged by inefficient, ineffective low-interest rural loan programs. The authors, each from his own viewpoint, tend to see that local people are better judges of how to provide and use credit than outsiders, and the task is to give them enough experience and chance to strengthen their own capacities against the traditional wealthy overclass. Otherwise, low-interest credit will almost inevitably benefit the more well-off and bypass the poor farmer. The volume deserves careful study.

The Zion Investment case is well presented in Ackerson et al., already cited.

Revolving loan and loan guarantee funds are described in detail in *Revolving Loan Fund Technical Manual,* prepared for the Program Evaluation Division, Economic Development Administration, 1980. Although the manual is designed to meet the U.S. federal program guidelines for EDA support, the descriptive material generalizes very well for any fund operated independently of a government connection. The Community Information Exchange of the National Urban Coalition (which has developed a systematic and computerized information bank for community groups) has available a sample "Feasibility Study and Program Design for a Revolving Loan Fund." The exchange is located at 1120 G Street, N.W., Washington, D.C. 20005.

The special form of U.S. credit union known as the Community Development Credit Union (CDCU) multiplied so quickly that a national association, the Federation of Community Development Credit Unions, was soon organized. The National Economic Development and Law Center (which changed its name a few years ago) has been a source of assistance to promote these financial tools, and it has published a technical handbook for local groups: Brad Caftel, *Community Development Credit Unions: A Self-Help Manual* (Berkeley, CA: National Economic Development Law Project, 1978). Growing fast, CDCUs have hundreds of millions of dollars in assets for reinvestment in their communities. In this activity, the United States has followed after a powerful and innovative type of credit union created in Quebec, *caisse d'entreaide economique* or CEE. The CEEs have the special task of providing entrepreneurial banking facilities for a local community, offering mainly long term commercial and industrial mortgages.

Iniquilinos Boricuas en Accion (IBA) is briefly described in Bratt et al., previously cited. MURAG is said, in another brief case study in the same publication, to be "the only organization of its type in the country."

The so-called Community Loan Funds (CLFs) have been vigorously promoted by the Institute for Community Economics (151 Montague City Road, Greenfield, MA 01301), which has offered valuable technical assistance. The fall 1985 issue of their publication, *Community Economics,* is devoted to CLFs, using information derived from the first national conference of the funds. Since that time, CLF capital has increased by several million dollars, and other CLFs have been started. For an introduction and update of the performance of these groups, see Michael Swack, "The Community Loan Fund," in Perry, *Cases and Issues in Community Economic Development,* forthcoming. The Mexican American Unity Council is described by Art Hochner in the same forthcoming book.

Chapter Eleven

Commenting on operational problems and making suggestions on their solutions is to teeter on the brink of cliches and generalities that do not hold or are just too vague. This is the weakness of any management manual. One can only hope that somehow what one says will connect with the reader's experience. I have not yet discovered a book that speaks enough to me to pass it on with confidence. However, *Steering Nonprofits,* a special issue of *Conserve Neighborhoods* (February, 1984) strikes me as eminently sensible. One comment from this publication illustrates its down-to-earth quality: "There is never a right time to bring a new policy or program to the board; it's always too early or too late. When presented with a new venture before it has been thought out, the board may seem puzzled or irritated and will request only fully developed ideas. However, when introduced to a coherent new policy or activity, the board then may see itself only as a rubber stamp" (p. 340).

Chapter Twelve

For further information on the ROTI method, contact Kentucky Highlands Investment Corporation, P.O. Box 628, London, KY 40741. My information on ROTI comes from an excellent but unpublished monograph on KHIC by Raymond Russell, Department of Sociology, University of California, Riverside, CA 92521.

Evaluations of New Dawn Enterprises were made successively by Professor Dorothy Butts and by Professor Marcel Leroy, both at University College of Cape Breton, P.O. Box 5300, Sydney, Nova Scotia B1P 6L2.

The final report of the three-way competition on the Special Impact Program was issued as Westinghouse Learning Corporation, *Evaluation of the Special Impact Program,* report under OEO Contract #B89-4532, July, 1970.

For the Abt evaluation, see *An Evaluation of the Special Impact Program: Final Report* (Cambridge, MA: Abt Associates, Inc., 1973). An early assessment of the Abt work can be found in Barry Stein, "How Successful Are the CDCs: An Interim Response," *Review of Black Political Economy* (1973) 3: 82–99. Later, the staff of the Center for Community Economic Development issued a major analysis: *A Review of the Abt Associates, Inc., Evaluation of the Special Impact Program* (Cambridge, MA: CCED, 1977).

Quotations from the evaluation of the early Ford Foundation program are taken from Harvey A. Garn, Nancy L. Tevis, and Carl E. Snead, *Evaluating Community Development Corporations—A Summary Report* (Washington, D.C.: The Urban Institute, 1976). Cf. Harvey A. Garn, "Program Evaluation and Policy Analysis of Community Development Corporations," in Gary Gappert and Harold M. Rose, eds., *Social Economy of Cities* (Beverly Hills, CA: Sage Publications, 1975).

The findings on the efficacy of community control are presented in Rita Mae Kelly, *Community Participation in Directing Economic Development* (Cambridge, MA: CCED, 1976); republished under the title *Community Control of Economic Development: Boards of Directors of Community Development Corporations* (New York, NY: Praeger, 1977).

For the assessment of the Special Impact Program, issued just as the sponsoring agency was abolished, see *Federal Assistance to Community Development Corporations: An Evaluation of Title VII of the Community Services Act of 1974* (Washington, D.C.: National Center for Economic Alternatives, 1981). I attended a meeting in which the director of the study presented his work just before the report appeared. Some interesting findings that he described then were not included in the report, and I cite a few of them here from my notes taken at the time. For example, CDC ventures in the service sector employed twice the number of people that the usual minority service business did; in general, CDC ventures paid more and had larger sales volume than those minority businesses aided by the Small Business Administration; and the income of nonmanagerial employees rose about 9 percent over their previous job salaries, and for managerial employees, about 12 percent. Regarding skill development and the improvement of human capital, 83 percent of nonmanagerial employees received some on-the-job training and 17 percent some formal training, while 32 percent of the managerial employees received some formal training. About 80 percent of managerial employees judged that they had improved their skills at the CDC, while the same percentage felt they still needed improvement. The study made an attempt to project whether the CDCs could, within fifteen years, reduce the gap in skill levels between their own neighborhoods and surrounding areas by as much as 50 percent; it concluded that they could in rural and smaller urban settings but not in larger urban settings. Projections for employment levels were even more positive for rural and small urban settings but negative for the larger urban neighborhoods. The data of this study, then, are only partly mined for their potential use in policy decisions.

The HUD program evaluation, sampling thirty of ninety-nine grantees, is reported in Neil Mayer, Sue Marshall, and Jennifer Blake, *Neighborhood Development Organizations: Why Their Projects Succeed or Fail and How They Grow in the Process* (Washington, D.C.: The Urban Institute, 1982). See also the same authors' *Who Is Doing Neighborhood-Based Development: Projects, Skills, Resources, and Limitations* (prepared under HUD contract H-5255; Washington, D.C.: The Urban Institute, 1982).

The quotations on the LISC evaluation are from Avis Vidal et al., *The Local Initiatives Support Corporation: Preliminary Findings of an Evaluation in Progress* (Cambridge, MA: State, Local and Intergovernmental Center, Kennedy School of Government, Harvard University, 1985).

Chapter Thirteen

The offices of the National Congress for Community Economic Development are located at 1612 K Street, N.W., Washington, D.C. 20006. The Federation of CDCs of Canada is reached at 182 George Street, Sydney, Nova Scotia B1P 1J3.

The Canadian report recommending a network of support institutions is by P.D. Brodhead, Michael Decter, and Ken Svenson, *Community-Based Development: A Development System for the 1980s* (Technical Study No. 3; Ottawa: Labour Market Development Task Force, Canada Employment and Immigration Commission, 1981).

A National Citizens Monitoring Project in the United States has been sponsored by the Center for Community Change to keep track of the use and abuse of the major potential source of federal assistance, the Community Development Block Grants (CDBGs).

Among its activites is a report by one of the collaborating groups in this project (The Working Group for Community Development Reform, 1615 Broadway, Oakland, CA 94612), which criticizes CDBG policies severely. See *Promoting Colonialism at Home: The Relationship of Subsidized Economic Development to Ten Low-Income Communities*, issued by the Working Group, 1985. Yearly reports have been issued by the group since 1980.

The concept of the enterprise zone has been popularized in the United States by Stuart Butler of the Heritage Foundation and taken up by the Reagan administration as well as by some congressional figures, including Jack Kemp, conservative Republican, and Robert Garcia, liberal Democrat. A full presentation is in Stuart Butler, *Enterprise Zones: Greenlining the Inner City* (New York: Universe Books, 1981). Enterprise zones and free-trade zones are a special interest of the Sabre Foundation, a policy research group (at 317 C Street, N.E., Washington, D.C. 20002) which began issuing a newsletter, *Enterprise Zone News* in 1982, including a bulletin, *Free Zone Update.* The foundation has a videotape that profiles some enterprise zone cases in the United States. CDCs have been attracted to the idea because it so clearly echoes their own concept of targeting the depleted community, and the National Congress for Community Economic Development has sponsored workshops on the topic. Since the tax incentive core of the concept conflicts so fundamentally with the movement to "simplify" the tax code and to remove from it any responsibility for promoting social policies, it is hard to see that federal enterprise zone legislation will move toward enactment in the United States in the near future.

The report and argument for the sectoral intervention approach as used by the Mountain Association for Community Economic Development (210 Center Street, Berea, KY 40403) is found in William A. Duncan, "Economic Development Strategy: What Next?" a paper prepared for a conference sponsored by the National Neighborhood Coalition, November, 1985. Incidentally, Duncan also insists that community economic development requires vigorous political intervention, and he describes a successful MACED campaign on bank lending policies in a situation in which the tools of the Community Reinvestment Act were not appropriate.

On the footloose factory, see Bennett Harrison, *The Deindustrialization of America* (New York: NY: Basic Books, 1982) and Gilda Haas and the Plant Closures Project, *Plant Closures: Myths,*

Realities, and Responses (Boston, MA: South End Press, 1985). Some current forms of local government support for community economic development are described in Thomas Burns and Carla Dickstein, "Building Capacity for Community Economic Development," *Economic Development and Law Center Report* (1985) 15, No. 3: 7-11. This work is based on the authors' "Building Capacity for Community Economic Development: A Micro and Macro Perspective," Community Economic Development Series Working Paper No. 5, The Wharton School, University of Pennsylvania, Philadelphia, PA.

For a valuable review of state economic development programs, see the forthcoming monograph prepared by David Osborne for the Economic Policy Institute of Washington, DC. See also David R. Jones, ed., Building the New Economy: States in the Lead (Washington, DC: Corporation for Enterprise Development, 1986). CfED is actively publishing other useful materials relevant to local economic development.

Index

For ease in identification, the location of CDCs listed here is indicated in parentheses after the name of the organization.